In Memory
of

CORINNE CORNISH

BY

PHYLLIS LOFTHOUSE

© 1987 GAYLORD

Steven Raichlen's

HIGH-FLAVOR, LOW-FAT ITALIAN COOKING

Steven Raichlen's

HIGH-FLAVOR,
LOW-FAT
ITALIAN COOKING

Photography by Greg Schneider

FOOD STYLING BY PATTY FORRESTEL

VIKING

VIKING
Published by the Penguin Group
Penguin Putnam Inc., 375 Hudson Street
New York, New York 10014, U.S.A.
Penguin Books Ltd, 27 Wrights Lane, London W8 5TZ, England
Penguin Books Australia Ltd, Ringwood, Victoria, Australia
Penguin Books Canada Ltd, 10 Alcorn Avenue,
Toronto, Ontario, Canada M4V 3B2
Penguin Books (N. Z.) Ltd, 182–190 Wairau Road,
Auckland 10, New Zealand

Penguin Books Ltd, Registered Offices:
Harmondsworth, Middlesex, England

First published in 1997 by Viking Penguin,
a member of Penguin Putnam Inc.

1 3 5 7 9 10 8 6 4 2

LIBRARY OF CONGRESS CATALOGING-IN-PUBLICATION DATA
Raichlen, Steven.
Steven Raichlen's high-flavor, low-fat Italian cooking/photography by Greg Schneider.
p.   cm.
ISBN 0-670-87443-4 (alk. paper)
1. Cookery, Italian.   2. Low-fat diet—Recipes.   I. Title.
TX723.R32   1997
641.5'638—dc21   97–14329

This book is printed on acid-free paper.

∞

Printed in the United States of America
Set in Goudy

To Barbara
con tutto il mio amore

ACKNOWLEDGMENTS

A book may bear the name of a single author, but it is never written alone. This one had the support of dozens of family members, friends, and colleagues.

First, I would like to thank Greg Schneider, who graced the book with his usual stunning photographs, and stylist Patty Forrestel, who made sure the food "tasted good" to the camera.

A huge thanks to my recipe testers: Sharon Marquedtson, Doris Porter, Elida Proenza, Alice Varga, and Wayne Vaughn, Jr. I'd also like to thank nutritionist Linda Yokum for the recipe analyses.

Another huge thanks to The Grand Bazaar and Norman Brother's Market, for providing such wonderful ingredients to cook with.

I'd also like to thank the Italian Trade Commission, International Olive Oil Council, and Tartuf-Langhe, for helping to expand my knowledge of Italian cooking.

Dawn Drzal at Viking Penguin polished the manuscript with her expert editing. I'd like to thank all my friends at Viking for their enthusiasm and support, including Barbara Grossman, Cathy Hemming, Paul Morris, Paul Slovak, Rachel Schnoll, and Roseanne Serra.

Above all, I want to thank my family: young chef Jake, basketball maven Betsy, and my lovely wife, Barbara, whose savvy, support, and love made this—and all my books—possible.

CONTENTS

INTRODUCTION

To eat well is to be close to God.
—ITALIAN SAYING

There are lots of places I could begin this book: In the Piedmont city of Alba at the odoriferous start of truffle season. By the fishing docks of Palermo, where the tuna boats come in. At a two-hundred-year-old pizzeria in Naples, where soft pillows of dough are transformed into airy, wood-oven-baked pizzas. At a family-run restaurant in a seventeenth-century hunting lodge in Umbria, where home-cured hams hang in the basement and the vegetables were still in the garden an hour before dinner.

But the best place to start might just be lunch at the home of my friend Pino Saverino. Pino is a chef from Chiavari, on the Ligurian coast, who lives and works in Miami. I've long enjoyed his food at Italian restaurants in this country. Last summer, my wife and I had the opportunity to meet his eighty-year-old mother and dine at their family home. Chiavari is a bustling banking town, but come 1:00 P.M., the sacrosanct lunch hour, shops are shuttered and traffic grinds to a halt. For the next three to four hours, the people of Chiavari do what Italians do best. They eat.

They eat in a simple, leisurely manner almost forgotten in the United States. They eat with friends and family, at home or in restaurants, as often as possible outdoors. They eat relatively small portions of delicious food that tastes homemade—even when

served in restaurants. They enjoy a diet rich in grains, beans, fresh fruits, and vegetables and they wash their meal down with what more and more medical researchers have come to realize is an essential part of a healthy diet: wine. They eat one of the most appealing cuisines on the planet—a fact attested to by the popularity of Italian restaurants all over the world.

We sat on a breezy terrace at the back of Mrs. Saverino's apartment. We crunched breadsticks made by a local bakery and savored astonishingly ripe melons with silk-soft, tissue-thin sliced prosciutto. We ate *trofie* (a short, stubby egg noodle) with a pesto so gossamer and delicate, it made most American versions seem like basil-flavored library paste. We ate *burrida*, a local fish stew made with *seppiolini* (cuttlefish) so tiny a half dozen could fit into a soup spoon. I don't remember everything we ate at Pino's that afternoon, but I know it was well after 4:00 P.M. when we left the table. I also know I felt sated, but not in the least bit stuffed.

Does the world need another Italian cookbook? Especially, a high-flavor, low-fat Italian cookbook? After all, isn't Italian cooking generally considered to be one of the healthiest cuisines in the world—especially as it's practiced on its home turf? Obesity doesn't seem to be a problem among younger Italians (although it's evident among older people). In any case, Italians are much less obsessed with obesity and heart disease than are their counterparts across the ocean.

Italian cuisine is a paragon of balance and moderation. I'm sure the notion of a high-flavor, low-fat cookbook would seem quite strange to most Italians. Why eliminate (or at least restrict) a whole class of ingredients (fats) that are an important part of Italian cooking and are generally eaten in moderation? Why focus a book on low-fat cooking when there are so many wonderful dishes to choose from in Italy?

Well, first of all, not all Italian cooking is automatically healthy. Not by a long shot. Think of the popularity of *fritto misto* and other deep-fried dishes. Think of the popularity of cheese and dairy products, of butter- and cream-based pasta sauces. Think of the oceans of olive oil, even if it is extra-virgin, poured over seafood, vegetables, and noodles.

We North Americans have always invented the Italian cuisine we need. In the 1950s and '60s, it was the comforting cooking of Naples and southern Italy, with its reliance on long-simmered tomato sauces. In the 1970s and '80s, it was the refined cuisine of northern Italy, with its emphasis on egg pasta and cream sauces. With each passing year, we discovered "new" Italian dishes (most of them actually centuries old), from risotto to focaccia.

And now we are about to discover the Italian cuisine we need for the twenty-first century: high-flavor, low-fat Italian cooking.

In crafting the recipes for this book, I've had three goals: First, to identify and present traditional Italian dishes that are naturally low in fat. Second, to rework higher-fat recipes, like pesto, to bring them in line with today's health-consciousness. And third, to create great-tasting low-fat dishes that are Italian in spirit, although they may never have been served in Italy.

To this end, I've used many techniques you'll be familiar with from my other high-flavor, low-fat cookbooks. For example, I still use chicken broth, fish broth, and vegetable broth in place of cream and butter in pasta dishes and casseroles and in place of some of the oil in sauces and salad dressings. I still use egg whites (or mostly egg whites) to set frittatas, custards, and flans. I still toast bread crumbs and nuts in the oven to intensify their flavor, so a little goes further.

I've also added some new techniques to the repertory in this book—for example, roasting vegetables in a super-hot oven to make a fat-free base for sauces. Roasting intensifies the flavor of a vegetable by evaporating the water in it. The high heat caramelizes the natural plant sugars, imparting a sweet, smoky taste.

Another technique I use extensively in this book is the surface application of butter or olive oil. The idea here is that in addition to the small amount of fat used for cooking the ingredients, a little is drizzled over or brushed on the finished dish. Thus, when you bite into the dish, the first thing you taste is olive oil (or butter). This gives your mouth the impression that there is more fat in the dish than there really is.

Having written at length about what this book is, I need to say a few words about what it is not. It's not, strictly speaking, an authentic Italian cookbook—although 95 percent of the recipes in the book are based on traditional Italian dishes. The author freely admits that he is not Italian. Even years of travel in Italy cannot replace the sort of culinary heritage that comes from being born into and growing up in a particular culture.

Nor is *High-Flavor, Low-Fat Italian Cooking* a diet book, in the strict sense of the word, although using the recipes can definitely help you—as it helped me—lose weight and lower cholesterol levels. I am a cookbook author, not a nutritionist. When I create a recipe, the foremost thing in my mind is taste. I try to write recipes that are great-tasting and that happen to be low-fat, not the other way around.

When it comes to the question of authenticity, there are two schools in writing cookbooks. The first holds that you must be scrupulously faithful to a dish you experienced at a particular time in a particular place. If the ingredients aren't available in this country, you shouldn't bother offering the recipe. Period.

The other school holds that recipes are a basic

guideline rather than a sacred text, that by following the general outlines of a dish you experienced abroad, you can create a very delicious, albeit different dish, one that is true in spirit to the original.

As you've probably gathered by now, I ascribe to the latter school. There is certainly an Italian school of cooking (or many schools of cooking). Over the past ten years, I've tried to evolve a high-flavor, low-fat school of cooking. The goal of this book is to bring them together.

Thus, you will find here many ingredients, recipes, and stratagems that most Italians would find quite bizarre. Consider the cannolis on page 215. In place of the traditional Sicilian deep-fried pastry shell, I've substituted crackling-crisp tubes made from baked, rolled wonton wrappers. The ricotta filling is the same (well, almost the same—I use low-fat ricotta, then bolster the flavor with rosewater).

Wontons certainly aren't Italian (although some food historians argue that the Italians learned to make pasta from the Chinese via Marco Polo). But the pastry shell still shatters into a million buttery flakes. My high-flavor, low-fat version contains only 142 calories and 4 grams of fat per cannoli. The spirit of the dish is the same, even though I've used an ingredient that couldn't be less Italian.

Or consider the Stuffed Zucchini Flowers on page 20. Fried zucchini flowers are a favorite Italian antipasto. To make a low-fat version, I brush the blossoms with lightly beaten egg white, then bake them in a bread-crumb crust. The result has the crispness of the original, with a fraction of the fat.

Of course, you need to replace the lost flavor and richness, and we do so with a generous—dare I say profligate?—use of herbs, spices, and condiments. Heretical? Some people may think so. But I ask you to judge these recipes not on the page but on the palate.

ABOUT THE HIGH-FLAVOR, LOW-FAT METHOD

As readers of the previous books in this series will know, my philosophy is simple: use intense flavor-

ings, not fat, to make food taste delicious. In this aspect, Italian cuisine readily lends itself to the high-flavor, low-fat method. For starters, fresh herbs—especially basil, rosemary, sage, and parsley—are cornerstones of Italian cooking. So are aromatic vegetables, like onions, garlic, peppers, celery, and carrots. Italians love the sharp flavors of wine, vinegar (especially balsamic vinegar), tomato paste, and lemon juice. These ingredients can go a long way toward creating a symphonic range of flavors with little or no fat.

The Italian larder is also full of tangy salty flavorings, such as prosciutto, olives, capers, anchovies, and dried tomatoes. Even a small amount of one of these ingredients can have an electrifying effect on a dish. Italian cheeses are generally quite flavorful, so a little goes a long way. Parmigiano-Reggiano, one of the world's most magnificent cheeses, is made with part-skim milk. One tablespoon freshly grated Parmigiano-Reggiano contains less than 2 grams fat.

And when Italians use fat for cooking, they often use the one fat that may actually help boost levels of HDL (the "good" cholesterol): olive oil. Unlike many fats used in North America (such as corn oil or canola oil), olive oil offers a flavorful dividend, providing not just the cooking properties and mouth feel of fat, but also a distinctive and pleasing flavor in its own right.

In more general terms, the Italian diet provides a compelling model for healthy eating. Grains, beans, and vegetables dominate the culinary landscape. As befits a country with 4,996 kilometers of coastline, seafood is enormously popular. There's no denying the popularity of meats in Italy, but the portions are generally of reasonable size.

ABOUT THE RECIPES

Most of the recipes in this book are designed to serve four people as a main course. When a range of servings is given (for example, 4 to 6 servings), the nutritional analysis refers to the smaller number of servings.

New in this book are listings of preparation and

cooking times and the notion of fat budgets. The former assume that you are a moderately experienced cook, that you know how to chop an onion or trim a chicken breast. If you're less experienced, take comfort in the fact that most of the recipes in this book are very easy. Just be prepared to spend a little more time chopping and prepping.

The notion of fat budgets arises out of letters I have received from my readers. (I welcome your letters, in care of my publisher, Viking, 375 Hudson Street, New York, NY 10014.) Some of you are on draconian diets that are intended to eliminate fat completely. Others of you are trying to reduce the overall fat in your diet while retaining a maximum of flavor. When a recipe calls for a range of ingredients (1 to 2 tablespoons olive oil, for example, or ¼ to ½ cup Parmigiano-Reggiano), know that the lower amount will give you a perfectly tasty, nutritional dish. (The nutritional analysis at the end of the recipe is based on this amount.) If you're a little more liberal or forgiving with your fat intake, however, use the higher amount and you'll wind up with an even more luscious dish.

Please note that my cooking is low-fat, not no-fat. In keeping with my emphasis on flavor, I've found, over the years, that a little fat can go a long way in making food taste great. Let's not forget that cooking isn't medicine. There's no sense making a no-fat dish that tastes that way and that no one likes or will eat again.

I've tried to keep the fat within current nutritional recommendations—that is, less than 10 to 15 grams fat for an entrée-size serving and less than 30 percent of the calories in the dish coming from fat. Below, you'll find a complete explanation of the numbers under the heading "Culinary Math."

One final bit of practical advice for the cook: Be organized. Read a recipe through from start to finish before you prepare it. Have all your ingredients out, measured, and prepped (chopped or whatever) before you start cooking. This will save you time in the long run and make cooking more enjoyable for you.

CULINARY MATH

The following numbers are given to help
interpret the nutritional analysis included with each recipe.

	Per day for a 120-pound person	Per day for a 170-pound person
Calories	1,800	2,550
Protein	Min. 44 g	Min. 62 g
Fat*	Max. 60 g	Max. 85 g
Carbohydrate	Min. 248 g	Min. 351 g
Sodium†	Max. 6,000 mg	Max. 6,000 mg
Cholesterol	Max. 300 mg	Max. 300 mg

*An easy way to limit fat consumption to the recommended 30 percent of calories is to divide your ideal weight in half. This number is an estimate of the allowed fat in grams per day for a moderately active person. The above values are given as a reference only, since calories needed to maintain ideal body weight vary from person to person.

†There is no general consensus for healthy people to reduce sodium below this moderate level.

Let me also say that cooking isn't brain surgery. Don't despair if you make a mistake. Most recipes are very forgiving. If you don't have or run short of a particular ingredient, chances are that somewhere in your kitchen there's a satisfactory substitute. Indeed, some of my best creations have resulted from a "mistake" in the kitchen.

A WORD ABOUT THE ITALIAN WAY OF EATING

Unlike most Italian cookbooks, this one is organized by types of dishes, not by the courses of an Italian meal. Like a piece of classical music, a traditional Italian meal comprises several movements: the antipasto (hors d'oeuvre), the pasta course, the *piatto primo* (first course, which might be seafood), the *piatto secondo* (second or main course), the *contorno* (vegetable course), the *formaggio* (cheese course), and the *dolci* (dessert). Few Italians, much less North Americans, have the time for such a substantial dining experience on a daily basis, although a typical Italian meal would include three or four of these courses.

By organizing the book by category of dishes, I've tried to make it easy to create the Italian meal that best suits the available time (both in the kitchen and at the table) and the occasion.

A NOTE ABOUT INGREDIENTS

Italian cooking is above all a cuisine based on good raw materials. The preparations are usually quite simple. The ingredients in a particular dish are often relatively few. But what makes Italian cooking so successful and irresistible is the fanatic attention Italians pay to quality when growing, producing, or buying ingredients. Garden-grown vegetables. Day-boat-fresh seafood. Hams that hang exposed to mountain breezes for six months. Cheese patiently aged for two to three years.

Truly top-notch Italian ingredients may cost a little more than mass-produced supermarket products and may require a special trip to an Italian market or gourmet shop (or use of the mail-order guide on page 248). The good news is that if you take the pains to ferret out top-quality ingredients, it's virtually impossible *not* to make great-tasting Italian food.

Here's a guide to some of the ingredients used in this book:

ANCHOVIES: These tiny cured fish can be thought of as the marine version of prosciutto. Its salty tang enlivens everything from pasta dishes to stuffings. Added judiciously, anchovies taste not in the least bit fishy. (Indeed, I've served them to people with a professed dislike for anchovies, only to be told that the particular dish is delicious.) Anchovies come in two forms: oil-packed or salt-packed. The former are readily available at the supermarket; the latter require a trip to an Italian market. To ready oil-packed anchovies for cooking, rinse them under warm water and blot dry. To ready salt-packed anchovies, rinse them in several changes of water. Whenever possible, buy an imported Italian brand. The best anchovies I have ever tasted are the olive oil–packed anchovies from Agostino Recca (available from Grand Bazaar —see mail-order sources, page 248).

ARBORIO RICE: This starchy, pearl-colored, short-grained rice from the Po Valley is the traditional grain for risotto. Arborio rice has a unique ability to absorb up to five times its volume in liquid without becoming mushy. As it cooks, the rice starches thicken the broth into a smooth, creamy sauce. Thanks to its newfound celebrity, you can buy arborio rice in virtually any supermarket. Look for the word *superfino* on the label: this signifies extra-large grains of rice. Good brands include Beretta and Amore. In a pinch, you can use the short-grain Valencia-style rice sold at Hispanic markets.

ARUGULA: A flavorful green in the radish family with a distinctive peppery bite. Once available only in Italian markets and specialty greengrocers, arugula can today be found at most supermarkets.

BALSAMIC VINEGAR: A thick, sweet, intensely flavored vinegar from the Emilia-Romagna province in north-central Italy. Unlike most vinegar, balsamic vinegar is made not from wine but from must (fresh or partially fermented grape juice). This gives it a fruity sweetness beloved by cooks on both sides of the Atlantic. The best balsamic vinegar comes from the town of Modena in the Reggio-Emilia district, where it is aged in a succession of fruitwood casks in farmhouse attics for years—sometimes for decades. The term *tradizionale* refers to a vinegar made this way and aged in wood for at least twelve years. Expect to pay dearly for it: up to $20 an ounce! Needless to say, you don't pour *tradizionale* into everyday salad dressings. (A few drops on a dish of strawberries is a more traditional use.) Vinegar companies in Modena make a respectable "industrial-grade" balsamic vinegar aged for three years that's fine for everyday use. One excellent brand of commercial balsamic vinegar is Cavalli. Recently, white balsamic vinegar has begun to turn up at Italian markets and gourmet shops. Its chief advantage is keeping dressings clear and white.

BEANS: Italians love beans and legumes. (Indeed, four of the most prominent ancient Roman families were said to be named for them: Piso for the pea, Lentulus for the lentil, Fabius for the fava bean, and Cicero for the chickpea.) Among the beans most beloved by Italians are *favas*, large pale-green or green-brown, broad, fleshy beans that are much sweeter than lima beans, which are often suggested as a North American substitute. *Cannellini* are white kidney beans. *Fagioli* (the generic term for beans in Italian) often refers to a medium-sized white bean similar to the North American Great Northern bean. If you live near an Italian market, you may be able to find fresh beans. If not, dried beans are widely available. Canned beans are the most convenient, of course. Their chief drawback is that most brands tend to be quite high in sodium. Try to choose a low-sodium brand and rinse the beans well in a colander before using.

BREAD CRUMBS: Used widely for stuffings, toppings, and even as a thickener for pasta dishes. I like to make my own bread crumbs, following the instructions on page 247.

BROTH (*BRODO*): As readers of my past cookbooks know, broth is one of the cornerstones of my high-flavor, low-fat cooking. It's particularly useful for making low-fat pasta sauces. On pages 239, 240, and 241, you'll find recipes for quick, easy chicken, fish, and vegetable broths. Acceptable results can be obtained with canned stock (but don't tell anyone I say so): try to choose a brand with reduced sodium. Bottled clam broth makes an acceptable substitute for fish broth.

CHEESES: As a rule, the high fat content of cheese limits its use in high-flavor, low-fat cooking. When I do use cheese, I prefer to use just a little of a full-flavored real cheese rather than a lot of a low-fat or no-fat cheese. Fortunately, Italian cheeses fit the full-flavor profile perfectly. Besides, Parmigiano-Reggiano and Pecorino Romano are such an essential part of Italy's culinary landscape, it's hard to imagine Italian cooking without them. Warning: Imitation is the highest form of flattery. Because of the universal popularity of Italian cheeses, copies of the best-known varieties are made in North America and elsewhere. None has the flavor of the Italian original. Be sure to buy imported.

GORGONZOLA: This soft, creamy, green-veined cheese is Italy's version of Roquefort. And a splendid version it is. Made near Milan, Gorgonzola has a distinctive, locker-roomish aroma and a blissful, salty, tangy flavor. A little goes a long way.

MASCARPONE: Italy's answer to clotted cream, mascarpone is a key ingredient in tiramisù. Its flavor is quite mild—even bland—but its silky texture is inimitable. Low-fat cream cheese can sometimes be used as a substitute.

PARMIGIANO-REGGIANO: This, the world's most famous grating cheese, comes from the province of Emilia-Romagna in northern Italy. In order to bear the name Parmigiano-Reggiano, it must be made from partially skim milk in a strictly delineated region following time-honored methods and aged for at least eighteen months. Parmigiano-Reggiano is expensive, but no other grating cheese is as rich, sweet, mild, and delicious. Buy it in wedges and grate it freshly as you need it. Many cheese are called Parmesan, but only the real McCoy will have the words *Parmigiano-Reggiano* stamped into the rind. This is what you should buy. (By the way, the rind makes a delicious flavoring for soups.)

PECORINO ROMANO: Italy's other great grating cheese is made from sheep's milk, which gives it a distinctive, sharp, earthy flavor. The best Pecorino comes from the Lazio region around Rome and from the island of Sardinia. Here, too, there are lots of imitations. Look for the words *Pecorino Romano* stamped into the rind.

SARDO: Another firm, piquant sheep's-milk cheese from Sardinia that's good for grating and eating out of hand. Look for the words *Fiore Sardo*. Beware of "Sardos" made in countries other than Italy. They may not even contain sheep's milk.

EGGS: All eggs used in the recipes are large eggs.

FRESH HERBS: An essential ingredient in both Italian cuisine and high-flavor, low-fat cooking. Among the most popular herbs in the Italian kitchen are fresh basil, rosemary, sage, bay leaf, spearmint, and parsley. All are widely available at the supermarket. Store fresh herbs wrapped in a damp but not wet paper towel—in an unsealed plastic bag to keep the herbs crisp and fresh longer, up to a week. (The moisture in a sealed bag hastens rot.) See also *Parsley*.

MILK AND CREAM: In the first six books in this series, I used only skim milk for high-flavor, low-fat cooking. It does have its limitations in terms of richness and mouth feel. More recently I've taken to using 2 percent milk or even whole milk in preparations requiring a little extra richness—béchamel sauce, for example. I find I can achieve better-tasting dishes with acceptable levels of fat. As with the other dairy products called for in this book, choose the product that best suits your fat budget. Sometimes, I'll even use a little heavy cream. Two tablespoons divided among four people will not cause a heart attack.

FAT FREE HALF & HALF: No, I'm not on the Land O Lakes payroll. Having pioneered low-fat and no-fat sour cream, this Minnesota dairy company has come up with a useful low-fat version of "cream": fat free half & half, which makes terrific cream sauces and pasta dishes. The bad news is that it's only available in limited markets. If it's unavailable, use evaporated skim milk.

OLIVE OIL: Olive oil is the heart, soul, and very lifeblood of Italian cooking. Besides its wonderful flavor and broad culinary applications, it's believed to help boost levels of HDL (high-density lipoproteins—the so-called good cholesterol), while reducing levels of LDL (low-density lipoproteins—the "bad cholesterol").

Like fine wine, olive oil varies widely in color, aroma, and flavor from region to region, year to year, and producer to producer. At its best, it will be golden-green, complex, and aromatic, with an intense, penetrating flavor that is at once earthy and fruity. You'll have to experiment to find the brand you like best: some of my favorites include Colavita and Alessi for everyday use, Badia a Coltibuono (especially good for salad dressings and drizzling), and for special occasions, any Tuscan oil bearing the word *Laudemio* on the label (indicative of an elite band of Tuscan producers). There are, of course, many fine oils from other Mediterranean countries, not to mention California, often at highly favorable prices.

When using olive oil as a flavoring (drizzled over beans or vegetables, for example), you want to choose the best extra-virgin brand you can find. When using olive oil for cooking, a less expensive oil will do, as heat tends to denature the flavor. One technique I use often in high-flavor, low-fat Italian cooking is adding half the oil at the beginning of a recipe for cooking, and pouring on the remaining oil for flavor at the end.

Most of the olive oil sold in America today is extra-virgin. Technically speaking, this means that its acidity level (its oleic free-fatty-acid content) is 1 percent or less. Practically speaking, this means that extra-virgin olive oil is made with the choicest olives, which are pressed in a machine designed to minimize heat (which denatures the flavor of the oil).

Plain old "olive oil" (formerly called "pure olive

oil") is a highly refined oil that, for reasons of excess acidity or a poor flavor, can't be sold in its natural state. After refining, the oil must have less than 1.5 percent acidity. Often, the manufacturers add virgin oil to bolster the flavor. Compared with extra-virgin, regular olive oil seems bland—even tasteless—but it's less expensive and it does have the health benefits of all monounsaturated oils.

PANCETTA: Italian "bacon." Pork belly cured with salt and pepper in the style of prosciutto. Unlike American bacon, pancetta (pronounced "pan-CHAY-ta") isn't smoked. To remove some of the excess fat for high-flavor, low-fat cooking, I like to blanch the pancetta in boiling water before using it.

PARSLEY: Because it's so widely used in Italian cooking, parsley is listed separately from the other herbs. Italian parsley (also known as flat-leaf parsley) has a much more profound and robust flavor than curly-leaf parsley, with overtones of celery and even a hint of spinach. Store flat-leaf parsley wrapped in a damp paper towel in an unsealed plastic bag, as described above for the other fresh herbs.

PINE NUTS: Known as *pignolia* in Italian, the small, sweet nut of a type of pine tree is widely used as a flavoring and garnish and a texture-adding ingredient in stuffings. To intensify the flavor of pine nuts (indeed of any nuts), lightly roast them in a dry skillet over medium heat or on a pan in a moderate, 350-degree oven.

PORCINI: The porcino is the king of Italian mushrooms, enjoyed fresh when in season, dried throughout the year, in dishes as varied as salads, pastas, soups, stews, and risotto. Known as the boletus mushroom in English (*cèpe* in French), the porcino is a large, fleshy mushroom with a barrel-shaped stem and a thick, round, light-brown cap with pores instead of gills. The texture is soft yet satisfyingly chewy; the flavor is earthy and meaty. In short, porcini are everything you want a wild mushroom to be. Dried porcini have an intense, concentrated, smoky flavor. Italians use them like vegetable bouillon cubes. Fresh porcini are sporadically available at Italian markets and specialty greengrocers. Fall is the prime season, but you

can also find them in June. There's no substitute for a porcino's taste, but fresh shiitakes have a similar intensity of flavor and texture and are widely available in the United States.

RICOTTA: The soft, sweet, creamy, white curds we know as ricotta are actually a by-product of the cheesemaking process, made from whole, partially skimmed, or skim milk whey. If your fat budget allows it, use low-fat, not no-fat, ricotta—the flavor and consistency are vastly superior.

SPINACH: So popular is spinach in Italy, the term *Florentine* refers to a garnish of spinach. For the best results, use young leaf spinach, which is sold in bunches of small, flat leaves. Cellopack spinach and frozen spinach are acceptable for stuffings.

TRUFFLES: The ancients believed truffles grew where lightning struck the earth. Today, we know that the aromatic fungus grows beneath oak and chestnut trees, but we're still figuring out how to cultivate it. There are many types of truffles in Italy, including summer truffles and black truffles, but the most famous is the white truffle from Piedmont. Actually more a beige or light brown in color, white truffles have a powerful earthy, cheesy, musty aroma (with a whiff of model-airplane glue thrown in) that endears them to epicures the world over. Fresh white truffles are in season September to December and can be purchased at Italian markets, gourmet shops, and via mail (see the mail-order guide on page 248). They should be intensely fragrant. The way to use a fresh truffle is to slice it paper-thin over pasta, risotto, or carpaccio. White truffles are rarely, if ever, cooked. Store white truffles in a jar of arborio rice until you're ready to use them (this keeps them dry and gives the rice a great aroma).

The simplicity and directness of Italian cooking are a marvelous help for today's frenzied lifestyle. As I set about testing the recipes in this book, I noticed that they are the quickest and easiest to prepare in the whole high-flavor, low-fat series. The vast majority can be prepared *and* cooked in less than thirty minutes. How appropriate that as we look to a new century and have less time than ever before, *High-Flavor, Low-Fat Italian Cooking* offers hundreds of great-tasting dishes that can be made in a matter of minutes.

Here, then, is an Italian cookbook that will help you eat more healthfully without sacrificing the flavors you have come to love in Italian cooking.

Unconventional? Sometimes. Authentic? In spirit, if not to the letter. I hope you enjoy cooking the recipes as much as I enjoyed creating them. Have a question or a comment? Feel free to E-mail me at 102333.1603@compuserve.com.

Buon appetito!

STEVEN RAICHLEN

COLD ANTIPASTI

CROSTINI WITH TOPPINGS

Crostini are the Italian equivalent of toast points. I like to brush or spray them with a little oil before baking, but you could certainly bake them dry. Crostini should be audibly crisp once they've emerged from the oven and cooled. Bruschetta is the cousin of crostini: a slice of bread that is grilled and drizzled with olive oil, not baked.

PREPARATION TIME: 10 MINUTES   COOKING TIME: 20 TO 30 MINUTES

1 Italian- or French-style baguette

1 tablespoon extra-virgin olive oil (or a can of spray olive oil)

1. Preheat the oven to 400°F. Cut the bread on the diagonal into ½-inch-thick slices. (If you prefer thinner crostini, cut into ¼-inch-thick slices.) Lightly brush or spray the bread slices with oil on both sides and arrange on a nonstick baking sheet.

2. Bake the crostini until crisp and golden brown, 8 to 12 minutes per side. Take care that they don't burn. Transfer the crostini to a wire rack to cool. Serve with one of the following toppings (see Yellow Tomato and Arugula Topping, Sardinian "Salsa," and Tuscan Mushroom Liver Pâté).

Makes 30 to 36 crostini, enough to serve 6 to 10

145 CALORIES PER SERVING;* 5 G PROTEIN; 3 G FAT; 23 G CARBOHYDRATE; 308 MG SODIUM; 0 MG CHOLESTEROL

*Analysis is based on 6 servings.

Crostini with Toppings

YELLOW TOMATO AND ARUGULA TOPPING

The Italian word for tomato is pomodoro, *literally "golden apple." The first tomatoes imported to Italy (or at least grown there) were probably a small yellow ancestor of the modern red tomato. That set me thinking about a gold-and-green topping made with yellow tomatoes and arugula. Yellow tomatoes can be found at gourmet shops, specialty greengrocers, and an increasing number of supermarkets.*

PREPARATION TIME: 10 MINUTES

3 ripe yellow tomatoes (enough to make about 2 cups diced) or 1½ pints yellow cherry tomatoes
1 bunch arugula, washed and stemmed (see box on page 43)

2 to 3 tablespoons minced red onion
1½ tablespoons balsamic vinegar
1 tablespoon extra-virgin olive oil
salt and freshly ground black pepper

1. If using large tomatoes, cut into ¼-inch dice, reserving the juices. If using cherry tomatoes, cut each in half lengthwise. Cut the arugula widthwise into ¼-inch slivers.

2. Not more than 20 minutes before serving, combine all the ingredients for the topping, adding enough strained tomato liquid to make a mixture that is moist but not wet. Correct the seasoning, adding vinegar or salt to taste.

Makes about 2¼ cups, enough for 1 recipe of crostini

40 CALORIES PER SERVING;* 0.7 G PROTEIN; 2.4 G FAT; 4 G CARBOHYDRATE; 7 MG SODIUM; 0 MG CHOLESTEROL

Analysis is based on 6 servings.

SARDINIAN "SALSA"

This fresh tomato topping makes me think of salsa. For a Sardinian touch, each crostino is topped with a shaving of Pecorino, the island's famous grating cheese, a firm, tangy sheeps'-milk cheese. Use a vegetable peeler to shave off broad, thin strips of cheese.

PREPARATION TIME: 10 MINUTES

3 ripe red tomatoes, cut into ¼-inch dice
6 pitted black olives, finely chopped
1 green onion or 3 scallions, finely chopped
3 tablespoons chopped flat-leaf parsley
2 anchovy fillets, finely chopped (optional)

1 tablespoon drained capers
1½ tablespoons balsamic vinegar, or to taste
1½ tablespoons extra-virgin olive oil
salt and freshly ground black pepper
a 1-ounce chunk of Pecorino cheese

1. Not more than 20 minutes before serving, combine the tomatoes, olives, scallions, parsley, anchovies, capers, vinegar, oil, salt, and pepper in a mixing bowl and gently toss to mix. Correct the seasoning, adding vinegar or salt to taste.

2. Mound the "salsa" on the crostini. Using a vegetable peeler, shave a thin slice of Pecorino on top of each crostini. *Makes about 2¼ cups, enough for 1 recipe of crostini*

70 CALORIES PER SERVING;* 2 G PROTEIN; 5 G FAT; 4 G CARBOHYDRATE; 174 MG SODIUM; 3 MG CHOLESTEROL

Analysis is based on 6 servings (without anchovy).

TUSCAN MUSHROOM LIVER PÂTÉ

The traditional topping for crostini in Tuscany is liver pâté. Liver is hardly what you'd call a low-fat or low-cholesterol ingredient. (Indeed, few foods could be worse in this respect.) My low-fat remake uses roasted mushrooms as the base of the pâté, with a little liver—just enough—for flavor. I think you'll be amazed at how "livery" this pâté actually tastes.

PREPARATION TIME: 15 MINUTES   COOKING TIME: 20 MINUTES

12 ounces portobello or button mushrooms,
    trimmed and quartered
½ medium onion, peeled and quartered
2 cloves garlic, peeled
1 tablespoon extra-virgin olive oil
salt and freshly ground black pepper

2 to 4 ounces chicken livers (from two birds),
    trimmed, rinsed and blotted dry
2 tablespoons finely chopped flat-leaf parsley
1 tablespoon brandy or to taste
1 to 2 tablespoons dried bread crumbs, as needed

1. Preheat the oven to 450°F. Place the mushrooms, onion, and garlic in a nonstick roasting pan. Toss with olive oil, salt, and pepper. Roast the mushrooms until beginning to brown, 5 to 10 minutes, stirring to ensure even cooking.

2. Add the livers and continue roasting until the mushrooms are well browned and flavorful and the liver is cooked but still pink in the center, 5 to 10 minutes more.

3. Purée the mushroom-and-liver mixture in a food processor, adding the parsley, brandy, and salt and pepper to taste. If the mixture seems watery, add a tablespoon or two of bread crumbs.

Makes 2 cups, enough for 1 recipe of crostini

60 CALORIES PER SERVING;* 5 G PROTEIN; 3 G FAT; 0.5 G SATURATED FAT; 5 G CARBOHYDRATE; 15 MG SODIUM; 35 MG CHOLESTEROL

Analysis is based on 6 servings.

OSTUNI CHICKPEA DIP

Ostuni is one of the most picturesque towns in southern Italy, a hilltop citadel with whitewashed stone homes and labyrinthine alleyways that recall the villages of the Greek islands. Food writers often depend on the kindness of strangers, and this particular night, a local physician who had done his residency in Boston invited our party to a restaurant we'd surely never have found on our own, as it possessed no sign or outward markings on the street. The meal opened with a tangy dip made with a local cheese called ricotta forte *("strong ricotta") that reminded me of feta. As feta is more readily available than* ricotta forte, *I call for it in this recipe. If you can find* ricotta forte, *all the better.*

PREPARATION TIME: 10 MINUTES

FOR THE DIP:
1½ cups cooked chickpeas (1 15-ounce can, drained and rinsed)
1 tomato, peeled and diced (with juices)
1 to 2 cloves garlic, minced
1 to 2 ounces feta cheese, crumbled, with 1 to 2 tablespoons brine
1½ tablespoons fresh lemon juice, or to taste

1 tablespoon extra-virgin olive oil, or to taste
salt and freshly ground black pepper
1 to 3 tablespoons Basic Vegetable Broth (page 241), chickpea cooking liquid, or water (optional)

crostini (page 1) for serving

Combine the chickpeas, tomato, garlic, and feta in a food processor and purée to a smooth paste. Still using the food processor, work in the lemon juice, olive oil, salt and pepper to taste. If the dip seems too thick, thin it with a little vegetable broth. Serve with crostini or bruschette.

Makes 1½ cups, enough to serve 6 to 8

96 CALORIES PER SERVING;* 4 G PROTEIN; 4 G FAT; 1 G SATURATED FAT; 12 G CARBOHYDRATE; 44 MG SODIUM; 3 MG CHOLESTEROL

*Analysis is based on 8 servings.

ROASTED VEGETABLE CAPONATA (EGGPLANT SALAD)

Most cultures have some sort of eggplant dip; consider Russian eggplant caviar or Middle Eastern baba ganooj. The Sicilian version, called caponata, is a cross between a salad and a spread. Traditionally, the vegetables would be sautéed in oceans of oil. My high-flavor, low-fat version calls for them to be roasted in a hot oven. Caponota can be served by itself as an antipasto, salad, or side dish. It would be delicious as a topping for the crostini on page 1. You may be surprised to find one ingredient here: a pinch of cocoa powder. Bitter, unsweetened chocolate has a curious way of bringing out a vegetable's sweetness.

PREPARATION TIME: 20 MINUTES   COOKING TIME: 1 HOUR

2 eggplants (about 1½ pounds)
5 cloves garlic, peeled
2 tomatoes, quartered
2 stalks celery, washed, trimmed, and cut into
    1-inch pieces
1 onion, peeled and cut into quarters
1 green bell pepper, cored, seeded, and cut into
    1-inch pieces
2 tablespoons olive oil
salt and freshly ground black pepper

TO FINISH THE CAPONATA:
3 tablespoons chopped flat-leaf parsley
2 tablespoons drained capers
1 tablespoon toasted pine nuts
8 pitted black olives, coarsely chopped
1 to 2 tablespoons balsamic vinegar
½ teaspoon unsweetened cocoa powder

1. Preheat the oven to 450°F. Prick the eggplant in several places with a fork. Place it on one side of a nonstick baking sheet. Combine the garlic, tomatoes, celery, onion, and bell pepper on the other side of the baking sheet and toss with 1 tablespoon of the olive oil, the salt and the pepper.

2. Roast the eggplant and vegetables until the former is very soft to the touch and the latter are tender and browned, 30 to 40 minutes. Stir the vegetables from time to time to ensure even cooking. If one becomes browned before the others are ready, transfer it with a slotted spoon to a platter. Transfer the vegetables with their juices to a platter to cool.

3. Cut the eggplants in half lengthwise and scrape out the flesh. Finely chop the eggplant and vegetables by hand or coarsely purée in a food processor. Stir in the parsley, capers, pine nuts, olives, vinegar, cocoa powder, remaining 1 tablespoon olive oil, and salt and pepper to taste. Toss well to mix. Correct the seasoning, adding salt or vinegar to taste: the caponata should be highly seasoned. (Eggplant is naturally bland, so you'll need a fair amount of seasoning.) Caponata will keep for several days. Just be sure to reseason it before serving.

Makes 3 to 4 cups, enough to serve 6 to 8

116 CALORIES PER SERVING;* 3 G PROTEIN; 7 G FAT; 1 G SATURATED FAT; 15 G CARBOHYDRATE; 152 MG SODIUM; 0 MG CHOLESTEROL

Analysis is based on 6 servings.

MELON, MINT, AND PROSCIUTTO

It's hard to imagine an appetizer that improves on melon with prosciutto. The following recipe retains the wonderful contrast of flavors and textures (sweet and salty, moist and dry), while reducing the overall ratio of ham to melon, so as not to tip the scales with fat grams. You could use almost any type of melon, as long as it's ripe. I like the color contrast provided by honeydew, but you can't go wrong with other old standbys, like cantaloupe or Cranshaw. To make an easy-to-eat finger food, serve the melon balls on toothpicks.

PREPARATION TIME: 20 MINUTES

1 very ripe melon
1 bunch mint, washed and stemmed

**1½ ounces very thinly sliced prosciutto, cut into
 1-inch squares**

Halve and seed the melon and cut it into 1-inch balls with a melon baller. Make a slit in each melon ball going halfway through to the bottom. Insert a mint leaf and a square of prosciutto in each melon ball.

Makes about 30 pieces, enough to serve 6

78 CALORIES PER SERVING; 3 G PROTEIN; 1 G FAT; 0.5 G SATURATED FAT; 16 G CARBOHYDRATE; 150 MG SODIUM; 6 MG CHOLESTEROL

TUNA CARPACCIO

Did you ever wonder how restaurants slice tuna carpaccio so marvelously thin? You may be surprised to learn that the secret isn't a razor-sharp knife. Nor is it partially freezing the tuna before slicing. Rather, the trick is to pound the slices between sheets of plastic wrap. You'll want to use sushi-quality tuna for this recipe, the sort you buy from a fishmonger or Japanese market. Salmon carpaccio would be made the same way.

PREPARATION TIME: 15 MINUTES

8 ounces fresh tuna
1 to 2 tablespoons fresh lemon juice (or to taste),
   plus 4 lemon wedges for garnish
1 tablespoon extra-virgin olive oil
salt and freshly ground black pepper

¼ red onion, minced (about 2 tablespoons)
1 tablespoon drained capers
1 tablespoon finely chopped fresh chives
1 tablespoon finely chopped flat-leaf parsley

1. Slice the fish across the grain as thinly as possible. If using a tuna steak, you may wish to cut it in half before slicing. Place the slices between 2 sheets of plastic wrap and gently flatten with the side of a meat cleaver to obtain paper-thin slices. Use these slices to carpet 4 dinner plates. (The easiest way to transfer the fish is to peel off one sheet of plastic wrap, invert the fish onto the plate, and peel off the second sheet of plastic wrap.)

2. Drizzle the lemon juice and olive oil over the fish and season with salt and pepper. Sprinkle the onion, capers, chives, and parsley on top. Gently pat the fish with your fingertips to work in the flavorings. Garnish each plate with lemon wedges and serve at once.

Serves 4

93 CALORIES PER SERVING; 13 G PROTEIN; 4 G FAT; 0.6 G SATURATED FAT; 1 G CARBOHYDRATE; 100 MG SODIUM; 25 MG CHOLESTEROL

VEAL CARPACCIO WITH WHITE TRUFFLES

This carpaccio, actually more a veal tartare, is a specialty of the restaurant Il Vicoletto in the city of Alba in Piedmont. Alba, of course, is the capital of Italy's white-truffle trade, and if you're lucky enough to be there during truffle season (October to January), you can order your carpaccio topped with paper-thin slices of white truffle. In this country, white truffles can be purchased at gourmet shops and Italian markets or ordered by mail from companies like Harvest Imports, Inc. (See mail-order sources, page 248.) Alternatively, you can sprinkle a few drops of truffle oil (also available at gourmet shops) on top of each. But even if you can't find fresh white truffles, this tangy carpaccio makes a delectably different antipasto. Buy the veal at a quality butcher shop that prizes freshness.

PREPARATION TIME: 15 MINUTES

1 pound veal loin or tenderloin, meticulously
    trimmed of all fat and sinew
1 to 2 anchovy fillets, rinsed, blotted dry, and
    finely chopped
1 large shallot or ¼ red onion, minced
    (about 3 tablespoons)
½ clove garlic, minced

1 to 2 tablespoons fresh lemon juice, or to taste
1½ tablespoons extra-virgin olive oil
salt and freshly ground black pepper
1 bunch arugula, stemmed, washed, and dried
    (see box on page 43)
¼ to ½ ounce fresh white truffle or ½ teaspoon
    truffle oil crostini (see page 1) or toast points

1. Finely chop the veal by hand using a cleaver or a sharp chopping knife. Hand chopping produces a much more pleasing texture than the food processor. Transfer the veal to a mixing bowl and stir in the anchovies, shallot, garlic, and lemon juice. Add half the olive oil and salt and pepper to taste.

2. Line 4 salad plates with arugula leaves and mound the veal mixture in the center. Drizzle the remaining olive oil over the veal and arugula. Season with more salt and pepper. If using fresh truffle, shave it as thinly as possible over the veal, using a truffle shaver (see Note). If using truffle oil, sprinkle a few drops on top. Serve the crostini or toast points on the side.

Note: White truffles taste best when sliced tissue-thin. The best way to do this is with a truffle shaver, a sort of hand-held mandoline with an adjustable blade that enables you to cut slices thin enough to read through. When you dine at a good restaurant in Alba during truffle season, you often find a truffle on a plate on your table. The waiter weighs the truffle before and after slicing. Guests are charged according to the amount of truffle used. Unlike black truffles, white are almost never cooked.

Serves 4

205 CALORIES PER SERVING; 23 G PROTEIN; 11 G FAT; 3 G SATURATED FAT; 2 G CARBOHYDRATE; 122 MG SODIUM; 90 MG CHOLESTEROL

SWEET AND SOUR ROASTED PEPPERS

Roasted peppers are such a part of Italy's culinary landscape, it's hard to imagine an antipasto spread without them. This recipe features one of my favorite techniques for high-flavor, low-fat cooking: high-heat roasting. The process is easier and cleaner than grilling peppers, but you still get the sweet, smoky flavor that comes from charring the pepper skins and caramelizing the natural sugars in the peppers.

PREPARATION TIME: 15 MINUTES   COOKING TIME: 20 MINUTES

2 red bell peppers
2 yellow bell peppers
2 green bell peppers
1½ tablespoons extra-virgin olive oil

2 sprigs fresh thyme or ½ teaspoon dried
salt and freshly ground black pepper
⅓ cup balsamic vinegar
1 to 2 tablespoons honey

1. Preheat the oven to 450°F. Cut the pepper flesh off the core and seeds. To do so, make four broad cuts from the top of the pepper to the bottom, one on each side. (The core and scraps can be saved for the Basic Vegetable Broth on page 241.) Cut each side in half lengthwise to obtain strips that are 3 inches long and 1 inch wide.

2. Place the peppers in a nonstick roasting pan and toss with 2 teaspoons of the olive oil, the thyme, salt, and pepper. Roast the peppers in the oven until nicely browned, 10 to 15 minutes, gently stirring from time to time to prevent burning. Remove the pan from the oven and let the peppers cool.

3. Prepare the sauce: Boil the balsamic vinegar until reduced by half. Whisk in the honey, the re-maining olive oil, any pepper juices that have accumulated in the roasting pan, and salt and pepper to taste. Cook for 1 minute. Correct the seasoning, adding salt or honey to taste.

4. To serve, arrange the peppers on a platter in rows or circles, with the pieces overlapping to create a colorful design. Spoon the sauce over the peppers and serve. The recipe can be prepared several hours ahead to this stage.

Note: You can make a virtually fat-free version of this dish by tossing the peppers with 1 teaspoon olive oil before roasting and omitting the remaining olive oil from the sauce.

Serves 6 to 8

104 CALORIES PER SERVING;* 2 G PROTEIN; 4 G FAT; 0.5 G SATURATED FAT; 18 G CARBOHYDRATE; 4 MG SODIUM; 0 MG CHOLESTEROL

Analysis is based on 6 servings.

STUFFED PEPPERS

Stuffed peppers are a perfect antipasto for a harried cook, requiring mere minutes to assemble. They can and should be made ahead of time. The stuffings are limited only to your imagination. I like to use small red bell peppers (about 3 inches long), which I cut in thirds, but you can also use the more widely available full-size peppers.

PREPARATION TIME: 15 MINUTES   COOKING TIME: 30 MINUTES

4 small red bell peppers or 3 large bell peppers
12 basil leaves
1 small onion, cut into 12 wedges
1 small tomato, cut into 12 wedges
2 cloves garlic, thinly sliced
1 tablespoon drained capers
salt and freshly ground black pepper

OPTIONAL GARNISH (CHOOSE ONE
OR MORE OF THE FOLLOWING):
    12 anchovy fillets, rinsed and drained
    12 pitted black olives
    12 thin shavings Pecorino Romano cheese
1 tablespoon extra-virgin olive oil

1. Preheat the oven to 400°F. Cut the stems out of the peppers. Cut small peppers lengthwise in thirds, large peppers in quarters. Remove the seeds and pith. Arrange the pepper pieces, skin side down, in a lightly oiled baking dish.

2. Place a basil leaf, an onion wedge, a tomato wedge, a slice of garlic, and a few capers in the hollow part of each pepper slice. Season with salt and pepper. Place one of the garnishes on top and drizzle the peppers with a little oil.

3. Roast the peppers until tender and lightly singed at the edges, 20 to 30 minutes. Let cool to room temperature before serving. Reseason with salt and pepper, if needed, and serve at once.

Makes 12 pieces, enough to serve 4 to 6

126 CALORIES PER SERVING;* 4 G PROTEIN; 4 G FAT; 0.5 G SATURATED FAT; 22 G CARBOHYDRATE; 82 MG SODIUM; 0 MG CHOLESTEROL

Analysis is based on 4 servings.

Hot Antipasti

Chicken, Prosciutto, and Sage Spedini

Spedini are Italian kebabs. Large ones are sold ready-made at Italian butcher shops, ready for home barbecues. Small ones make a great antipasto. Here's a bite-size spedini inspired by the classic Roman dish saltimbocca. Veal or pork spedini would be made the same way—you just substitute meat for the chicken.

PREPARATION TIME: 20 MINUTES   COOKING TIME: 6 TO 8 MINUTES

1 pound boneless, skinless chicken breasts
12 pearl onions, unpeeled
salt
2 very thin slices prosciutto, cut into ½-inch strips
1 bunch sage leaves, stemmed
12 stiff sprigs fresh rosemary or bamboo skewers,
    each about 5 inches long
freshly ground black pepper

FOR BASTING:
1 tablespoon extra-virgin olive oil
1 teaspoon grated lemon zest

1. Trim any fat or sinew off the chicken breasts and cut each half breast lengthwise into finger-thick strips. (Each strip should be about 4 inches long and ½ inch wide.)

2. Place the onions in a saucepan in cold salted water to cover. Bring to a boil. Cook the onions until just tender, about 5 minutes. Drain well, refresh under cold water, and drain again. Peel the onions.

3. Assemble the spedini: Place a strip of prosciutto and a sage leaf on top of each strip of chicken. Skewer the chicken on the rosemary sprig, curving it into an S shape as pictured on page 12. Skewer an onion on the end. If the rosemary sprigs are too flexible for skewering, make holes in the chicken with a

bamboo skewer, then insert the rosemary. (It helps to strip the leaves off the bottom 2 inches of each rosemary sprig.) Season the spedini with salt and pepper. The recipe can be prepared several hours ahead to this stage.

4. Just before serving, preheat the grill or broiler to high. Combine the oil and lemon zest in a small bowl and stir to mix. Brush the spedini with the lemon oil and grill or broil until the chicken is cooked, 2 to 3 minutes per side. Baste with the lemon oil as the spedini cook.

Makes 12 spedini, enough to serve 6 as an appetizer, 4 as an entrée

63 CALORIES PER 1 PIECE SPEDINI; 9 G PROTEIN; 2 G FAT; 0.5 G SATURATED FAT; 1 G CARBOHYDRATE; 65 MG SODIUM; 23 MG CHOLESTEROL

Spedini

SHRIMP SPEDINI WITH BASIL AND PEPPERS

These shrimp spedini are packed with flavor, thanks to their skewers—sprigs of fresh rosemary. You'll need fairly stiff rosemary branches: the sort you find on a small rosemary bush at a plant shop. (Besides, this is a more economical way to buy rosemary than in the plastic bags in the supermarket produce section. It helps to strip the leaves off the bottom 2 inches of each rosemary sprig.) Scallops could be prepared the same way.

PREPARATION TIME: 20 MINUTES   COOKING TIME: 6 TO 8 MINUTES

24 large shrimp, peeled and deveined
1 tablespoon fresh lemon juice
1 tablespoon extra-virgin olive oil
1 clove garlic, minced
1 red bell pepper, cut into 1-inch triangles

1 bunch fresh basil, washed and stemmed
1 yellow bell pepper, cut into 1-inch triangles
12 stiff sprigs fresh rosemary, each about 5 inches long
salt and freshly ground black pepper

1. Combine the shrimp, lemon juice, olive oil, and garlic in a glass bowl and toss to mix. Marinate for 15 minutes.

2. Skewer the shrimp on the rosemary sprigs, placing 2 shrimps head to head on each skewer, as pictured on page 12. Place a red pepper triangle on one end, a fresh basil leaf and a yellow pepper triangle on the other. If the rosemary sprigs are too flexible for skewering, make holes in the shrimp with a bamboo skewer, then insert the rosemary.

3. Just before serving, preheat the grill or broiler to high. Generously season the shrimp with salt and pepper. Grill or broil the spedini until cooked, about 2 minutes per side. Baste with any excess marinade as the spedini cook.

Makes 12 spedini, enough to serve 4 to 6

33 CALORIES PER 1 PIECE SPEDINI; 3 G PROTEIN; 1 G FAT; 0.2 G SATURATED FAT; 3 G CARBOHYDRATE; 25 MG SODIUM; 22 MG CHOLESTEROL

BAKE-FRIED SAGE LEAVES

I first had fried sage leaves about fifteen years ago at a restaurant called Upstairs at the Pudding at the Hasty Pudding Club in Cambridge, Massachusetts. I never forgot the interplay of flavors and textures—even after I embraced high-flavor, low-fat cooking. I've come up with several versions of this recipe: one using a flour coating (the sage leaves will blister like potato chips), one with a bread-crumb coating (the leaves will become crisp like crackers). Sometimes, I'll press two leaves together, with a sliver of cheese or prosciutto in between. Bake-fried sage leaves make a great and unexpected antipasto, not to mention an interesting garnish for a main course.

PREPARATION TIME: 10 MINUTES   COOKING TIME: 10 TO 12 MINUTES

spray olive oil
1 bunch fresh sage leaves (choose the largest
    leaves you can find)
1 egg plus 2 whites, or ½ cup egg substitute,
    lightly beaten with a fork

salt and freshly ground black pepper
¾ cup fine toasted bread crumbs (preferably
    homemade; see page 247) or flour, in a
    shallow bowl

1. Preheat the oven to 400°F. Spray a nonstick baking sheet with spray olive oil. Using a pastry brush, brush the sage leaves on both sides with the egg mixture and season with salt and pepper. Dip each in bread crumbs or flour, turning to coat on all sides, shaking off the excess.

2. Arrange the sage leaves on the prepared baking sheet. Spray the tops of the leaves with oil and re-season with salt and pepper. Bake the sage leaves until crisp and nicely browned, 10 to 12 minutes. Serve at once.   *Makes 20 to 24 sage leaves,*
enough to serve 4 to 6 as an antipasto

23 CALORIES PER LEAF; 1 G PROTEIN; 0.5 G FAT; 0.1 G SATURATED FAT; 3 G CARBOHYDRATE; 44 MG SODIUM; 11 MG CHOLESTEROL

VARIATION: STUFFED SAGE LEAVES

To make a more substantial antipasto, cut 1 ounce smoked mozzarella, bel paese, or Italian fontina cheese into flat thin strips a little smaller than the sage leaves. Brush 2 sage leaves with egg mixture on both sides. Season with salt and pepper. Press the leaves together, sandwiching a strip of cheese between them. Dip the leaves in bread crumbs or flour, turning to coat on all sides, shaking off the excess. Spray with oil and bake as described above.

GRILLED PORTOBELLO MUSHROOMS WITH GARLIC AND SAGE

The Italian food revolution of the 1980s introduced many new ingredients to the American larder, including the portobello mushroom, a jumbo, dark-gilled cousin of Agaricus bisporus, the common white mushroom. Portobellos are great for grilling, thanks to their large size, and they acquire a smoky, meaty flavor when cooked over fire. The antipasto version of this dish calls for the portobellos to be cut into triangles and served at the end of bamboo skewers. I like to top them with strips of grilled red peppers. You can also serve the portobellos sliced into strips in salads or whole as a first course.

PREPARATION TIME: 15 MINUTES   COOKING TIME: 10 MINUTES

4 large portobello mushrooms (4 inches across)
4 cloves garlic, cut into slivers
4 sage leaves, cut widthwise into thin strips
1½ tablespoons extra-virgin olive oil

1 tablespoon balsamic vinegar or fresh lemon juice
salt and freshly ground black pepper
1 red bell pepper (optional)

1. Cut the stems off the mushrooms (reserve for stock). Using the tip of a paring knife, make 10 to 12 narrow slits in the top (rounded part) of each portobello. Insert a sliver of garlic and a strip of sage leaf into each slit. Combine the olive oil and vinegar in a mixing bowl and whisk in salt and pepper to taste. Add any leftover garlic or sage. Place the portobellos in a baking dish and brush or spoon the marinade over the mushrooms, turning to coat both sides. Let marinate for 1 hour.

2. Preheat the grill to medium-high. Grill the portobellos until nicely charred on the outside and cooked through, 3 to 4 minutes per side. (Start grilling with the rounded part down.) Brush the bell pepper, if using, with any leftover marinade and grill it until nicely charred, about 2 minutes per side. Transfer the vegetables to a plate to cool.

3. Cut the portobellos into bite-size wedges or triangles. Core and seed the pepper, if using, and cut into wedges, strips, or triangles smaller than the mushrooms. Place a piece of pepper on top of each portobello and impale with a small bamboo skewer.

Makes 24 to 32 pieces, enough to serve 8 to 12

47 CALORIES PER SERVING;* 2 G PROTEIN; 3 G FAT; 0.3 G SATURATED FAT; 3 G CARBOHYDRATE; 4 MG SODIUM; 0 MG CHOLESTEROL

Analysis is based on 8 servings.

STUFFED MUSSELS

No antipasto spread would be complete without stuffed shellfish. These mussels can be prepared ahead of time and are equally tasty served hot or at room temperature. There are a couple of options for cheese. For a sweeter stuffing, you could use Parmigiano-Reggiano. For a sharper stuffing, you could use Pecorino Romano. Or you could omit the cheese entirely.

PREPARATION TIME: 30 MINUTES   COOKING TIME: 20 MINUTES

2 pounds mussels
1 cup dry white wine
1 small onion, peeled and quartered

FOR THE STUFFING:
1½ tablespoons extra-virgin olive oil
3 to 4 shallots or 1 small onion, minced
   (about ¾ cup)

1 celery stalk, minced
2 cloves garlic, minced
1¼ cups fine dry bread crumbs
2 tablespoons finely chopped flat-leaf parsley
1 teaspoon finely grated lemon zest
2 tablespoons grated Parmigiano-Reggiano or
   Pecorino Romano cheese (optional)

1. Scrub the mussels, discarding any with cracked shells or shells that fail to close when tapped. Bring the wine and quartered onion to a boil in a large, heavy saucepan. Add the mussels and tightly cover the pot. Cook the mussels until the shells open wide, about 8 minutes, stirring once or twice to give the mussels on the bottom room to open. Transfer the cooked mussels to a colander to drain, discarding any that do not open. (Strain the broth through cheesecloth and set aside.) When the mussels are cool enough to handle, remove the top shell. Arrange the bottom shells with the mussels on a heatproof platter.

2. Prepare the stuffing: Heat half the olive oil in a nonstick frying pan. Add the shallots, celery, and garlic and cook over medium heat until just beginning to brown, about 5 minutes. Stir in the bread crumbs,

parsley, lemon zest, and cheese, if using. Add 6 to 8 tablespoons mussel liquid—enough to moisten the stuffing but not so much that it will make the stuffing soggy. (Save extra mussel liquid for one of the fish soups on pages 145–51.) Place a spoonful of stuffing in each mussel shell, smoothing the top with the back of a spoon. The recipe can be prepared ahead to this stage.

3. Preheat the oven to 400°F. or preheat the broiler. Bake the mussels until thoroughly heated and the top is lightly browned, about 15 minutes, or broil for 2 minutes. Just before serving, drizzle the remaining olive oil over the mussels or spray with spray oil.

*Makes 40 to 50 pieces, enough
to serve 6 to 8 as an appetizer*

42 CALORIES PER EACH OF 40 PIECES; 4 G PROTEIN; 1 G FAT; 0.1 G SATURATED FAT; 4 G CARBOHYDRATE; 95 MG SODIUM; 13 MG CHOLESTEROL

STUFFED CLAMS WITH PROSCIUTTO AND OREGANO

When I was growing up, stuffed clams—loaded with butter and bacon—were part of any self-respecting antipasto platter. Here's a low-fat version that uses prosciutto and fresh oregano for flavor, with a fraction of the fat found in the original. I like the delicacy of littleneck or cherrystone clams, but you could make the recipe with a dozen large clams.

PREPARATION TIME: 20 MINUTES   COOKING TIME: 30 MINUTES

24 littleneck or cherrystone clams
  (1½ to 2 inches across)
2 cups dry white wine
1 tablespoon extra-virgin olive oil, plus ½ to 1
  tablespoon for drizzling
1 medium onion, finely chopped
2 stalks celery, finely chopped
2 cloves garlic, minced

1 ounce prosciutto, minced
3 tablespoons finely chopped flat-leaf parsley
2 teaspoons chopped fresh oregano, plus 24 leaves
  or tiny sprigs for garnish
1¾ cups fresh bread crumbs, lightly toasted
1 teaspoon fresh lemon juice, or to taste
salt and freshly ground black pepper

1. Scrub the clams with a stiff brush under cold water to remove any grit or sand. Bring the wine to a boil in a large pot. Add the clams, tightly cover the pot, and cook over high heat until the shells just begin to open, 6 to 8 minutes. Transfer the clams with a slotted spoon to a plate to cool. Strain the broth (the cooking liquid) through cheesecloth or strainer lined with a paper towel and set aside 1½ cups. (Any excess can be saved for the Umbrian Clam "Chowder" on page 151.)

2. Remove the meat from the clamshells, reserving the bottoms of the shells. Finely chop the clam meat in a food processor or by hand, reserving the juices.

3. Heat the olive oil in a large nonstick frying pan. Cook the onion, celery, garlic, and prosciutto over medium heat until just beginning to brown,

about 5 minutes. Add the chopped clams, parsley, and chopped oregano and cook for 1 minute. Remove the pan from the heat.

4. Stir in the clams, the bread crumbs, and enough reserved broth to obtain a moist but not wet filling. Add lemon juice, salt, and pepper to taste: the mixture should be highly seasoned. Spoon the mixture into the clamshells, mounding it high in the center. The clams can be prepared ahead to this stage. Preheat the oven to 450°F. or preheat the broiler.

5. Drizzle a little of the ½ to 1 tablespoon olive oil over each clam. Bake or broil the clams until thoroughly heated and browned on top, about 15 minutes. Garnish each clam with an oregano sprig or leaf and serve at once.   *Makes 24 pieces*

37 CALORIES PER CLAM; 2 G PROTEIN; 1 G FAT; 0.2 G SATURATED FAT; 3 G CARBOHYDRATE; 48 MG SODIUM; 4 MG CHOLESTEROL

EGGPLANT CHIPS

"There's no such thing as a mistake in the kitchen, just a new dish waiting to be discovered." Such is the advice I give my cooking students, and while working on this book, I had occasion to follow it myself. I was experimenting with ways to make "crêpes" from thinly sliced vegetables. These chips were a failure in the sense that they proved impossible to roll. But they sure were tasty to munch by themselves. I like to serve them with the Neapolitan Tomato Sauce on page 60 as a dip.

PREPARATION TIME: 20 MINUTES   COOKING TIME: 15 MINUTES

1 medium eggplant (about 1 pound—try to choose a long, uniformly slender eggplant, rather than one that swells to a large bulb at one end)
coarse sea salt and freshly ground black pepper
spray olive oil or 1 tablespoon extra-virgin olive oil for brushing

1¾ cups all-purpose unbleached white flour
2 eggs plus 4 egg whites, lightly beaten with a fork
¾ cup fine cornmeal

1. Preheat the oven to 400°F. Cut the eggplant crosswise into the thinnest possible (not more than ⅛-inch) slices. The easiest way to do this is on a mandoline, but you can also do it by hand if you're careful. Season each slice on both sides with salt and pepper. Spray or brush 2 or 3 nonstick baking sheets with oil.

2. Place 1 cup of the flour in a shallow bowl. Place the egg mixture in a second shallow bowl. Combine the remaining ¾ cup flour and the cornmeal in a third bowl and whisk to mix. Dip each eggplant slice first in the flour mixture, shaking off the excess, then in the egg mixture, shaking off the excess, and finally in the cornmeal mixture, shaking off the excess. (Use a pair of tongs or forks for dipping to keep the breading mixture off your fingers.)

3. Arrange the eggplant slices on the prepared baking sheets. Spray or brush the tops of the slices with oil. Season again with salt and pepper. Place the eggplant in the oven and bake until the slices are crusty and dark golden brown, 6 to 8 minutes per side. They should almost look burnt. Transfer the chips to a wire rack to cool and become crisp. If desired, sprinkle with a little more salt before serving.

Makes 50 to 60 chips

122 CALORIES PER SERVING;* 5 G PROTEIN; 1 G FAT; 0.3 G SATURATED FAT; 22 G CARBOHYDRATE; 77 MG SODIUM; 35 MG CHOLESTEROL

Analysis is based on a serving of 4 chips.

STUFFED ZUCCHINI FLOWERS

Crisply fried squash or zucchini blossoms are one of the happiest harbingers of summer in Italy—enjoyed as an antipasto in May and June, when the zucchini crop flowers. I never expected to include a recipe for this tasty but oil-laden treat until I began experimenting with Bake-Fried Sage Leaves (see page 15). I discovered that audibly crisp and delectable crunchy zucchini flowers could be made by brushing the blossoms with beaten eggs and baking them with toasted bread crumbs.

PREPARATION TIME: 15 MINUTES   COOKING TIME: 10 TO 12 MINUTES

2 dozen zucchini or squash blossoms
1 ounce smoked mozzarella, Bel Paese, or
  Parmigiano-Reggiano cheese, cut into
  24 matchstick slivers
1 thin slice prosciutto, cut into 24 matchstick
  slivers
6 fresh basil or sage leaves, cut lengthwise into
  matchstick slivers (optional)

1 egg plus 2 whites, or ½ cup egg substitute,
  lightly beaten with a fork
salt and freshly ground black pepper
1 cup fine toasted bread crumbs (preferably
  homemade), in a shallow bowl (page 247)
spray olive oil

1. Preheat the oven to 400°F. Check the zucchini flowers to be sure they are free of bugs. Carefully insert a sliver of cheese, a sliver of prosciutto, and a sliver of basil, if using, in each flower. Using a pastry brush, brush the blossoms on both sides with the egg mixture and season with salt and pepper. Dip each in the bread crumbs, turning to coat on all sides, shaking off the excess.

2. Arrange the squash blossoms on a nonstick baking sheet sprayed with oil. Spray the tops of the blossoms with oil and reseason with salt and pepper. Bake the squash blossoms until crisp and nicely browned, 10 to 12 minutes. Serve at once.

*Makes 24 blossoms, enough to
serve 4 to 6 as an antipasto*

28 CALORIES PER BLOSSOM; 2 G PROTEIN; 0.8 G FAT; 0.3 G SATURATED FAT; 4 G CARBOHYDRATE; 67 MG SODIUM; 10 MG CHOLESTEROL

BAKE-FRIED SQUID

If squid has gone from being a geek food to a chic food, it is largely thanks to a single Italian dish: calamari fritti *(fried squid).*
My low-fat version uses a technique I call "bake-frying": the squid is breaded as it would be for frying, but is then
cooked in a hot oven rather than in oil. The Neapolitan Tomato Sauce on page 60 would make a
good dipping sauce. Instructions for cleaning squid are found in the box on page 158.

PREPARATION TIME: 15 MINUTES   COOKING TIME: 10 MINUTES

2 pounds cleaned squid
salt and freshly ground black pepper
1¾ cups all-purpose unbleached white flour

1 egg, plus 2 egg whites
¾ cup very fine white cornmeal
2 tablespoons extra-virgin olive oil or spray oil

1. Preheat the oven to 450°F. Cut the squid bodies widthwise into ¼-inch rings. Blot dry. Leave the tentacles whole. Season the squid with salt and pepper.

2. Place 1 cup of the flour in a shallow bowl and season with salt and pepper. Place the egg and whites in another bowl and beat well with a fork. Combine the remaining ¾ cup flour with the cornmeal in a third shallow bowl. Add salt and pepper and whisk to mix.

3. Use about ⅔ tablespoon of the oil to oil a large nonstick baking sheet. Dip each piece of squid first in flour, shaking off the excess, then in the egg mixture, and finally in the cornmeal, again shaking off the excess. Place the squid in a single layer on the baking sheet. Drizzle or spray the remaining oil on top.

4. Bake the squid until crisp and golden-brown, 8 to 10 minutes, turning with a spatula to ensure even browning. Serve at once. *Serves 6 to 8*

385 CALORIES PER SERVING;* 31 G PROTEIN; 8 G FAT; 2 G SATURATED FAT; 44 G CARBOHYDRATE; 101 MG SODIUM; 388 MG CHOLESTEROL

Analysis is based on 6 servings.

FRITTATAS, CUSTARDS, AND SAVORY TARTS

NOODLE FRITTATA

A frittata is a cross between an omelet and a Spanish tortilla (the egg dish, not the Mexican cornmeal flatbread). Like the former, it's started on the stove and the main ingredient is eggs; like the latter, it's finished in the oven and cut into wedges for serving. My low-fat version uses mostly egg whites, with a few whole eggs for richness. Egg substitute produces a fine frittata (after all, the main ingredient in egg substitute is egg whites), although the idea may be unsettling for a purist. Necessity may be the traditional mother of invention, but some of my best ideas come from leftovers. This colorful frittata was inspired by a bowl of leftover angel-hair pasta! The idea isn't as strange as it sounds: consider kugel (Jewish noodle pudding).

PREPARATION TIME: 20 MINUTES   COOKING TIME: 10 MINUTES

¼ pound angel-hair pasta
salt
1½ tablespoons extra-virgin olive oil
1 small onion, thinly sliced
1 clove garlic, minced
1 red bell pepper, cut into matchstick slivers
1 yellow bell pepper, cut into matchstick slivers
1 small zucchini, cored and cut into matchstick slivers

2 eggs plus 8 egg whites, or 12 egg whites, or 1½ cups egg substitute
3 tablespoons finely chopped flat-leaf parsley
3 to 4 tablespoons freshly grated Parmigiano-Reggiano cheese
freshly ground black pepper

1. Cook the pasta in 3 quarts rapidly boiling salted water until al dente, about 5 minutes. Drain in a colander, rinse under cold water, and drain again. Blot the pasta dry with a paper towel. Preheat broiler.

2. Heat half the olive oil in a 12-inch nonstick frying pan. Add the onion, garlic, red and yellow pepper, and zucchini and cook over medium heat until soft and translucent but not brown, about 4 minutes.

3. Lightly beat the eggs and whites in a large mixing bowl. Stir in the sautéed vegetables, parsley, cheese, and angel-hair. Add salt and pepper to taste: the mixture should be highly seasoned.

4. Heat the remaining olive oil in a 12-inch nonstick frying pan. Add the frittata mixture and cook over medium heat until the mixture is set on the bottom, 3 to 5 minutes. Place the frittata under the broiler and continue cooking until the frittata is set and the top is lightly browned, 2 to 4 minutes. Let the frittata cool for a few minutes. Using a spatula or thin flexible knife, loosen the frittata from the sides of the pan. Invert it onto a round platter and cut into wedges for serving. The frittata can be served either hot or at room temperature.

Serves 6 as an appetizer, 4 as a light entrée

180 CALORIES PER 4 APPETIZERS; 12 G PROTEIN; 7 G FAT; 2 G SATURATED FAT; 18 G CARBOHYDRATE; 162 MG SODIUM; 90 MG CHOLESTEROL

MARK MILITELLO'S VEGETABLE AND EGG-WHITE FRITTATA

Mark Militello is best known for his cutting-edge Floridian cuisine, but in many ways the Miami chef remains true to his Italian heritage. This egg-white frittata offers a colorful assortment of vegetables in a frittata entirely devoid of egg yolks. Feel free to vary the vegetables according to what's available and looks fresh.

PREPARATION TIME: 30 MINUTES   COOKING TIME: 10 TO 15 MINUTES

6 ounces slender asparagus, snapped (see step 2, page 35)
salt
1 yellow or red bell pepper, grilled or roasted
1 grilled or roasted portobello mushroom (4 inches across) or 4 grilled shiitakes

1½ tablespoons extra-virgin olive oil
2 roma (plum) tomatoes
12 egg whites, or 1½ cups egg substitute
8 fresh basil leaves, thinly slivered
1 clove garlic, minced (optional)
salt and freshly ground black pepper

1. Cut the asparagus into 3-inch lengths. Cook in 1 quart rapidly boiling salted water until tender, about 4 minutes. Drain in a colander, rinse under cold water, drain again, and blot dry.

2. Grill or roast the bell pepper. Core and seed it and cut the flesh into ¼-inch strips. Roast or grill the portobello, brushing with 1 teaspoon of the olive oil and seasoning with salt and pepper. Cut into ¼-inch strips. Peel, seed, and coarsely dice the tomatoes. Preheat the broiler.

3. Combine the egg whites, basil leaves, garlic, salt, and pepper in a mixing bowl and whisk just to mix. Stir in the vegetables. Correct the seasoning,

adding salt and pepper to taste. The mixture should be highly seasoned.

4. Heat the remaining olive oil in a large nonstick frying pan. Add the frittata mixture and cook over medium heat until the mixture is set on the bottom, 3 to 5 minutes. Place the frittata under the broiler and continue cooking until set and the top is lightly browned, 2 to 4 minutes. Let the frittata cool for 3 minutes. Using a spatula or thin flexible knife, loosen the frittata from sides of the pan. Invert it onto a round platter and cut into wedges for serving. This frittata is best served hot.

Serves 6 as an appetizer; 4 as a light entrée

94 CALORIES PER SERVING;* 9 G PROTEIN;* 4 G FAT; 0.5 G SATURATED FAT; 6 G CARBOHYDRATE; 116 MG SODIUM; 0 MG CHOLESTEROL

Analysis is based on 6 servings as an appetizer.

ROASTED SWEET POTATO AND GARLIC SFORMATO (CUSTARD)

Sformati (custards or timbales) are a popular primo piatto (first course) in Italy, and the flavorings are limited only to your imagination. This one owes rich flavor to the high-heat roasting of its main ingredients: garlic and sweet potatoes. As you've probably gathered by now, roasting is one of my favorite low-fat cooking methods: it evaporates the water in a vegetable, concentrating the flavor and caramelizing the natural sugars.

PREPARATION TIME: 20 MINUTES   COOKING TIME: 1 HOUR

spray oil
1½ pounds sweet potatoes (2 or 3 large)
1 medium head garlic
⅓ cup grated Parmigiano-Reggiano cheese
2 tablespoons chopped flat-leaf parsley

1 egg plus 2 egg whites, or ½ cup egg substitute
salt, freshly ground black pepper, and a little
    freshly grated nutmeg

8 ½-cup timbale molds or ramekins

1. Preheat the oven to 400°F. Spray the timbale molds or ramekins with oil and freeze. Place the sweet potatoes and garlic in a nonstick roasting pan. Roast until soft, about 20 minutes for the garlic, 40 to 60 minutes for the potatoes. Transfer the vegetables to a plate to cool. Peel the sweet potatoes with the help of a paring knife. Squeeze the roasted garlic out of the skins.

2. Combine the sweet potatoes, garlic, cheese, and parsley in a food processor and purée until smooth. While still using the food processor, work in the egg and egg whites. Add salt, pepper, and nutmeg to taste: the mixture should be highly seasoned.

3. Reduce the oven temperature to 350°F. Bring 3 cups water to a boil. Remove the timbale molds from the freezer and line the bottom of each mold with an oval of baking parchment or foil. Spray the mold again. (The freezing and double oiling helps prevent sticking.) Spoon the sweet potato mixture into the molds. Set the molds in a roasting pan with 1 inch boiling water.

4. Bake the timbales until set (an inserted skewer will come out clean), 20 to 30 minutes. (If the water in the roasting pan evaporates, add more.) Transfer the timbales to a wire rack and let cool for 3 minutes. Place a plate over each one, invert, and give the mold a little shake: the timbale should slide right out.

You don't really need a sauce, but if you'd like one, the Sugo di Pomodoro on page 59 would be a nice accompaniment.   *Serves 8*

103 CALORIES PER SERVING; 5 G PROTEIN; 2 G FAT; 1 G SATURATED FAT; 17 G CARBOHYDRATE; 108 MG SODIUM; 30 MG CHOLESTEROL

SPINACH OR SWISS CHARD SFORMATI

Puréed ricotta cheese gives these delicate spinach custards the lightness of soufflés. If your fat budget allows it, use low-fat, not no-fat, ricotta—the flavor will be richer. For the best results, use fresh bunch spinach (the sort sold in bunches, not the kind in the cello bag).

PREPARATION TIME: 20 MINUTES   COOKING TIME: 30 MINUTES

spray oil
1 pound fresh spinach or 1 10-ounce package
    frozen
salt
1 pound low-fat or no-fat ricotta cheese
1 clove garlic, minced
¼ cup freshly grated Parmigiano-Reggiano cheese
1 egg plus 4 whites, or 6 egg whites, or ¾ cup egg
    substitute

2 teaspoons fresh lemon juice
freshly ground black pepper
a pinch of freshly grated nutmeg

6 ½-cup timbale molds or ramekins
baking parchment or foil

1. Spray the timbale molds or ramekins with oil and freeze. If using fresh spinach, stem and wash it. Bring 1 cup salted water to a boil. Add the spinach and cook until tender and greatly reduced in volume, about 2 minutes. If using frozen spinach, cook it following the directions on the package. Drain the spinach in a colander, rinse under cold water, and drain again. Grab handfuls of spinach and squeeze tightly to wring out the excess water. Preheat the oven to 350°F.

2. Place the spinach, ricotta, garlic, and Parmesan in a food processor fitted with a chopping blade. Purée until very smooth, scraping down the sides of the processor bowl. Add the egg and whites, lemon juice, pepper, and nutmeg and salt to taste. Purée until smooth. Bring 3 cups water to a boil.

3. Remove the timbale molds from the freezer and line the bottom of each mold with an oval of baking

parchment or foil. Spray the mold again. (The freezing and double oiling helps prevent sticking.) Spoon the spinach mixture into the molds. Set the molds in a roasting pan with 1 inch boiling water.

4. Bake the timbales until set (an inserted skewer will come out clean), 20 to 30 minutes. (If the water in the roasting pan evaporates, add more.) Transfer the timbales to a wire rack and let cool for 5 minutes. Place a plate over each one, invert, and give the mold a little shake: the timbale should slide right out. As an accompaniment, you could serve the pumpkin sauce on page 77, the Sugo di Pomodoro on page 59, or the Fresh (Uncooked) Tomato Sauce on page 58.

Note: To make Swiss chard *sformati*, start with 1 pound trimmed Swiss chard leaves.

Serves 6

120 CALORIES PER SERVING; 14 G PROTEIN; 4 G FAT; 1 G SATURATED FAT; 7 G CARBOHYDRATE; 226 MG SODIUM; 49 MG CHOLESTEROL

SWISS CHARD TART

TORTA DI BIETE

Swiss chard isn't a particularly popular vegetable in North America. Italians use it with such enthusiasm, it perhaps should be called Italian chard, not Swiss. This handsome vegetable, with its broad, crinkly, reddish-green leaves, turns up in tarts (both savory and sweet), in fillings for ravioli and other pasta, and sautéed or steamed as a vegetable. Loaded with vitamins and minerals (especially iron, calcium, and vitamin C), it possesses a robust, earthy flavor that may remind you of beet greens. The following tart, which is popular in northern Italy, is a cousin of frittata. Roasting the onions and garlic enables you to slash the amount of oil in traditional recipes, saving the fat grams for the cheese.

PREPARATION TIME: 25 MINUTES   COOKING TIME: 40 MINUTES

2 medium onions, peeled and quartered
1 teaspoon extra-virgin olive oil
4 cloves garlic, in the skin
1 large bunch of Swiss chard (about 1½ pounds)
salt

spray oil
½ cup fine dry bread crumbs
½ cup freshly grated Parmigiano-Reggiano cheese
1 egg plus 2 egg whites, or ½ cup egg substitute
freshly ground black pepper

1. Preheat the oven to 400°F. Toss or brush the onion quarters with the olive oil. Place the onions and garlic in a nonstick roasting pan and roast until soft, about 20 minutes. Remove the pan from the oven and let cool. Squeeze the roasted garlic out of the skins.

2. Meanwhile, wash, stem, and thinly slice the chard (slice the leaves crosswise). Place the chard in a large pot with ¼ inch salted water. Cook over high heat until the chard has cooked down to a compact mass, about 3 minutes. Drain the chard and let cool. (You can save the cooking liquid for soups.) Squeeze the chard between your fingers to wring out all the liquid.

3. Spray the bottom and sides of a 7-inch spring-form pan (or 8-inch pie pan) with oil and sprinkle with 1 tablespoon bread crumbs.

4. Place the chard, onions, garlic, cheese, and remaining bread crumbs in a food processor and finely chop. Work in the eggs and egg whites. Correct the seasoning, adding salt and pepper to taste: the mixture should be highly seasoned. Spoon this mixture into the springform pan.

5. Bake the tart until set, about 20 minutes. Transfer the tart to a wire rack and let cool. Swiss chard tart is usually served at room temperature (although you can certainly serve it hot). If using a springform pan, remove the sides. If using a pie pan, invert the tart onto a plate. Cut into wedges for serving.

Serves 8

108 CALORIES PER SERVING; 7 G PROTEIN; 4 G FAT; 2 G SATURATED FAT; 13 G CARBOHYDRATE; 350 MG SODIUM; 32 MG CHOLESTEROL

TOMATO AND ONION TART

This explosively flavorful tart—a sort of tomato quiche—is part of a trio of savory pies served as a first course at the Ristorante Dorando in San Gimignano, Tuscany. The tomatoes are roasted in the oven to concentrate the flavor and evaporate some of the excess liquid. The tart makes a lovely appetizer or light entrée for brunch or lunch.

PREPARATION TIME: 30 MINUTES (EXCLUDING THE CRUST)   COOKING TIME: 40 MINUTES

1 prebaked Enlightened Tart Shell (page 29)
4 ripe tomatoes, stemmed and cut into ¼-inch
   slices
salt and freshly ground black pepper
1 tablespoon extra-virgin olive oil, plus a little oil
   for the baking sheets
1 large onion, finely chopped

¼ cup all-purpose unbleached white flour
2⅔ cups skim milk
6 egg whites, lightly beaten with a fork, or ¾ cup
   egg substitute
6 fresh basil leaves, slivered, plus sprigs of basil for
   garnish, or 3 tablespoons chopped fresh flat-leaf
   parsley

1. Preheat the oven to 400°F. Prepare the tart shell, following the recipe below. Season the tomato slices with salt and pepper and arrange them on a lightly oiled baking sheet (preferably nonstick). Bake the tomatoes until most of the liquid has evaporated, 15 to 20 minutes. Let the tomatoes cool on the baking sheet. Leave the oven on.

2. Heat the olive oil in a large, nonstick sauté pan. Add the onion and cook over medium heat until soft and translucent but not brown, about 5 minutes. Stir in the flour and cook for 1 minute. Stir in the milk, increase the heat to high, and bring to a boil. Reduce the heat back to medium and gently simmer the mixture until thick and flavorful, about 5

minutes. Add a little salt and pepper. Remove the pan from the heat and let cool to tepid, then stir in egg whites and basil.

3. Spread one-third of the onion custard mixture in the tart shell. Arrange a layer of roasted tomatoes on top. Spread another third of the custard mixture on top, and top with tomatoes. Spread a final layer of custard on top, and top with the remaining tomatoes.

4. Transfer the tart to the oven and bake until the custard is set, puffed, and lightly browned, about 30 minutes. Let the tart cool for 10 minutes, then unmold and transfer it to a platter. Cut into wedges for serving. Garnish with sprigs of basil.

Serves 8

232 CALORIES PER SERVING; 9 G PROTEIN; 9 G FAT; 3 G SATURATED FAT; 29 G CARBOHYDRATE; 297 MG SODIUM; 10 MG CHOLESTEROL

ENLIGHTENED TART SHELL

You can't make a crisp, flaky pastry without using at least a little fat. I've replaced some of the butter in the traditional recipe with olive oil, which is a better type of fat. The cake flour has a softening effect on the dough.

PREPARATION TIME: 20 MINUTES   COOKING TIME: 20 MINUTES

1¼ cups all-purpose unbleached white flour
¼ cup cake flour
¾ teaspoon salt
2 tablespoons cold unsalted butter (if using salted
  butter, reduce the salt above to ½ teaspoon)

1 egg white
2 tablespoons extra-virgin olive oil
2 to 3 tablespoons ice water

1 12-inch tart pan with removable sides

1. Place the all-purpose flour, cake flour, salt, and butter in a food processor fitted with a chopping blade. Run the machine to cut in the butter: the mixture should feel crumbly, like sand.

2. Add the egg white, oil, and ice water. Run the machine in short bursts until the dough comes together into a smooth ball. (If the mixture looks too dry, add a little more ice water.) Flatten the ball of dough into a disk, wrap in plastic, and refrigerate until firm, about 1 hour.

3. Preheat the oven to 400°F. If you're experienced working with dough, roll it into a 13-inch circle on a lightly floured work surface, flouring the rolling pin as well. Keep the dough moving, flouring as needed. If you're less comfortable working with dough, roll it out between 2 sheets of plastic wrap.

Peel off the top sheet of plastic and invert the dough into the pie pan. (The dough is quite fragile and tears easily. That's why less experienced bakers may wish to roll it out between sheets of plastic wrap.) Use the dough circle to line a 12-inch tart pan (bottom and sides) with removable sides. Prick the bottom of the crust with a fork and line with a sheet of foil. Freeze the crust for 5 minutes.

4. Fill the foil-lined crust with dried beans or rice and bake for 15 minutes. (The beans/rice hold the crust in shape during baking.) Remove the beans and foil and continue baking the crust until golden brown on the sides and bottom, 5 to 10 minutes more. Remove the crust from the oven and let cool to room temperature before filling.

Makes 1 12-inch pie shell, enough to serve 8 to 10

142 CALORIES PER SERVING;* 3 G PROTEIN; 7 G FAT; 2 G SATURATED FAT; 18 G CARBOHYDRATE; 208 MG SODIUM; 8 MG CHOLESTEROL

Analysis is based on 8 servings.

SALADS

A VENETIAN SALAD OF BITTER GREENS

Of the four basic types of tastes recognized by physiologists (sweet, sour, salty, and bitter), bitter flavors are perhaps the least appreciated by North Americans. We don't generally like bitter flavors—which is not surprising, given our collective sweet tooth. A very different sensibility reigns in Italy, where bitter flavors are not only accepted but prized. Consider the Italian love of bitter apéritifs, like Campari and Cynar (the latter made from artichokes). Consider the Italian love for bitter greens, like escarole and broccoli rabe. This salad was inspired by an open-air market in Venice, where a staggering assortment of bitter greens was on display: purple and white veined radicchio, red-leafed treviso, slender jagged-leafed chicory, fleshy escarole. Combined, they make an intriguing, pleasantly bitter salad that is unexpectedly refreshing. The fennel adds a counterpoint of sweetness.

PREPARATION TIME: 15 MINUTES

5 cups bitter greens, including chicory, escarole, radicchio, treviso (a red-leaf chicory with cream-colored veins), arugula, young dandelions, Belgian endive, etc.
1 small or ½ large bulb fennel, thinly sliced crosswise
2 stalks celery, thinly sliced

FOR THE DRESSING:
1½ tablespoons balsamic vinegar
salt and freshly ground black pepper
1½ tablespoons extra-virgin olive oil

1 ounce Parmigiano-Reggiano cheese

1. Wash and dry the greens and combine with the fennel and celery.

2. In the bottom of a large salad bowl, combine the vinegar, salt, and pepper and whisk until the salt crystals are dissolved. Whisk in the olive oil in a thin stream to make a smooth emulsion.

3. Just before serving, add the greens and vegetables and gently toss to mix. Shave curls of Parmesan over the salad, using a vegetable peeler. Serve at once.

Serves 4 to 6

105 CALORIES PER SERVING;* 4 G PROTEIN; 7 G FAT; 2 G SATURATED FAT; 6 G CARBOHYDRATE; 173 MG SODIUM; 6 MG CHOLESTEROL

Analysis is based on 4 servings.

A Venetian Salad of Bitter Greens

Tuscan Bean Salad

Visit a restaurant in the Italian countryside and the chances are that you'll find a grandmother or grandfather sitting at a table in the kitchen or dining room shelling fagioli (white beans). North Americans tend to become obsessed with the nutritional benefits of particular foods. But I believe that the cohesiveness of the Italian family does as much to foster health and well-being in that country as does diet. If you live in an area with a large Italian community, you may be able to find fresh fagioli. If not, use dried or canned beans. If using the former, cook according to the instructions on page 244. If using the latter, rinse well before using.

PREPARATION TIME: 10 MINUTES

2 cups cooked cannellini beans
1 gorgeous ripe tomato, peeled, seeded, and diced
1½ tablespoons top-quality Tuscan extra-virgin
   olive oil
1 tablespoon toasted pine nuts

¼ red onion, minced (3 to 4 tablespoons)
¼ cup chopped flat-leaf parsley
salt and freshly ground black pepper
lemon wedges for garnish

1. If using canned beans, rinse well under cold water. Drain well and blot dry. Warm the beans and tomato in a nonstick frying pan over medium heat. They should be warm but not hot.

2. Remove the pan from the heat and stir in the oil, pine nuts, red onion, parsley, and salt and pepper to taste. The salad should be highly seasoned. Serve the salad with lemon wedges for squeezing.

Serves 4 to 6

193 CALORIES PER SERVING;* 10 G PROTEIN; 7 G FAT; 1 G SATURATED FAT; 25 G CARBOHYDRATE; 11 MG SODIUM; 0 MG CHOLESTEROL

Analysis is based on 4 servings.

BABY ARTICHOKE SALAD

I first tasted this salad at the restaurant Fantino in the Ritz-Carlton Hotel, New York. The fact that artichokes (at least baby artichokes) could be eaten raw came as a revelation. And raw they are eaten by the truckload in Italy, when the first of the crop comes into season. Baby artichokes have a crisp, snappy texture and a sweetness that will remind you of licorice or basil. Once hard to find, baby artichokes are readily available in gourmet shops, Italian markets, and many supermarkets in this country. Look for them in late spring and summer. The best are the size of a walnut.

PREPARATION TIME: *20 MINUTES*

3 tablespoons fresh lemon juice, or to taste
1½ pounds baby artichokes (6 to 8 per person)
1½ tablespoons extra-virgin olive oil
2 tablespoons chopped fresh chives or shallots

1 ripe tomato, peeled, seeded, and cut into ¼-inch dice (optional)
salt and freshly ground black pepper

1. Place the lemon juice in a large nonreactive mixing bowl. Pull off the tough outside leaves of the artichokes. (You'll need to remove 4 or 5 leaves in all.) Using a sharp paring knife, cut the top third and stem off the artichoke and pare off any tough sections on the bottom, rotating the artichoke as you pare it. Cut the artichoke lengthwise into the thinnest possible slices. This is most easily done on a mandoline, but you can also use a sharp knife. Immediately add the slices to the lemon juice and toss. The lemon juice serves two purposes: it marinates the artichokes and keeps them from discoloring. It's important to finish with one artichoke and toss it in lemon juice before starting with the next.

2. Just before serving, stir in the olive oil, chives, and tomato. Add salt and pepper to taste: the salad should be highly seasoned.   *Serves 4*

82 CALORIES PER SERVING; 2 G PROTEIN; 5 G FAT; 0.7 G SATURATED FAT; 9 G CARBOHYDRATE; 65 MG SODIUM; 0 MG CHOLESTEROL

CAPRI SHRIMP AND BEAN SALAD

Call me a sucker for street life, but my favorite part of Capri wasn't the upper village, with its picture-perfect narrow streets and expensive boutiques. I preferred the hurly-burly of the docks in the lower village, where the ferries and fishing boats come in. I wandered in and out of trattorie, chatting with cooks (no one would be so pretentious as to call himself a chef here), sampling simple fare and supremely fresh seafood, including the following salad.

PREPARATION TIME: 15 MINUTES   COOKING TIME: 5 MINUTES

1½ tablespoons extra-virgin olive oil
1 clove garlic, crushed with the side of a cleaver
  and peeled
½ teaspoon curry powder
¼ to ½ teaspoon hot pepper flakes
1 pound large shrimp, peeled and deveined

salt and freshly ground black pepper
2 cups cooked cannellini beans
10 black olives
3 tablespoons chopped flat-leaf parsley
1 tablespoon red wine vinegar, or to taste
lemon wedges for garnish

1. Heat 1 tablespoon oil in a nonstick frying pan over a medium flame. Add the garlic, curry powder, and pepper flakes and sizzle in the oil until fragrant, about 30 seconds to a minute. Add the shrimp and sauté until cooked (they'll be firm and pink), 2 to 3 minutes, seasoning with salt and pepper.

2. Remove the pan from the heat and let cool.

Stir in the beans, olives, parsley, and vinegar. Correct the seasoning, adding salt or vinegar to taste: the salad should be highly seasoned. Transfer the salad to a shallow serving bowl or to plates, drizzle the remaining ½ tablespoon olive oil on top, and garnish with lemon wedges for serving.

Serves 4 to 6

275 CALORIES PER SERVING;* 28 G PROTEIN; 8 G FAT; 1 G SATURATED FAT; 24 G CARBOHYDRATE; 253 MG SODIUM; 175 MG CHOLESTEROL

Analysis is based on 4 servings.

ITALIAN FLAG SALAD #2

GRILLED VEGETABLE SALAD

History neglects to tell us who first cooked a vegetable on a grill. I bet it was a Tuscan. Nothing brings out the sweetness of a vegetable like grilling. And nowhere do grilled vegetables taste better than in Tuscany. This attractive salad features grilled green asparagus, white Belgian endive, and red bell peppers: the colors of the Italian flag. (The first Italian Flag Salad—orzo, green beans, and sun-dried tomatoes—appears in my book High-Flavor, Low-Fat Vegetarian Cooking.*)*

PREPARATION TIME: 15 MINUTES   COOKING TIME: 10 MINUTES

1 pound asparagus
4 Belgian endives
2 red bell peppers
1½ tablespoons extra-virgin olive oil

salt and freshly ground black pepper
1 to 1½ tablespoons balsamic vinegar (preferably white balsamic vinegar) or tarragon vinegar
3 tablespoons finely chopped flat-leaf parsley

1. Preheat the grill to high.
2. Snap the asparagus stalks: Hold each stalk firmly by the stem end in one hand. Bend the stalk with the other hand—the asparagus will break at its natural point of tenderness. Cut the endives in half lengthwise. Brush the asparagus, endives, and peppers with 1 to 2 teaspoons oil and season with salt and pepper.
3. Grill the vegetables until nicely charred on all sides. It will take 2 to 3 minutes per side for the asparagus, 4 minutes per side for the endive, and 2 min-utes per side for the peppers. Transfer the grilled vegetables to a plate to cool. Cut the flesh of the peppers off the core and cut it into strips.
4. Arrange the grilled vegetables on a platter, like the Italian flag: green asparagus on the left, red peppers on the right, white endive in the center. Drizzle the remaining oil and the vinegar on top. Season with salt and pepper and sprinkle with the parsley. The salad can be prepared up to 4 hours ahead but dress at the last minute.   *Serves 4 to 6*

115 CALORIES PER SERVING;* 5 G PROTEIN; 6 G FAT; 0.7 G SATURATED FAT; 15 G CARBOHYDRATE; 17 MG SODIUM; 0 MG CHOLESTEROL

Analysis is based on 4 servings.

FENNEL AND BEET SALAD WITH MINT

This Apulian salad offers a stunning contrast of colors and flavors. I particularly like the way the licoricy sweetness of the fennel offsets the earthy flavor of the beets. For the sake of convenience, the recipe calls for cooked beets, but you can certainly cook raw ones from scratch. You'll need about 1 pound. Simmer the beets until tender in 1½ cups water and ½ cup white (distilled) vinegar, with salt and pepper to taste.

PREPARATION TIME: 15 MINUTES   COOKING TIME: 5 MINUTES

FOR THE DRESSING:
1 clove garlic, minced
¼ cup balsamic vinegar
1½ tablespoons extra-virgin olive oil
1 tablespoon Chicken Broth (page 239) or Basic
    Vegetable Broth (page 241)
salt and freshly ground black pepper

1 large or 2 small bulbs fennel (stems cut off)
1 bunch arugula or tender leaf spinach, stemmed,
    washed, and spun dry (see boxes on pages 43
    and 37)
1 pound cooked beets, cut into ½-inch dice (about
    1½ cups)
⅓ cup chopped fresh spearmint or peppermint

1. Prepare the dressing: Combine the garlic and vinegar in a small, heavy saucepan. Boil until reduced to 1½ tablespoons. Whisk in the olive oil, broth, and salt and pepper to taste. Let the dressing cool.

2. Thinly slice the fennel widthwise. Carpet plates or a platter with the arugula leaves and arrange the fennel slices on top. Spoon one-third of the dressing over the salad.

3. Stir the beets and most of the mint leaves into the remaining dressing. Toss to mix. Correct the sea-soning, adding salt or vinegar to taste. Mound the beet mixture on top of and in the center of the fennel slices. Sprinkle the remaining mint leaves over the salad and serve at once.   *Serves 4*

Note: In this and some of the following recipes, broth is added to the dressing to provide richness and flavor without fat. (I learned this trick from the great French chef Joël Robuchon.) For convenience, freeze one of the broths in ice-cube trays, so you always have a tablespoon quantity on hand.

55 CALORIES PER SERVING; 1 G SODIUM; 3 G FAT; 6 G CARBOHYDRATE; 106 G SODIUM; 0 MG CHOLESTEROL

❧

NINO'S FENNEL, TOMATO, AND SPINACH SALAD

Nino Pernetti runs the popular Caffe Abbracci in Coral Gables. His simple, tasty food—epitomized by this salad—is always served with style and generosity. For the best results buy young leaf spinach. You could also use arugula.

PREPARATION TIME: 15 MINUTES

1 bunch tender, young leaf spinach
2 ripe tomatoes
1 small bulb fennel or ½ large bulb (reserve the
    feathery leaves for garnish)

FOR THE DRESSING:
1½ tablespoons balsamic vinegar (preferably
    white)
1½ tablespoons extra-virgin olive oil
1½ tablespoons Chicken Broth (page 239) or
    Basic Vegetable Broth (page 241)
2 tablespoons minced red onion or shallot
salt and freshly ground black pepper

1. Wash and stem the spinach. Thinly slice the tomatoes. Thinly slice the fennel crosswise, discarding the fibrous core.

2. Combine the ingredients for the dressing (the vinegar, oil, broth, onion, salt, and pepper) in a bowl and whisk until smooth. Correct the seasoning, adding vinegar or salt to taste.

3. Carpet four salad plates or a platter with spinach leaves. Arrange the tomato slices in a circle on top and mound the sliced fennel in the center. Spoon the dressing over the salads and serve at once, garnished with feathery fennel leaves.

Serves 4

75 CALORIES PER SERVING; 2 G PROTEIN; 5 G FAT; 0.7 G SATURATED FAT; 6 G CARBOHYDRATE; 58 MG SODIUM; 0 MG CHOLESTEROL

How to Wash Spinach

The easiest way to wash spinach is to immerse the spinach leaves in a bowl of cold water, holding the bunch by the stems. Agitate it vigorously. Keep changing the water and washing until the water runs clear. Shake the spinach dry and remove the stems.

PEAR SALAD WITH WATERCRESS AND GORGONZOLA

This attractive salad is bursting with autumnal flavors: the sweetness of ripe pear, the woodsy flavor of walnuts, the salty tang of Gorgonzola. The latter is Italy's Roquefort, a pungent, creamy blue cheese (actually more green than blue) from a village near Milano. The use of Gorgonzola in this recipe reflects my philosophy about the role of cheese in high-flavor, low-fat cooking—namely, it is better to use a little bit of an intensely flavored real cheese than a lot of a low-fat or no-fat cheese that tastes waxy and insipid.

PREPARATION TIME: 10 MINUTES

1 bunch watercress, washed, spun dry, and torn
   into sprigs
4 ripe pears (preferably bosc)
½ lemon
8 walnuts, toasted and coarsely chopped

FOR THE DRESSING:
1 ounce Gorgonzola cheese, crumbled
1 tablespoon extra-virgin olive oil
2 to 3 tablespoons Chicken Broth (page 239) or
   Basic Vegetable Broth (page 241)
2 to 3 teaspoons white wine vinegar
freshly ground black pepper and salt as needed

1. Arrange a bed of watercress on each of 4 salad plates. Peel the pears (if desired), cut in quarters lengthwise, remove the cores, and rub with cut lemon to prevent discoloring.

2. Arrange the pears on top of the watercress, narrow ends facing out, like the points of a compass. Sprinkle the walnuts on top.

3. Prepare the dressing: Combine the cheese, oil, broth, vinegar, and pepper in a bowl and whisk to mix. Correct the seasoning, adding salt or vinegar to taste.

4. Spoon the dressing over the pears and watercress and serve at once.   *Serves 4*

188 CALORIES PER SERVING; 4 G PROTEIN; 10 G FAT; 2 G SATURATED FAT; 23 G CARBOHYDRATE; 134 MG SODIUM; 6 MG CHOLESTEROL

SICILIAN ORANGE SALAD

This offbeat recipe comes from a former cooking student, who learned to make it from his Sicilian grandfather.
(The grandfather claimed his longevity came from a generous diet of garlic, hot peppers, and wine.)
This salad is incredibly easy to make and is wonderfully refreshing in warm weather.

PREPARATION TIME: 15 MINUTES

4 plump, juicy oranges, preferably seedless
1 clove garlic
1½ tablespoons extra-virgin olive oil
1½ tablespoons dry red wine
1½ tablespoons toasted pine nuts

½ teaspoon red wine vinegar or balsamic vinegar
¼ teaspoon hot pepper flakes (or to taste)
salt and freshly ground black pepper
2 tablespoons chopped flat-leaf parsley

1. Cut the rind and white pith off the oranges as neatly as possible, leaving only the orange flesh. At this stage, there are two ways you can cut the oranges: either in slices or segments. (For the latter, cut between the membranes. Remove all membranes and discard.) Remove any seeds with a fork.

2. Cut the garlic in half and use one half to rub the inside of a nonreactive mixing bowl. Mince the other half and add it to the bowl with the olive oil, wine, pine nuts, vinegar, pepper flakes, salt, and pepper. Gently stir in the oranges. Let the oranges marinate for 5 to 10 minutes before serving. The recipe can be prepared up to 1 hour ahead. Just before serving, stir in the parsley.   *Serves 4 to 6*

132 CALORIES PER SERVING;* 2 G PROTEIN; 7 G FAT; 1 G SATURATED FAT; 16 G CARBOHYDRATE; 5 MG SODIUM; 0 MG CHOLESTEROL

Analysis is based on 4 servings.

FELIDIA'S BLOOD ORANGE SALAD

Felidia Bastianich is one of the foremost Italian chefs in New York, the owner of three restaurants (Felidia, Becco, and the Frico Bar), as well as the author of an acclaimed cookbook. What I come away with whenever I dine at one of her restaurants is her uncanny ability to create amazingly complex dishes with a few simple ingredients. Consider this simple but stunning salad, which she inspired. Blood oranges are a traditional southern Italian citrus fruit with striking red color and intense strawberry-orange flavor. Blood oranges are in season primarily in winter, although they turn up sporadically throughout the year. Look for them in gourmet shops, Italian markets, and specialty greengrocers. If unavailable, use regular oranges.

PREPARATION TIME: 15 MINUTES

8 blood oranges
3 Belgian endives
1 bunch watercress, washed, stemmed, and torn
   into sprigs

2 to 3 teaspoons white wine vinegar
salt and freshly ground black pepper
1½ tablespoons extra-virgin olive oil
4 sprigs flat-leaf parsley

1. Using a sharp paring knife, cut the rind and white pith off the oranges to expose the red flesh. Cut each orange, crosswise, into ¼-inch slices. Remove the seeds with a fork without breaking the slices. Work over a bowl or on a grooved cutting board to collect the juices. Cut the endives on the diagonal into ¼-inch slices.

2. Combine the vinegar, salt, and pepper in a shallow bowl and whisk until the salt is completely dissolved. Whisk in the olive oil and any reserved orange juice.

3. Arrange the orange slices around the outside edge of 4 salad plates or a platter. Spoon a little of the salad dressing over the oranges. Gently toss the endive and watercress with the remaining dressing and mound the mixture in the center. Garnish with parsley sprigs and serve at once. *Serves 4*

173 CALORIES PER SERVING; 3 G PROTEIN; 5 G FAT; 0 G SATURATED FAT; 32 G CARBOHYDRATE; 9 MG SODIUM; 0 MG CHOLESTEROL

RICE SALAD WITH SPICY PICKLED VEGETABLES

Visit an Italian salumeria (delicatessen) and you will see huge, colorful jars of pickled vegetables. Smaller bottles are available at gourmet shops and supermarkets, and they're just the thing for electrifying a rice salad. If Italian pickled vegetables aren't available, you could use Mexican or Latin American–style pickled vegetables, which are sold at most supermarkets. Rice salad is quick and easy and makes a great party dish. Feel free to vary the vegetables.

PREPARATION TIME: 15 MINUTES

1 cup diced pickled vegetables (should include carrots, celery, cauliflower, and/or peppers), with juices
1 red ripe tomato
3 or 4 thinly sliced pickled peperoncini, or jalapeños or other hot peppers (optional—use only if the pickled vegetables contain no peppers), plus 2 or 3 tablespoons juice from the jar

12 fresh basil leaves, thinly slivered, or ¼ cup chopped flat-leaf parsley
12 black olives
½ cup cooked chickpeas (optional)
5 to 6 cups cooked rice
2 tablespoons extra-virgin olive oil
salt and freshly ground black pepper

1. Cut the pickled vegetables into ¼-inch slices or ½-inch dice. Cut the peel off the tomato in a continuous 1-inch strip. Roll the strip up on itself and set on its side to make a tomato rose. Cut the tomato into ½-inch dice.

2. Combine the pickled vegetables, the diced tomato, the sliced peperoncini, the basil, most of the olives, most of the chickpeas, the rice, the oil, and the salt and pepper in a mixing bowl and toss to mix. Add the pickled vegetable juice by way of a souring agent. Correct the seasoning, adding salt or pepper to taste: the salad should be highly seasoned.

3. Transfer the salad to an attractive bowl or platter and garnish with the tomato rose and the remaining olives and chickpeas. *Serves 6 to 8*

252 CALORIES PER SERVING;* 4 G PROTEIN; 6 G FAT; 0.9 G SATURATED FAT; 0 G CARBOHYDRATE; 141 MG SODIUM; 0 MG CHOLESTEROL

Analysis is based on 6 servings.

BREAD SALAD

Like many classic Italian dishes, panzanella was born of frugality—as a way to use up stale bread. It remains one of the quickest, easiest, and most satisfying salads I know of, yet it's substantial enough to be served as a light entrée. For the best results, use a firm, dense, country-style bread that's a day or two old.

PREPARATION TIME: 15 MINUTES

6 to 8 cups country-style bread cubes (the bread should be cut into 1-inch dice)

2 juicy, red ripe tomatoes, cut into ½-inch dice (work over a bowl to catch the juices)

2 stalks celery, thinly sliced

1 English-style cucumber, peeled, seeded, and cut into ½-inch dice (or 2 American-style cucumbers)

½ red onion, finely chopped

3 tablespoons finely chopped flat-leaf parsley

12 basil leaves, thinly slivered, plus whole sprigs of basil for garnish

1 tablespoon drained capers

2 tablespoons extra-virgin olive oil

2 tablespoons red wine vinegar

2 tablespoons Chicken Broth (page 239) or Basic Vegetable Broth (page 241) or water (or as needed)

salt and freshly ground black pepper

8 pitted black olives

1. In a large mixing bowl, combine the bread, tomatoes with juices, celery, cucumber, onion, parsley, slivered basil leaves, capers, oil, vinegar, stock, salt, and pepper. Toss to mix. Let the salad stand for 10 minutes to allow the liquid ingredients to moisten the bread. If the bread still seems dry, add a little more stock.

2. Correct the seasoning, adding salt or vinegar to taste. Garnish the salad with the basil sprigs and black olives. Serve at once. *Serves 6 to 8*

153 CALORIES PER SERVING;* 4 G PROTEIN; 7 G FAT; 1 G SATURATED FAT; 20 G CARBOHYDRATE; 271 MG SODIUM; 0 MG CHOLESTEROL

Analysis is based on 6 servings.

ARUGULA, TOMATO, AND ENDIVE SALAD WITH SHAVED PARMESAN

This salad is a standby at our house. My wife and I enjoy a variation of it several times a week. Sometimes we substitute watercress or spinach for the arugula. Sometimes we omit the endive. Usually, we simply toss the ingredients together, but sometimes, when we're feeling fancy, we'll carpet salad plates or a platter with arugula leaves and pile the tossed endive and diced tomato in the center.

PREPARATION TIME: 10 MINUTES

1 large or 2 medium juicy, red ripe tomatoes
2 Belgian endives, thinly sliced crosswise
1 bunch arugula, washed, dried, and stemmed
1½ tablespoons extra-virgin olive oil

1 to 1½ tablespoons balsamic vinegar
salt and freshly ground black pepper
1 ounce Parmigiano-Reggiano cheese

1. Cut the tomatoes into ¼-inch dice and add them with the juices to a salad bowl. Just before serving, add the endive, arugula, oil, vinegar, salt, and pepper to the bowl. Gently toss to mix. Correct the seasoning, adding salt or vinegar to taste.

2. Transfer the salad to plates or a platter. Shave a few curls of Parmigiano-Reggiano cheese over each and serve at once. *Serves 4*

90 CALORIES PER SERVING; 3 G PROTEIN; 7 G FAT; 2 G SATURATED FAT; 3 G CARBOHYDRATE; 140 MG SODIUM; 6 MG CHOLESTEROL

How to Wash Arugula

The easiest way to wash arugula is to agitate the leaves in a bowl of cold water, holding the bunch by the stems. Change the water two or three times, or until grit no longer appears; arugula tends to be very gritty, so wash well before using.

How to Shave Parmesan

The easiest way to shave Parmesan is to use a swivel-bladed vegetable peeler. Hold the block of cheese in your left hand (or right hand if you're left-handed) and pull the vegetable peeler over it with your left. Long, thin shavings of Parmesan will land on the salad. It's easier to start with a larger block of cheese than you actually need for serving four people.

SOUPS

REAL RIBOLLITA

TUSCAN TWICE-COOKED BEAN AND VEGETABLE SOUP

Don't tell Carlo Cioni that you know about ribollita. The proprietor of the restaurant Delfina in the hamlet of Atimino outside Florence will roll his eyes at the mention of Tuscany's most famous soup—or, more accurately, at the thought of the "citified" version of that soup. Not that there's anything wrong with the ribollita found in most Florentine restaurants—a brimming bowl of beans and vegetables thickened with slices of saltless Tuscan bread. It's just that, according to Carlo Cioni, real ribollita isn't really soup at all, but the sort of pan-fried vegetable mush that has well-heeled Florentines flocking in droves to the hilltop restaurant founded by his mother in 1961. Ribollita means "reboiled" or "twice cooked," explains Cioni. In the old days, peasants would make a large batch of soup on Sundays, storing the leftovers in the cellar. It didn't become the ribollita until said leftovers were pan-fried in olive oil. And to judge from Delfina's ribollita, glorious leftovers they were. Here's a recipe for the soup, with instructions on how to turn it into a ribollita of which even Carlo Cioni would approve.

PREPARATION TIME: 40 MINUTES   COOKING TIME: 30 TO 40 MINUTES,
PLUS THE TIME NEEDED TO COOK THE BEANS (IF YOU START WITH DRIED BEANS)

1½ tablespoons extra-virgin olive oil

1 onion, finely chopped

1 leek, trimmed, washed, and thinly sliced (see box on page 46)

2 celery stalks, cut into ½-inch chunks

2 large carrots, cut into ½-inch chunks

½ head cabbage, cored and cut crosswise into ¼-inch strips

1 bunch kale, collard greens, or Swiss chard, stemmed, washed, and cut crosswise into ¼-inch strips

2 large ripe tomatoes, cut into ½-inch chunks

1 large baking potato, peeled and cut into ½-inch chunks

6 to 8 cups bean cooking liquid, if cooking beans from scratch (do not use the liquid from canned beans), Chicken Broth (page 239), or Basic Vegetable Broth (page 241), or water

1 prosciutto bone (available at an Italian deli) (optional)

1 herb bundle made by tying together 1 bay leaf, 1 sprig of rosemary, 1 sprig of basil, and 1 sprig of parsley

salt and freshly ground black pepper

3 cups cooked cannellini beans (If using canned beans—you'll need 2 15-ounce cans—rinse and drain well. If using dried beans, start with 1½ cups.)

6 thick slices Tuscan or dense country-style bread (preferably a little stale)

Ribollita

45

1. Heat the olive oil in a large pot. Add the onion, leek, celery, and carrots and cook over medium heat until onions are soft and translucent but not brown, about 5 minutes. Add the cabbage, kale, tomatoes, potatoes, bean cooking liquid, prosciutto bone (if using), and herb bundle. Bring the soup to a boil.

2. Reduce the heat and gently simmer the soup until the vegetables are tender, 20 to 30 minutes. Gradually add salt and pepper to taste. Add the cannellini beans and continue cooking until the beans and vegetables are very soft. Remove and discard the ham bone and herb bundle. Correct the seasoning, adding salt and pepper to taste. Meanwhile, lightly toast the bread slices.

3. To serve, place a slice of bread in each soup bowl and ladle the broth and vegetables on top. Let stand for a few minutes to soften. (The bread will absorb the broth and thicken the soup.) Serve at once.

4. To make real ribollita (the sort of which Carlo Cioni would approve), toast and dice the bread and stir it into the soup. Let the soup cool to room temperature, then refrigerate overnight. It should be as thick as porridge. Just before serving, heat a little olive oil in a nonstick frying pan. Add ladlefuls of the soup and pan-fry over medium heat until crusty on the bottom. Turn and fry until crusty on top. This sort of ribollita should be served in a shallow dish with a fork, not a spoon.

Note: In the interest of time and convenience, this recipe calls for cooked beans. A respectable ribollita can be made with canned beans. The soup will be better, of course, if you take the time to make them from scratch. Instructions on cooking beans are found on page 244. Also, to be strictly authentic, you'd use Tuscan black kale (*cavolo nero*), a dark-leafed, highly flavorful member of the cabbage family. If you live near a large Italian community, you may be able to find *cavolo nero*. If not, use regular kale or collard greens. *Serves 6*

322 CALORIES PER SERVING; 15 G PROTEIN; 5 G FAT; 0.8 G SATURATED FAT; 57 G CARBOHYDRATE; 231 MG SODIUM; 0 MG CHOLESTEROL

How to Trim and Wash Leeks

Cut off and discard the dark green leaves, furry root end, and outer layer of the white part. Cut the leek in four lengthwise—to but not through the base. Holding the uncut end with one hand, plunge each leek up and down in a bowl of cold water, as you would a plunger, to remove any grit.

MINESTRONE WITH PESTO

Italy meets Provence in this recipe—vegetable, bean, and pasta soup with pesto. Feel free to vary the vegetables according to what's in season and what looks good. If using canned beans, choose a low-sodium brand. This recipe may look complicated because it contains a lot of ingredients, but it's actually quick and easy to make.

PREPARATION TIME: 30 MINUTES   COOKING TIME: 30 MINUTES

1 medium onion, finely chopped
1 medium leek, trimmed, washed, and finely chopped (see box on page 46)
3 cloves garlic, thinly sliced
3 stalks celery, thinly sliced
1 large or 2 medium potatoes (about 12 ounces), peeled and cut into ¼-inch dice
3 medium zucchini (about 1 pound), cut into ¼-inch dice
3 carrots (about 8 ounces), peeled and cut into ¼-inch dice
2 ripe tomatoes (about 1 pound), peeled, seeded, and cut into ¼-inch dice

4 ounces green beans, ends snapped, cut into ¼-inch pieces
½ cup green peas (ideally freshly shucked) (optional)
1 herb bundle made by tying together 2 bay leaves, 2 sprigs fresh or dried thyme, and 2 sprigs fresh or dried rosemary)
6 to 8 cups water
1½ cups cooked cannellini beans (1 15-ounce can)
2 ounces thin spaghetti, broken into ½-inch pieces
salt and freshly ground black pepper
¾ cup Enlightened Pesto (page 57)

1. In a large pot combine the onion, leek, garlic, celery, potatoes, zucchini, carrots, tomatoes, green beans, peas (if using), and herb bundle and 6 cups water and bring to a boil. Briskly simmer the soup until the vegetables are almost cooked, about 15 minutes.

2. Add the cannellini beans, spaghetti, and a little salt and pepper and simmer until the pasta and vegetables are tender, 10 to 15 minutes. Add 1 to 2 cups water (or more) if necessary to keep the soup soupy. Discard the herb bundle and correct the seasoning, adding salt and pepper to taste: the soup should be highly seasoned.

3. To serve, ladle the soup into bowls, Serve the pesto on the side. Have each eater stir a tablespoon of pesto into his soup before eating.

Note: For a quicker, easier version of this soup, omit the pesto and add 1 bunch washed, stemmed, thinly slivered basil leaves. Of course, it will be minestrone with basil, not pesto.

Makes 10 cups, enough to serve 8 to 10

190 CALORIES PER SERVING;* 7.6 G PROTEIN; 4.6 G FAT; 1 G SATURATED FAT; 31 G CARBOHYDRATE; 350 MG SODIUM; 0 MG CHOLESTEROL

Analysis is based on 8 servings.

Zuppa di Ceci

Tuscan Chickpea Soup

Chickpeas (ceci) occupy a privileged place in Italian social history. So highly esteemed were they in Roman times that Cicero is said to have been named for them. The following smooth chickpea soup is a rib-sticking Tuscan specialty. The combination of beans (chickpeas) and grains (pasta) is an age-old strategy for providing nutritionally complete protein without meat. The soup tastes best when made with dried chickpeas, but a very tasty soup can be made with canned. See Note for instructions on using canned chickpeas.

PREPARATION TIME: 20 MINUTES   COOKING TIME: 1¾ HOURS (15 MINUTES IF YOU START WITH CANNED BEANS)

1½ cups dried chickpeas
1 small onion, peeled and quartered
1 bay leaf
1 sprig rosemary, or 1 teaspoon dried
10 cups water

TO FINISH THE SOUP:
1½ tablespoons extra-virgin olive oil
1 onion, finely chopped
1 carrot, finely chopped

2 cloves garlic, minced
2 to 3 teaspoons chopped fresh rosemary
    (or 1 teaspoon dried), plus rosemary sprigs
    for garnish
5 to 6 cups Chicken Broth (page 239) or Basic
    Vegetable Broth (page 241)
1 bay leaf
salt and freshly ground black pepper
2 ounces spaghetti or fettuccine, broken into
    1-inch pieces

1. Soak the chickpeas in cold water to cover for at least 4 hours, preferably overnight. Drain well. Place the chickpeas in a large pot with the quartered onion, bay leaf, and rosemary. Add 10 cups water and bring to a boil. Reduce the heat, cover the pot, and simmer the chickpeas until soft enough to crush between your thumb and forefinger, about 1½ hours. Drain the chickpeas before adding them to the soup. The cooking time can be shortened to about 30 minutes by using a pressure cooker.

2. Heat the oil in a large saucepan (preferably nonstick). Add the onion, carrot, garlic, and rosemary and cook over medium heat until soft and translucent but not brown, about 4 minutes. Stir in the chickpeas, 5 cups of the broth, the bay leaf, and salt and pepper. Simmer the soup until richly flavored and the chickpeas are very soft, 10 to 15 minutes. If

the mixture becomes too thick, add another cup of broth.

3. Remove ½ cup chickpeas with a slotted spoon and set aside. Discard the bay leaf. Purée the soup in a blender and return it to the saucepan.

4. Meanwhile, cook the pasta in 2 quarts boiling salted water until al dente, about 8 minutes. Rinse under cold water and drain well.

5. Stir the pasta and reserved chickpeas into the soup. Correct the seasoning, adding salt and pepper to taste. Ladle the soup into bowls and garnish with sprigs of rosemary.

Note: To make this soup with canned chickpeas, use 2 15-ounce cans (about 3 cups cooked chickpeas). Omit step 1. Rinse the chickpeas well before adding.

Makes 7 to 8 cups, enough to serve 6 to 8

303 CALORIES PER SERVING;* 14 G PROTEIN; 8 G FAT; 1 G SATURATED FAT; 46 G CARBOHYDRATE; 844 MG SODIUM; 15 MG CHOLESTEROL

Analysis is based on 6 servings.

CHARRED YELLOW PEPPER BISQUE

Sweet and smoky is this satiny soup of charred yellow peppers. There are two options for cooking the peppers. My favorite is to char them on the grill. But you can also roast them in the oven, following the high-heat method outlined on page 10. The bisque can be served hot or chilled—the latter is great in the summer. Yogurt isn't a particularly traditional Italian ingredient, but it goes well with the peppers and it contains a lot less fat than cream does.

PREPARATION TIME: 20 MINUTES   COOKING TIME: 30 MINUTES

6 large yellow peppers
1 tablespoon extra-virgin olive oil
3 to 4 shallots or ½ large red onion, finely chopped
  (¾ cup)
1 clove garlic, minced
4 cups Basic Vegetable Broth (page 241) or
  Chicken Broth (page 239)

salt and freshly ground black pepper
½ cup plain nonfat yogurt or no-fat sour cream,
  plus 2 to 4 tablespoons for garnish
1 tablespoon balsamic vinegar, or to taste
1 teaspoon sugar or honey (optional)
12 fresh basil leaves, thinly slivered

1. Preheat the grill to high. Grill the peppers until charred on all sides, turning with tongs. This will take 3 to 4 minutes per side. Transfer the peppers to a large bowl, cover with plastic wrap, and let cool. If roasting the peppers, preheat the oven to 450°F. Lightly brush or spray the peppers with oil. Roast on a nonstick baking sheet until the skins are browned and blistered, 15 to 25 minutes, turning with tongs to ensure even cooking. Let cool in a covered bowl as described above.

2. Meanwhile, heat the olive oil in a large, heavy saucepan. Add the shallots and garlic and cook over medium heat until soft and translucent but not brown, about 3 minutes. Scrape the burnt skin off the peppers with a paring knife. (It's okay for a few burnt spots to remain.) Core and seed the peppers and add the flesh to the shallots. Add the broth and salt and pepper and gently simmer the soup until peppers are soft, 5 to 10 minutes. Stir in ½ cup of the yogurt and the vinegar.

3. Purée the soup in a blender. If serving the soup cold, strain it into a bowl and let cool to room temperature, then refrigerate for at least 4 hours. If serving the soup hot, strain it back into the saucepan. (Straining is optional, but it will produce a more silken-textured soup.) Correct the seasoning, adding salt or vinegar to taste. If a touch of sweetness is desired, you can add a teaspoon of sugar or honey.

4. To serve, stir half the slivered basil into the soup. Ladle it into bowls and garnish with a dollop of the remaining yogurt in the center and the remaining slivered basil sprinkled on top.   *Serves 4*

185 CALORIES PER SERVING; 6 G PROTEIN; 4 G FAT; 0.5 G SATURATED FAT; 34 G CARBOHYDRATE; 113 MG SODIUM; 0 MG CHOLESTEROL

PUMPKIN FENNEL SOUP WITH FRIED SAGE LEAVES

This soup is a study in sweet harvest flavors: the earthy sweetness of pumpkin, the anisy sweetness of fennel, the pungent sweetness of sage leaves. Yet the end result is not in the least bit saccharine. Roasting the pumpkin may take more time than simmering it, but the flavor will be more concentrated. Don't worry about the seemingly large amount of oil: most of it is used for frying the sage leaves, then reserved for later use or discarded. For an even leaner soup, you could skip frying the sage leaves or make the Bake-Fried Sage Leaves on page 15.

PREPARATION TIME: 15 MINUTES   COOKING TIME: 40 MINUTES FOR BAKING THE PUMPKIN,
PLUS 30 MINUTES FOR COOKING THE SOUP

a 2-pound piece of pumpkin or butternut squash, peeled and seeded (enough to make 2 cups pulp)
1 tablespoon extra-virgin olive oil, plus ¼ cup oil for frying the sage leaves
1 medium onion, finely chopped
½ large or 1 small fennel, trimmed and diced (save the feathery leaves for garnishing the soup, the stalks for stews and salads)

4 to 5 cups Chicken Broth (page 239) or Basic Vegetable Broth (page 241)
1 cup 2 percent, 1 percent, or skim milk
salt and freshly ground black pepper
16 to 20 fresh sage leaves, stemmed, washed, and patted dry

1. Preheat the oven to 400°F. Loosely wrap the pumpkin in foil and bake until soft, 40 to 60 minutes. Transfer to a plate and let cool. Cut the pumpkin into ½-inch dice.

2. Heat the 1 tablespoon oil in a large saucepan. Add the onion and fennel and cook until soft and translucent but not brown, about 5 minutes. Add 4 cups of the broth and the milk, salt, pepper, and roasted pumpkin and gently simmer the soup until the fennel is soft, about 20 minutes. Transfer the soup to a blender and purée until smooth, adding broth as needed to obtain a souplike consistency. Return the soup to the saucepan and reheat, adding salt and pepper to taste.

3. Just before serving, heat the remaining ¼ cup oil to 350°F. in a small frying pan or saucepan. Add the sage leaves and fry until lightly browned and crisp, about 1 minute. Transfer the sage leaves with a wire skimmer to paper towels to drain. Blot dry with more paper towels.

4. To serve, ladle the soup into bowls and garnish with the fried sage leaves and the feathery fennel leaves.

Makes 7 to 8 cups, enough to serve 6 to 8

104 CALORIES PER SERVING;* 4 G PROTEIN; 5 G FAT; 1 G SATURATED FAT; 13 G CARBOHYDRATE; 489 MG SODIUM; 15 MG CHOLESTEROL

Analysis is based on 6 servings.

EMMER OR WHEAT BERRY SOUP

ZUPPA DI FARRO

Grain soups are enjoyed throughout Italy. This version comes from Tuscany, where it is made with a grain called farro (emmer in English), an ancestor of modern wheat. You may be able to find emmer in a natural-foods store; if not, use wheat berries. Part of the soup is puréed in the blender to serve as a natural thickener.

PREPARATION TIME: 25 MINUTES   COOKING TIME: 40 MINUTES

1 cup emmer or wheat berries
1 tablespoon extra-virgin olive oil
1 onion, finely chopped
2 cloves garlic, minced
2 carrots, cut into ¼-inch dice
2 stalks celery, cut into ¼-inch dice
1 ounce prosciutto, minced
¼ cup finely chopped flat-leaf parsley
1 tablespoon tomato paste

6 cups Chicken Broth (page 239) or Basic Vegetable Broth (page 241)
an herb bundle made by tying together a bay leaf, a sprig of fresh thyme, and a sprig of fresh rosemary
1 large or 2 small potatoes, cut into ¼-inch dice
1 large or 2 small zucchini, cut into ¼-inch dice
salt and freshly ground black pepper

1. Cook the emmer in a pressure cooker until tender, about 15 minutes. Alternatively, soak the grain overnight in cold water to cover, then cook in 3 quarts briskly simmering water until tender, about 1 hour. Drain well.

2. Heat the olive oil in a large pot. Add the onion, garlic, carrots, celery, and prosciutto and half the parsley and cook over medium heat until soft but not brown, about 4 minutes, stirring occasionally with a wooden spoon. Stir in the tomato paste and cook for 1 minute.

3. Add the broth and herb bundle and bring to a boil. Add the wheat berries and potatoes and cook until the potatoes are tender, about 15 minutes. Add the zucchini and cook until tender, another 3 minutes. Discard the herb bundle. Season the soup to taste with salt and pepper. Garnish with the remaining parsley and serve at once.

Serves 6 as an appetizer, 4 as a light entrée

196 CALORIES PER SERVING;* 8 G PROTEIN; 6 G FAT; 1 G SATURATED FAT; 32 G CARBOHYDRATE; 1,128 MG SODIUM; 22 MG CHOLESTEROL

Analysis is based on 6 servings as an appetizer.

SAUCES

ROASTED VEGETABLE SAUCE

This recipe was created for the vegetarians in my family. It's a rich, rib-sticking sauce that will remind you of a bolognese, yet it contains not one iota of meat and virtually no fat. The secret is to roast the vegetables in a super-hot oven to concentrate their flavor.

PREPARATION TIME: 15 MINUTES   COOKING TIME: 40 MINUTES

1 medium onion, peeled and quartered
1 carrot, peeled and cut into 1-inch pieces
1 stalk celery, cut into 1-inch pieces
1 zucchini or yellow squash, cut into 1-inch pieces
2 cloves garlic, peeled
4 ounces button mushrooms
1 to 2 teaspoons extra-virgin olive oil
salt and freshly ground black pepper

4 large red ripe tomatoes (about 2½ pounds) or
   1 28-ounce can imported peeled plum tomatoes
1 tablespoon tomato paste
1 to 2 teaspoons balsamic vinegar
½ teaspoon sugar or honey
6 fresh basil leaves
8 fresh oregano leaves, or 1 teaspoon dried
½ teaspoon hot pepper flakes (optional)

1. Preheat the oven to 450°F. Place the onion, carrot, celery, zucchini, garlic, and mushrooms on a baking sheet or in a shallow roasting pan. Toss the vegetables with the oil and season with salt and pepper. Roast the vegetables until a deep golden brown, 20 to 30 minutes, stirring occasionally to ensure even browning.

2. If using fresh tomatoes, remove the cores and cut each in 8 pieces. Add the tomatoes to the vegetable pan and roast for 10 minutes to evaporate some of the tomato water. If using canned tomatoes, you don't need to roast them.

3. Transfer the roasted vegetables and the toma-toes to a food processor with the tomato paste, vinegar, sugar, basil, oregano, and pepper flakes and grind to a coarse purée. Place the sauce in a saucepan and simmer for 5 minutes to blend the flavors. Correct the seasoning, adding salt, vinegar, or sugar to taste.

Note: If your fat budget allows it, whisk 2 to 3 tablespoons extra-virgin olive oil into the sauce at the end. This will give you a lovely olive-oil flavor. Even with an extra 3 tablespoons oil, you wind up with only about 6 grams of fat per person.

Makes about 5 cups, enough to serve 8 to 10

59 CALORIES PER SERVING;* 2.2 G PROTEIN; 1.2 G FAT; 0.2 G SATURATED FAT; 12 G CARBOHYDRATE; 38 MG SODIUM; 0 MG CHOLESTEROL

Analysis is based on 8 servings.

Roasted Vegetable Sauce

REDUCED-FAT BÉCHAMEL

The creamy white sauce known as balsamella *(béchamel) is, of course, one of the cornerstones of Italian cooking. Trying to create a credible low-fat version nearly drove me crazy. My first attempts involved combinations of skim milk and roasted vegetables. One batch was reasonably tasty, but no one would have called it béchamel. The breakthrough came from a reader in Louisiana, curiously enough, who wrote me about a butterless, oven-baked roux she uses for making low-fat gumbo. That gave me the idea to dry-roast the flour in a saucepan before adding the milk, producing a béchamel with the requisite thickness and cooked-flour taste but without all the customary butter. (I do like to add a tiny piece of butter at the end, however, just for flavor.) I also found that 2 percent milk produced much better results than skim, without unduly tipping the fat scales.*

PREPARATION TIME: 5 MINUTES   COOKING TIME: 15 MINUTES

3 tablespoons all-purpose unbleached white flour
2¼ cups 1 percent or 2 percent milk
1 bay leaf
½ small onion
1 clove
a 2-inch piece of celery (optional)

1 clove garlic, peeled
4 blades mace or ⅛ teaspoon ground mace or nutmeg
½ to 1 tablespoon unsalted butter (optional)
salt, white pepper (preferably freshly ground), and a pinch of cayenne pepper

1. Have ready a large bowl of cold water. Place the flour in a 1-quart saucepan (preferably nonstick) over medium heat. Cook the flour, stirring with a whisk or wooden spoon, until it smells cooked, 3 to 5 minutes (quite suddenly, you'll notice a pronounced toasted smell). Do not let the flour brown. Place the bottom of the saucepan in the bowl of cold water to stop the cooking of the flour. Set the pan aside until it and the flour are cool.

2. Add ½ cup of the milk to the flour and whisk to a smooth paste. Gradually whisk in the remaining milk. Pin the bay leaf to the onion with a clove and add it to the milk with the celery, garlic, and mace. Gradually bring the mixture to a boil over medium-high heat, whisking steadily. The sauce will thicken.

3. Reduce the heat to medium-low and gently simmer the sauce until thick and flavorful, about 10 minutes, whisking occasionally.

4. Strain the sauce into another saucepan, pressing the vegetables with the back of a wooden spoon to extract the juices. Whisk in the butter (if using). Correct the seasoning, adding salt, pepper, and cayenne pepper to taste.

Makes 2 cups, enough to serve 8

41 CALORIES PER SERVING; 3 G PROTEIN; 0.8 G FAT; 0.5 G SATURATED FAT; 6 G CARBOHYDRATE; 35 MG SODIUM; 3 MG CHOLESTEROL

PARMESAN CHEESE SAUCE

Cheese isn't normally an ingredient one associates with high-flavor, low-fat cooking. But real Parmigiano-Reggiano has so much flavor (thanks to the lengthy aging) that just a little will give you a satisfying cheese flavor. Another plus: Parmigiano-Reggiano is made with part-skim milk.

PREPARATION TIME: 5 MINUTES   COOKING TIME: 15 MINUTES

1 recipe Reduced-Fat Béchamel (page 54)
6 to 8 tablespoons freshly grated Parmigiano-Reggiano cheese

1 to 2 teaspoons mustard (nonsweetened or Dijon-style)

Prepare the béchamel sauce. Whisk all but 1 tablespoon cheese into the sauce. Whisk the mustard in. Just before serving, sprinkle the remaining cheese over the sauce. That way, the first taste that hits your tongue will be cheese, and it will trick your mouth into thinking there's more cheese in the sauce than there really is.

Makes 2 cups, enough to serve 8

70 CALORIES PER SERVING; 5 G PROTEIN; 2 G FAT; 1.7 G SATURATED FAT; 6 G CARBOHYDRATE; 130 MG SODIUM; 9 MG CHOLESTEROL

GORGONZOLA SAUCE

Gorgonzola is Italy's Roquefort, a pungent, creamy cow's-milk cheese with delicate blue-green veining.
Once again, because it's so full-flavored, a little goes a long way.

PREPARATION TIME: 5 MINUTES   COOKING TIME: 15 MINUTES

1 recipe Reduced-Fat Béchamel (page 54), using leek instead of onion
1 leek, trimmed and washed (optional) (see box on page 46)

6 to 8 tablespoons crumbled Gorgonzola cheese

Prepare the béchamel sauce, substituting the leek for the onion. Whisk all but 1 tablespoon cheese into the sauce. Just before serving, sprinkle the remaining cheese over the sauce. That way, the first taste that hits your tongue will be cheese and it will trick your mouth into thinking there's more cheese in the sauce than there really is.

Makes 2 cups, enough to serve 8

63 CALORIES PER SERVING; 4 G PROTEIN; 3 G FAT; 2 G SATURATED FAT; 6 G CARBOHYDRATE; 123 MG SODIUM; 8 MG CHOLESTEROL

ENLIGHTENED PESTO

Like most Americans who came of culinary age in the 1970s, I cut my teeth on pesto. I remember it as a thick, garlicky paste, rich with cheese and chunky with pine nuts. My first taste of pesto in its birthplace, Genoa, came as a shock. It was a smooth, thin, emerald-colored elixir. It was much lighter than the North American version—made with very little cheese and no pine nuts. Traditionally, the ingredients for pesto were pounded to a smooth paste in a marble mortar and pestle. Nothing produces a smoother, more mellow-tasting pesto than this method. (Realizing this, restaurateurs in northern Italy have devised a mechanized version of a mortar and pestle: a rotating drum with a heavy marble tumbler to crush the basil leaves.) But delicious results can be obtained by puréeing the ingredients in a blender. To further lighten the pesto, I've substituted broth for some of the olive oil.

PREPARATION TIME: 10 MINUTES

4 cloves garlic, peeled, trimmed, and sliced
½ teaspoon salt, or to taste
1 large or 2 medium bunches fresh basil, washed, stemmed, and blotted dry (about 4 cups leaves)
2 tablespoons freshly grated Parmigiano-Reggiano cheese

2 tablespoons extra-virgin olive oil
3 to 4 tablespoons Basic Vegetable Broth (page 241) or Chicken Broth (page239)
½ teaspoon freshly ground black pepper, or to taste

With a mortar and pestle, pound the garlic and salt to a smooth paste. Add the basil leaves and pound to a smooth paste. Pound in the cheese. Work in the olive oil, broth, and pepper, stirring the pestle in a circular motion. The pesto can also be made in a blender. Correct the seasoning, adding salt and pepper to taste.

Makes ¾ to 1 cup, enough to serve 4

88 CALORIES PER SERVING; 3 G PROTEIN; 8 G FAT; 2 G SATURATED FAT; 3 G CARBOHYDRATE; 196 MG SODIUM; 2 MG CHOLESTEROL

FRESH (UNCOOKED) TOMATO SAUCE

Here's a fresh uncooked tomato sauce for dishes and occasions when you simply don't feel like cooking. The sauce can literally be made in a matter of minutes. It's delicious with frittatas, sformati (savory custards), and grilled seafood. For the best results, use tomatoes so ripe and juicy, they would go splat if you dropped them.

PREPARATION TIME: 10 MINUTES

2 large, juicy, red ripe tomatoes (about
    1¼ pounds), quartered (reserve juices)
1 clove garlic, minced
8 fresh basil leaves, thinly slivered

4 fresh oregano leaves, or ¼ teaspoon dried
1½ tablespoons extra-virgin olive oil
1 tablespoon balsamic vinegar
salt and freshly ground black pepper

Place all the ingredients in a blender or food processor and grind to a coarse or smooth purée. Correct the seasoning, adding salt or vinegar to taste.

Makes 2 cups, enough to serve 4 to 6

83 CALORIES PER SERVING;* 1 G PROTEIN; 6 G FAT; 0.7 G SATURATED FAT; 8 G CARBOHYDRATE; 14 MG SODIUM; 0 MG CHOLESTEROL

Analysis is based on 4 servings.

SMOOTH TOMATO SAUCE

SUGO DI POMODORO

Sugo di pomodoro (literally, "tomato juice") is the simplest of all Italian tomato sauces, a smooth, light, velvety sauce perfect for spooning over spaghetti, gnocchi, and other simple pastas. What's remarkable about this recipe is that it is virtually fat-free. Traditionally, the onion and garlic would be sautéed in a generous amount of olive oil. Here they're roasted in a hot oven. But if your fat budget allows it, add one or two tablespoons of extra-virgin olive oil at the end for extra flavor.

PREPARATION TIME: 15 MINUTES   COOKING TIME: 30 MINUTES

1 small onion, peeled and quartered
3 cloves garlic, in their skins
½ teaspoon extra-virgin olive oil, plus (optional)
   1 to 2 tablespoons for adding at end
salt and freshly ground black pepper

1 28-ounce can imported peeled plum tomatoes,
   with their juices
6 basil leaves, thinly slivered, or ½ teaspoon dried
½ teaspoon sugar (optional)

1. Preheat the oven to 400°F. Toss or brush the onion and garlic with ½ teaspoon olive oil and season with salt and pepper. Roast the onion in a roasting pan for 10 minutes. Add the garlic and continue roasting until both onion and garlic are soft and golden-brown, an additional 10 to 15 minutes. Turn once or twice to ensure even roasting.

2. Grind the onion, garlic, and tomatoes with their juices through a vegetable mill or purée in a food processor or blender until smooth. Strain the mixture through a strainer or sieve back into the saucepan. (Straining is not necessary if you use a vegetable mill.)

3. Add the basil and sugar (if using), and simmer the sauce, uncovered, over medium heat, stirring occasionally, until it is well flavored and slightly thickened, 4 to 6 minutes. Correct the seasoning, adding salt and pepper to taste. If using additional oil, add it 1 minute before you remove the sauce from the heat.

Makes 3½ cups, enough to serve 8 to 10

26 CALORIES PER SERVING;* 1 G PROTEIN; 0.3 G FAT; 0 G SATURATED FAT; 6 G CARBOHYDRATE; 162 MG SODIUM; 0 MG CHOLESTEROL

*Analysis is based on 8 servings.

NEAPOLITAN TOMATO SAUCE

Here's another simple red sauce—the sort that simmers away in huge pots in steamy kitchens in Naples and in Italian-American kitchens in North America. I've streamlined the procedure to give you a flavor-packed sauce that can be prepared in fifteen minutes. The easiest way to chop the tomatoes is to purée them, juices and all, in a food processor.

PREPARATION TIME: 15 MINUTES   COOKING TIME: 20 MINUTES

2 tablespoons extra-virgin olive oil
1 large onion, finely chopped
3 cloves garlic, finely chopped
1 stalk celery, finely chopped
½ green bell pepper, finely chopped
¼ to ½ teaspoon hot pepper flakes (optional)
1 28-ounce can imported peeled plum tomatoes,
  with their juices, finely chopped or puréed

2 tablespoons finely chopped flat-leaf parsley
½ teaspoon dried oregano
½ teaspoon dried thyme
½ teaspoon sugar
salt and freshly ground black pepper

1. Heat the olive oil in a large, heavy saucepan. Add the onion, garlic, celery, bell pepper, and pepper flakes (if using) and cook over medium heat until the vegetables are soft but not brown, about 5 minutes.

2. Stir in the tomatoes, parsley, oregano, thyme, sugar, salt, and pepper and gently simmer the sauce until thick and flavorful, about 15 minutes. Correct the seasoning, adding salt and pepper to taste.

Makes about 4 cups, enough to serve 8 to 10

84 CALORIES PER SERVING;* 3 G PROTEIN; 5 G FAT; 1 G SATURATED FAT; 7 G CARBOHYDRATE; 255 MG SODIUM; 4 MG CHOLESTEROL

Analysis is based on 8 servings.

TOMATO "CREAM" SAUCE

Cream has a mellowing effect on tomatoes, a property appreciated by anyone who has tasted a panna rossa *(literally, "pink cream"), tomato cream sauce. My low-fat version uses an ingredient that might shock an Italian—evaporated skim milk—but I think you'll find the sauce quite creamy and tasty. I like the way the slight sweetness of this product cuts the acidity of the tomatoes. Tomato cream sauce is great on ravioli and other stuffed pasta and smooth noodles, like bucatini.*

PREPARATION TIME: 15 MINUTES   COOKING TIME: 15 MINUTES

1½ tablespoons extra-virgin olive oil
1 medium onion, finely chopped
1 clove garlic, finely chopped
1 stalk celery, finely chopped
1 carrot, finely chopped
salt and freshly ground black pepper

1 28-ounce can imported peeled plum tomatoes,
    with their juices, finely chopped or puréed
6 fresh basil leaves, thinly slivered, or ½ teaspoon
    dried
½ teaspoon sugar
½ cup evaporated skim milk

1. Heat the olive oil in a large, heavy saucepan. Add the onion, garlic, celery, carrot, and a little salt and pepper. Cook over medium heat until the vegetables are soft but not brown, about 4 minutes.

2. Stir in the tomatoes, basil, and sugar and gently simmer the sauce until thick and flavorful, about 10 minutes. Add the evaporated skim milk the last 3 minutes.

3. Purée the mixture in a blender or food processor. Strain the sauce through a strainer or sieve back into the saucepan. Correct the seasoning, adding salt and pepper to taste.

Makes about 4 cups, enough to serve 8 to 10

70 CALORIES PER SERVING;* 2 G PROTEIN; 3 G FAT; 0.4 G SATURATED FAT; 10 G CARBOHYDRATE; 36 MG SODIUM; 0 MG CHOLESTEROL

Analysis is based on 8 servings.

FRESH TOMATO SAUCE WITH CAPERS AND OLIVES

This sauce is more robust than the preceding ones—a rich, chunky tomato sauce made with fresh tomatoes and loaded with flavorful bits of capers and olives. I make this sauce when tomatoes are in season: in the winter here in Florida, in late summer up North. If you can't find luscious ripe fresh tomatoes, use good imported canned plum tomatoes. (You'll need a 28-ounce can.) If you like anchovies, you can always chop a few and add them to the sauce.

PREPARATION TIME: 15 MINUTES   COOKING TIME: 20 MINUTES

1 tablespoon extra-virgin olive oil
1 to 2 cloves garlic, smashed with the side of a
  cleaver and peeled
1 small onion, finely chopped
2 tablespoons tomato paste
½ teaspoon dried oregano (or 8 fresh oregano
  leaves)

3 to 4 large ripe tomatoes (about 2 pounds), peeled
  and finely chopped (with their juices)
½ teaspoon sugar (optional)
2 tablespoons capers, undrained
4 pitted black olives, finely chopped
salt and freshly ground black pepper

1. Heat the olive oil in a large nonstick frying pan. Add the garlic and cook over medium heat until fragrant, about 1 minute. Reduce the heat to medium-low and add the onion. Cook until a rich golden-brown, 8 to 10 minutes. Add the tomato paste and oregano and cook for 2 minutes.

2. Add the tomatoes with their juices and the sugar, capers, olives, salt, and pepper and gently simmer the sauce, stirring often with a wooden spoon, until thick and richly flavored, about 10 minutes. Correct the seasoning, adding salt or sugar as needed.
Makes 3 to 4 cups sauce, enough to serve 6 to 8

66 CALORIES PER ½-CUP SERVING; 2 G PROTEIN; 3 G FAT; 0.4 G SATURATED FAT; 10 G CARBOHYDRATE; 175 MG SODIUM; 0 MG CHOLESTEROL

BOLOGNESE MEAT SAUCE (RAGÙ)

This rich, meaty sauce is one of the glories of Bolognese cooking. The traditional version would contain butter, cream, liver, and other fat-laden ingredients. My low-fat version uses lean cuts of veal, pork, and/or turkey, which I chop at home to make sure they're completely devoid of fat. (For the richest flavor, use 4 ounces of each type of meat.) In place of the traditional cream, I enrich this sauce, too, with a thoroughly non-Italian ingredient, evaporated skim milk. I like the way the slight sweetness of this product cuts the acidity of the tomatoes. The easiest way to chop the tomatoes is in a food processor.

PREPARATION TIME: 15 MINUTES   COOKING TIME: 40 MINUTES

1 tablespoon extra-virgin olive oil
1 medium onion, finely chopped
2 stalks celery, finely chopped
2 small or 1 large carrot, finely chopped
12 ounces lean veal, pork, and/or turkey, minced
    with a cleaver or in the food processor
1 ounce prosciutto, minced
1 tablespoon tomato paste
1 cup dry white wine
1 cup evaporated skim milk

1 28-ounce can imported peeled plum tomatoes,
    with their juices, finely chopped
3 tablespoons finely chopped flat-leaf parsley
2 fresh basil leaves, or ½ teaspoon dried
1 bay leaf
salt and freshly ground black pepper
1 cup Chicken Broth (page 239) or veal broth
    (page 239) (optional)
a little freshly grated nutmeg

1. Heat the olive oil in a large, heavy saucepan (preferably nonstick). Add the onion, celery, and carrot and cook over medium heat until lightly browned, about 5 minutes.

2. Stir in the meat and prosciutto and cook until crumbly and browned, 5 to 10 minutes, breaking the meat apart with the edge of a metal spatula or with a wooden spoon. Add the tomato paste after 4 minutes. Add the wine and bring to a boil. Reduce the heat and simmer the sauce until the wine is completely absorbed, about 5 minutes. Add ½ cup of the evaporated skim milk and simmer until completely absorbed, about 5 minutes.

3. Stir in the chopped tomatoes with their juices and the parsley, basil leaves, bay leaf, salt, and pepper. Reduce the heat and gently simmer the sauce until it is well reduced and richly flavored, 30 to 40 minutes. If the sauce becomes too thick, add a little chicken broth or water. Stir in the remaining ½ cup of evaporated skim milk and continue simmering the sauce until the milk is absorbed and reduced. Correct the seasoning, adding salt and pepper to taste. Add a hint, just a hint of freshly grated nutmeg. Discard the bay leaf before serving.

Makes 4 cups, enough to serve 6 to 8 people

226 CALORIES PER SERVING;* 20 G PROTEIN; 6 G FAT; 2 G SATURATED FAT; 17 G CARBOHYDRATE; 437 MG SODIUM; 55 MG CHOLESTEROL

Analysis is based on 6 servings.

FRESH PASTA

HOMEMADE EGG PASTA

Is there any dish that better epitomizes the glory and comfort of the Italian table than fresh pasta? Soft yet chewy, velvety and smooth, it's the very soul of Italian cooking. Traditional egg pasta is made with only eggs and flour, of course, but it's still not what I'd call bad for you. An appetizer-size portion of egg pasta rings in at about 3.3 grams of fat per serving; a main-course portion, at about 4.4 grams per serving. Tolerable. So our master recipe follows the traditional proportions. You can trim the fat by about 30 percent by substituting 2 egg whites for 1 of the whole eggs. Or by making one of the vegetable pastas on page 68. On page 70 you'll find a recipe for a fat-free pasta made with egg substitute or egg whites. I also offer three methods for making pasta: one by hand, one in the food processor, and one in the mixer. But even when mixing by machine, I like to knead the dough for a minute or two by hand to give it a "human" touch.

PREPARATION TIME: 30 TO 40 MINUTES   COOKING TIME: 4 TO 6 MINUTES

MAKING THE DOUGH

3 large eggs

approximately 2 cups all-purpose unbleached white flour

HAND METHOD

1. Place the flour in a mound on a clean work surface. Make a 3-inch "well" (depression) in the center, using your hands or the bottom of a cup. Place the eggs in the well and beat with a fork until smooth. Using the tips of your fingers, gradually work enough flour into the eggs to form a thick paste. Using both hands, mix in the remaining flour to form a compact mass. Scrape the crumbs off your hands and the work surface and add them to the dough. If the dough is too wet (that is, if it sticks to your hands), add a little more flour. Wash and dry your hands.

2. Lightly flour the work surface. Turn dough 90°, fold over. Using the heels of your palms, knead the dough until smooth and satiny, about 8 minutes. Use as little flour as possible—just enough to keep the dough from sticking to your hands. When ready, it will feel dense, smooth, and elastic. Wrap it in plastic wrap until you're ready to roll it out. It is best to roll out the dough within 10 minutes of making it.

FOOD PROCESSOR METHOD

1. Crack the eggs into a food processor fitted with a dough blade (or metal blade, if you don't have a dough blade). Process until smooth. Mix in the flour, running the machine in bursts. The dough should form a smooth ball. If it is too wet, add a little more flour. Knead the dough in the food processor until smooth and pliable, about 3 minutes.

2. Transfer the dough to a lightly floured work surface and knead by hand for a minute or two, as described in the hand-method instructions. Wrap it in

Making Homemade Egg Pasta

plastic wrap until you're ready to roll it out. It is best to roll out the dough within 10 minutes of making it.

MIXER METHOD

1. Crack the eggs into a mixer fitted with a dough hook. Mix until blended. Add the flour and mix at low or medium-low speed until the ingredients come together into a soft ball. If dough is too wet, add a little more flour. Knead the dough in the mixer until smooth and pliable, about 10 minutes.

2. Transfer the dough to a lightly floured work surface and knead by hand for a minute or two. Wrap it in plastic wrap until you're ready to roll it out. It is best to roll out the dough within 10 minutes of making it.

MAKING PASTA WITH AN EXTRUDER-TYPE MACHINE

Extruder-type pasta machines are based on industrial pasta presses in Italy. They vary in their quality and their success with particular types of noodles. I'm not a big fan of extruder-type machines: I find the noodles tend to clump together. But many people swear by them. Follow the manufacturer's instructions.

ROLLING OUT THE DOUGH

HAND METHOD

Rolling the dough is the only hard part about making pasta. Pat the dough into a disk. Using a long, slender rolling pin, roll the dough into as large and thin a circle as you can, rotating the dough and lightly flouring the work surface as needed. Begin rolling from the center of the dough circle and roll toward the edge. Keep the dough moving.

The trick to obtaining really thin pasta is to stretch the dough with the heels of your palms as you roll it. Continue turning, rolling, and stretching the dough until it's a little thinner than a dime.

MACHINE METHOD

Divide the dough into 2 balls. Open the rollers of the pasta machine to their widest setting. Run each ball through the rollers 4 or 5 times. Close the setting a notch and crank the dough through again. Continue closing the rollers and rolling the dough until you obtain the desired thickness.

Note: If you plan to make cannelloni, ravioli, agnolotti, tortellini, or other stuffed pasta, cover the resulting dough sheets with plastic wrap, then a slightly damp dish towel, to keep them from drying out. If you plan to make noodles, hang the sheets on a rack or hanger until they just begin to feel dry, 10 to 15 minutes. Do not let the pasta dry so much that it cracks when you try to fold it.

CUTTING THE PASTA INTO NOODLES

HAND METHOD

To cut the pasta into noodles, fold the sheet of pasta like a business letter. Using a large chopping knife, cut the dough perpendicular to the folds into strips of uniform thickness. Cut 2-inch strips to make lasagne, 1-inch strips to make pappardelle, ½-inch strips for tagliatelle, ¼-inch strips for fettuccine, ⅛-inch strips for tarelli (flat spaghetti), and ¹⁄₁₆-inch strips for capelli d'angelo (angel hair). To give lasagna or pappardelle a rippled edge, cut the pasta with a fluted pastry wheel. Maltagliati (literally, "badly cut" noodles) are made by cutting the dough into irregular parallelograms.

MACHINE METHOD

Feed the long dough sheets through the cutting rollers of the pasta machine, using cutters of the desired size. Hang the noodles on a pasta rack or loosely coil them on a wire rack to dry. The pasta can be dried completely and stored in plastic bags, or frozen, for later use.

Instructions for making filled pastas will be found in the respective recipes.

COOKING THE PASTA

Pasta should be cooked in rapidly boiling water—at least 4 quarts for every pound of pasta. The water should be lightly salted. Depending on the size of the noodle and the freshness of the pasta, you'll need 4 to 6 minutes of cooking. Italians have a wonderful term for describing properly cooked pasta: al dente (literally "to the tooth"). That is, the pasta should be tender, but still a little firm.

Serves 4

274 CALORIES PER SERVING; 11 G PROTEIN; 3 G FAT; 0.8 G SATURATED FAT; 68 G CARBOHYDRATE; 60 MG SODIUM; 107 MG CHOLESTEROL

Additional Tips for Making Homemade Pasta

Of all the people who have written about making pasta, no one is so eloquent or expert as Giuliano Bugialli. Here are some of his tips.

- Let the flour stand in a bowl for 1 hour before making the pasta, to allow the air to escape. Airless flour produces a denser, sturdier pasta.

- When mixing the dough by hand, sift any dough crumbs in a strainer to remove the excess flour. Specks of undissolved flour can weaken the dough.

- Roll the dough as soon as it's kneaded. When you let the dough rest, the gluten expands, and the resulting pasta will be starchy.

- To achieve a uniform consistency, roll the pasta out in 1 or 2 long strips.

- Beware of pasta machines with plastic rollers. They have a hard time rolling the dough to the proper thinness.

VARIATIONS ON THE BASIC PASTA

SPINACH PASTA

PREPARATION TIME: 30 MINUTES   COOKING TIME: 4 TO 6 MINUTES

¼ cup cooked fresh or frozen spinach (tightly squeeze it between your fingers to wring out all excess water)

1 egg, plus 2 egg whites
about 2 cups all-purpose unbleached white flour

Purée the spinach, egg, and egg whites in a blender. Use this mixture, in place of the plain eggs in the basic recipe, to make pasta dough, following one of the procedures outlined above.   *Serves 4*

TOMATO PASTA

PREPARATION TIME: 30 MINUTES   COOKING TIME: 4 TO 6 MINUTES

2 eggs, plus 2 egg whites
1 tablespoon tomato paste

about 2 cups all-purpose unbleached white flour

Combine the eggs, whites, and tomato paste in a bowl and whisk until smooth. Use this mixture to make pasta dough, following one of the procedures outlined above.   *Serves 4*

LEMON PEPPER PASTA

Prepare the basic pasta recipe, adding 1 to 2 teaspoons finely grated lemon zest and ½ teaspoon freshly ground black pepper. One easy way to grate lemon zest is to peel off strips with a vegetable peeler, then grind them in a spice mill.

PREPARATION TIME: 30 MINUTES   COOKING TIME: 4 TO 6 MINUTES

Serves 4

YOLKLESS PASTA

Okay, I know I'll really come under fire for this one. But egg substitutes (which are basically egg whites and flavorings) can be used to make a credible pasta dough—without a trace of fat from the yolk.

PREPARATION TIME: 30 TO 40 MINUTES   COOKING TIME: 4 TO 6 MINUTES

¾ cup egg whites (6 large) or egg substitute   **about 2 cups all-purpose unbleached white flour**

Prepare as described in the basic recipe (page 65).   *Serves 4*

253 CALORIES PER SERVING; 12 G PROTEIN; 0.6 G FAT; 0.1 G SATURATED FAT; 48 G CARBOHYDRATE; 83 MG SODIUM; 0 MG CHOLESTEROL

WHOLE-WHEAT ORECCHIETTE

Many fancy restaurants and hotels in Italy have the sense to hire local housewives to make their pasta. Which is how I met Antonia Chiarappa, pastamaker at the luxurious Melograno ("Pomegranate") resort in Apulia. Working with a dexterity that borders on legerdemain, Antonia transforms a simple whole-wheat dough into delicate orecchiette (tiny pasta disks—the name literally means "little ears"). Don't be discouraged if your first few orecchiette look misshapen. With a little practice, you'll be turning them out the way Antonia does. Orecchiette are traditionally served with broccoli rabe sauce (page 81), cauliflower sauce (page 82), or any of the tomato sauces on pages 58–62.

PREPARATION TIME: 30 MINUTES   COOKING TIME: 5 MINUTES

1 cup whole-wheat flour
1 cup all-purpose unbleached white flour
1 egg or 2 egg whites

about ½ cup hot water
1 scant teaspoon salt

1. **Hand method:** Mix the flours in a bowl and dump them in a mound on a smooth work surface. Make a depression in the center, using your hands or the bottom of a measuring cup. Place the egg or whites, water, and salt in the center and beat with a fork. Gradually incorporate the flour, working with your fingertips. Knead the mixture into a firm but pliable dough. (If the dough looks too dry, add a little more water.) You'll need 6 to 8 minutes kneading by hand in all. Wrap the dough in plastic wrap and let stand for 30 minutes.

1a. **Food processor method:** Place the flours in a processor bowl fitted with a dough blade. With the machine running, add the egg or whites, water, and salt. Knead the mixture into a firm but pliable dough, about 3 minutes. Wrap the dough in plastic wrap and let stand for 30 minutes.

1b. **Mixer method:** Place the flours in the bowl of a mixer fitted with a dough hook. With the machine running, add the egg or whites, water, and salt. Knead

the mixture into a firm but pliable dough, about 8 minutes. Wrap the dough in plastic wrap and let stand for 30 minutes.

2. Divide the dough into 4 even portions. Roll each under the palms of your hands to form a cylinder ½ inch in diameter. Cut the cylinder into ¼-inch pieces. Lightly flour your fingers. Roll each small piece of dough into a ball with your fingers, then flatten it against your thumb by pressing with your forefinger. Peel the dough off your thumb. It should look like a tiny concave disk (or, with a little imagination, a little ear). Transfer to a lightly floured baking sheet or screen to dry. Continue making the orecchiette until all the dough is used up. Let the orecchiette dry for 30 minutes.

3. Bring 4 quarts salted water to a rolling boil. Add the orecchiette and boil until al dente, 5 to 8 minutes. Drain well before adding to the sauce.

Serves 4 to 6

234 CALORIES PER SERVING;* 9 G PROTEIN; 2 G FAT; 0.5 G SATURATED FAT; 46 G CARBOHYDRATE; 444 MG SODIUM; 53 MG CHOLESTEROL

Analysis is based on 4 servings.

PUMPKIN AGNOLOTTI

Agnolotti are round ravioli. This version features a savory pumpkin filling I first sampled in Parma. The crumbled amaretti (almond cookies) provide a sweet, nutty touch. Amaretti are available at Italian markets and most gourmet shops.

PREPARATION TIME: 40 MINUTES   COOKING TIME: 40 TO 60 MINUTES
FOR BAKING THE SQUASH, PLUS 10 MINUTES FOR THE PASTA

FOR THE FILLING:
1½ pounds trimmed fresh pumpkin or butternut
    squash (1½ cups puréed cooked flesh)
2 to 3 amaretti, crumbled (about 2 tablespoons)
3 tablespoons freshly grated Parmigiano-Reggiano
    cheese
1 egg white
salt and freshly ground black pepper

a whisper of nutmeg
3 to 5 tablespoons toasted bread crumbs (or as
    needed)

TO FINISH THE AGNOLOTTI:
1 recipe any of the homemade pastas on pages
    65–70
1 egg white, lightly beaten

1. Prepare the filling: Preheat the oven to 400°F. Loosely wrap the pumpkin in foil and bake until soft, about 40 minutes. Transfer to a plate and let cool. Purée the pumpkin and amaretti in a food processor or mash with a fork in a mixing bowl. Still using the processor, work in the cheese, egg white, salt, pepper, and nutmeg to taste: the filling should be highly seasoned. Add enough bread crumbs to obtain a soft but dry filling: it should be the consistency of soft ice cream.

2. Roll out the pasta dough through the thinnest setting on your machine to make 2 sheets about 40 inches long and 5 inches wide. Lay one of these sheets on a work surface and brush the top with the beaten egg white. Using a piping bag fitted with a ½-inch round tip or using a spoon, place small mounds of the filling (about 1 tablespoon each) in 2 neat rows on top of the dough strip, 1½ inches apart.

Bring 4 quarts lightly salted water to a boil in a large pot.

3. Lay the second sheet of pasta on top. Press with your fingertips between the mounds of filling to seal the two pasta sheets together. Using a fluted round pastry cutter (1½ inches in diameter), cut out the agnolotti and transfer them to a wire rack. Pasta scraps can be gathered together and rerolled. (If you wish to freeze the agnolotti for later use, place them on a baking sheet in the freezer. Once frozen, pack in a zip-top plastic bag.)

4. Cook the agnolotti in rapidly boiling water until they are al dente, about 6 minutes. Drain in a colander and serve at once. I like to serve these agnolotti in bowls with chicken broth or vegetable broth to cover and a grating of Parmesan cheese.

*Makes 32 to 40 agnolotti, enough to
serve 6 to 8 as an appetizer, 4 to 5 as an entrée*

283 CALORIES PER SERVING;* 12 G PROTEIN; 5 G FAT; 1 G SATURATED FAT; 45 G CARBOHYDRATE; 161 MG SODIUM; 73 MG CHOLESTEROL

Analysis is based on 6 servings as an appetizer.

EXOTIC MUSHROOM RAVIOLI

In Italy these ravioli would be made with fresh porcini mushrooms. While it's possible to find fresh porcini in the United States, shiitakes have a similar pungency and are much more readily available, so I've called for shiitakes in this recipe. If you can find porcini, by all means, use them. Another way to beef up the mushroom flavor would be to use ½ to 1 ounce dried porcini or 2 to 3 teaspoons porcini powder. For that matter, you could use 3 ounces of any exotic mushroom instead of the shiitakes, or even 8 to 10 dried Chinese black mushrooms soaked in hot water to soften.

PREPARATION TIME: 40 MINUTES   COOKING TIME: 20 MINUTES

FOR THE FILLING:
½ to 1 ounce dried porcini mushrooms (optional)
   or 2 to 3 teaspoons porcini mushroom powder
3 ounces shiitake mushrooms
1 tablespoon extra-virgin olive oil
1 small onion, finely chopped
¼ cup dry white wine
1 cup low-fat or no-fat ricotta cheese (if your fat budget allows it, use the low-fat—it has a much better flavor)

1 egg white
salt, freshly ground black pepper, and a pinch of cayenne pepper

TO FINISH THE RAVIOLI:
1 recipe any of the homemade pastas on pages 65–70
1 egg white, lightly beaten

1. If using dried porcini, soak them in 1 cup hot water until soft, about 20 minutes. Drain the porcini, reserving the soaking liquid for soups or risotto (strain it through a coffee filter to remove any grit). Transfer the porcini to a bowl with fresh water and agitate with your fingers to remove any remaining grit. Wring the porcini dry with your fingers and finely chop.

2. Stem and finely chop the shiitakes. Heat the oil in a nonstick frying pan. Add the onions and cook over medium heat for 2 minutes. Add the shiitakes (and soaked porcini or porcini powder, if using) and continue cooking until the mushrooms are soft and the onions are just beginning to brown, about 3 minutes more. Add the wine and boil until all the liquid is evaporated or absorbed by the mushrooms. Transfer the mushroom mixture to a mixing bowl and let cool. Stir in the ricotta, egg white, and salt, pepper, and cayenne to taste: the filling should be highly seasoned.

3. Roll out the pasta dough through the thinnest setting on your machine to make 2 sheets about 40 inches long and 5 inches wide. Lay one of these sheets on a work surface and brush the top with egg white. Using a piping bag fitted with a ½-inch round tip or a spoon, place small mounds of the filling (about 1 tablespoon each) in 2 neat rows on top of the dough strip, 2 inches apart. Bring 4 quarts lightly salted water to a boil in a large pot.

4. Lay the second sheet of pasta on top. Press with your fingertips between the mounds of filling to seal the two pasta sheets together. Using a fluted pastry wheel, cut the pasta into 2-inch squares, each containing a mound of filling. As you cut the ravioli, transfer them to a wire rack to dry. (If you wish to freeze the ravioli for later use, place them on a baking sheet in the freezer. Once frozen, pack in a zip-top plastic bag.)

5. Cook the ravioli in rapidly boiling water until the pasta is al dente, about 6 minutes. Drain in a colander and serve at once. There are lots of good sauce possibilities for mushroom ravioli, including

the Parmesan Cheese Sauce on page 55, the Pumpkin Sauce on page 77, or the Tomato "Cream" Sauce on page 61. Alternatively, you can serve the ravioli in bowls with Chicken Broth (page 239) or Basic Vegetable Broth (page 241) to cover and a grating of Parmesan cheese.

Makes about 32 to 40 ravioli, enough to serve 6 to 8 as an appetizer, 4 to 5 as an entrée

268 CALORIES PER SERVING;* 13 G PROTEIN; 6 G FAT; 0.8 G SATURATED FAT; 38 G CARBOHYDRATE; 235 MG SODIUM; 71 MG CHOLESTEROL

*Analysis is based on 6 servings as an appetizer.

RAVIOLI RAPIDISSIMO

Authenticity versus convenience. Nutrition versus taste. As an author writing about low-fat cooking in a hurried age, I constantly wrestle with conflicting values. On the one hand, I certainly strive to chronicle the proper way to cook a particular dish. On the other, I want to write recipes that people will actually cook. While writing my High-Flavor, Low-Fat Pasta book, I discovered that Italian ravioli could be made with Chinese eggroll wrappers and dumpling skins. The result isn't really Italian, of course, but it's quite tasty. Wonton wrappers enable you to enjoy traditional Italian fillings, such as the mushroom filling on page 73 and the pumpkin filling on page 72, in a fraction of the time that it would take to make Italian pasta from scratch. I offer the following recipe to the time-harried cook who doesn't mind mixing cultures. A replacement for real ravioli? No. But my wife and I enjoy ravioli rapidissimo from time to time, and so will you.

PREPARATION TIME: 15 MINUTES   COOKING TIME: 5 MINUTES

salt
40 3-inch Chinese dumpling wrappers or wonton wrappers (round or square) or 10 large eggroll wrappers (if using eggroll wrappers, cut each in quarters)

1 egg white, lightly beaten
one of the following fillings:
    pumpkin filling (page 72)
    mushroom filling (page 73)

1. Bring 4 quarts salted water to a boil. Lay the wrappers out on a work surface. Very lightly brush the edges of each wrapper with egg white. Place a small spoonful of filling in the center of each. Fold the wrapper in half and pinch the edges, starting at one side and working around to the other, to seal in the filling. (If using a square wrapper, fold it in half on the diagonal.)

2. Cook the ravioli in boiling water until tender, about 2 minutes. Drain in a colander and serve with any of the sauces on pages 53–63.

*Makes 40 ravioli, enough to serve
8 to 10 as an appetizer, 4 to 5 as an entrée*

171 CALORIES PER SERVING;* 6 G PROTEIN; 3 G FAT; 1 G SATURATED FAT; 28 G CARBOHYDRATE; 93 MG SODIUM; 3 MG CHOLESTEROL

Analysis is based on 8 servings as an appetizer.

PASTA WITH SAUCE

PICI WITH PUMPKIN SAUCE

This ancient Tuscan sauce contains only three main ingredients—pumpkin, broth, and onions (plus a little oil to fry them in)—but the resulting flavor is deeply satisfying and mouth-filling to the max. The secret is to caramelize the onions by long, slow, gentle cooking. For an extra splurge, you could thinly shave white or summer truffles on top. Pici is a Tuscan pasta that looks like flat spaghetti. If unavailable, use spaghetti, spaghettini, or fedelini.

PREPARATION TIME: 20 MINUTES   COOKING TIME: 45 MINUTES

2 tablespoons extra-virgin olive oil
2 large red onions, thinly sliced
1½ pounds trimmed fresh pumpkin or butternut
  squash
1 bay leaf
2 to 3 cups Basic Vegetable Broth (page 241) or
  Chicken Broth (page 239)

salt and freshly ground black pepper
1 pound fresh pici or ½ pound dried
½ ounce white or summer truffle (optional)
2 tablespoons finely chopped flat-leaf parsley

1. Heat the oil in a large nonstick frying pan. Cook the onions until nicely caramelized (a rich golden-brown). Start cooking the onions over high heat, then lower the heat to medium, then to low, lowering the flame as the onions cook to prevent them from burning. The whole process will take 20 to 30 minutes.

2. Add the pumpkin, the bay leaf, broth just to cover, and a little salt and pepper. Simmer the mixture until the pumpkin is very soft, about 15 minutes. Add broth as necessary to keep the mixture from drying out. Discard the bay leaf.

3. Purée the sauce in a blender, adding salt and pepper to taste. Return the sauce to the pan and keep warm.

4. Just before serving, cook the pasta until al dente, 3 to 4 minutes for fresh pasta, 8 to 10 minutes for dried pasta. Drain well in a colander. Transfer the pasta to plates or a platter and spoon the hot sauce on top. If using truffles, shave them on top and serve at once. Otherwise, sprinkle the pasta with parsley.

Makes 2½ cups sauce, enough to serve 5 to 6 as an appetizer, 4 as an entrée

471 CALORIES PER SERVING;* 14 G PROTEIN; 7 G FAT; 1 G SATURATED FAT; 88 G CARBOHYDRATE; 39 MG SODIUM; 0 MG CHOLESTEROL

Analysis is based on 5 servings as an appetizer.

❦

Pici with Pumpkin Sauce

SPAGHETTINI WITH RED CLAM SAUCE

When most Americans hear the words "spaghettini with clam sauce," they think of a white butter- or oil-based sauce.
Fresh tomato gives this version an inviting red color and so much flavor that you don't need a lot of fat. Buy the tiniest
clams you can find for this recipe. The shellfish of choice in Italy would be a vongole, a small clam with a brown-striped shell.

PREPARATION TIME: 20 MINUTES   COOKING TIME: 10 MINUTES

36 littleneck or 24 cherrystone clams in the shell
   (see Note)
1½ tablespoons extra-virgin olive oil
3 cloves garlic, thinly sliced
¼ to ½ teaspoon hot pepper flakes
1 cup dry white wine

1 ripe tomato, peeled, seeded, and puréed in a food
   processor
½ cup chopped flat-leaf parsley
salt and freshly ground black pepper
10 ounces spaghettini (thin spaghetti)

1. Scrub the clam shells with a stiff brush, discarding any clams with cracked shells or shells that fail to close when tapped. Put 4 quarts salted water on to boil for the pasta.

2. Heat the oil in a large nonstick frying pan. Add the garlic and pepper flakes and cook over medium heat until the garlic begins to turn golden, about 2 minutes. Add the wine, tomato, and half the parsley and bring to a boil. Tightly cover the pan and cook the clams over high heat until the shells open, 6 to 8 minutes. Uncover the pan and season the sauce to taste with salt, pepper, and additional pepper flakes. Discard any clams that do not open.

3. Meanwhile, put the spaghettini on to boil. Cook until al dente, about 7 minutes. Drain the pasta in a colander and stir it into clam sauce. Cook until thoroughly heated, about 2 minutes. Sprinkle the remaining parsley on top and serve at once.

Note: If fresh clams aren't available, substitute 2 6.5-ounce cans of canned.

Serves 4

462 CALORIES PER SERVING; 20 G PROTEIN; 7 G FAT; 1 G SATURATED FAT; 68 G CARBOHYDRATE; 52 MG SODIUM; 26 MG CHOLESTEROL

EGG NOODLES WITH PESTO, POTATOES, AND PEAS

TROFIE CON PESTO

Pesto has been part of the North American culinary repertory since the 1970s. We make it with lots of cheese (Pecorino Romano), lots of pine nuts, lots of garlic, and lots of olive oil. So I was surprised to find out how light, almost gossamer, pesto is in the land of its birth: the rugged coast of Liguria. Pine nuts are used sparingly, if at all. The cheese is a whisper of Parmigiano-Reggiano. In short, pesto is a light herb sauce, not a heavy paste, which, of course, is good news for the healthy eater. Another surprise is the traditional garnish of boiled potato and fresh peas. The traditional way to enjoy pesto in the towns around Genoa is with a short, stubby egg noodle called trofie. *You may be able to find* trofie *at an Italian market or gourmet shop; alternatively, you could use fettuccine or twisted egg noodles.*

PREPARATION TIME: 10 MINUTES   COOKING TIME: 10 MINUTES

salt
8 ounces *trofie* or other short, stubby dried pasta
1 potato (8 to 10 ounces), peeled and cut into
¼-inch dice

¾ cup shucked peas (preferably fresh)
1 recipe Enlightened Pesto (page 57)

1. Bring 4 quarts lightly salted water to a boil in a large pot. Add the pasta and potato. Cook until the pasta is al dente and the potatoes are soft, about 8 minutes. Add the peas after 4 minutes. Drain the pasta and vegetables well in a colander, reserving ¼ cup cooking liquid.

2. Return the pasta, potatoes, and peas to the pot and stir in the pesto. Cook over high heat until the sauce boils, about 1 minute. If the pesto looks too thick, add 1 to 2 tablespoons pasta cooking liquid. Serve at once.

Serves 4

398 CALORIES PER SERVING; 15 G PROTEIN; 10 G FAT; 2 G SATURATED FAT; 63 G CARBOHYDRATE; 211 MG SODIUM; 52 MG CHOLESTEROL

VARIATION

In Portofino and Santa Frutosa, pesto is served with wide, flat egg noodles similar to lasagne. Prepare the preceding recipe substituting 1 pound fresh lasagna-width noodles or pappardelle.

Spaghetti *Sciue Sciue*

Spaghetti with Tomatoes, Basil, and Garlic

This is about the quickest pasta dish I know of, containing only six ingredients, which are combined at the last minute.
Sciue means quickly in the Sicilian dialect, although I first tasted this dish in Capri.
The food processor works great for chopping the tomatoes and garlic.

PREPARATION TIME: 10 MINUTES   COOKING TIME: 10 MINUTES

8 ounces spaghetti or spaghettini
salt
2 large red ripe tomatoes, finely chopped, with
    their juices
12 large basil leaves, thinly slivered, plus 4 whole
    sprigs for garnish

2 cloves garlic, minced
1 tablespoon drained capers (optional)
1½ tablespoons extra-virgin olive oil
freshly ground black pepper
2 to 4 tablespoons freshly grated Parmigiano-
    Reggiano for serving

1. Cook the spaghetti in 4 quarts rapidly boiling salted water until al dente, about 8 minutes for spaghetti, 6 minutes for spaghettini. Drain the pasta in a colander and return it to the pot.

2. Stir in the chopped tomatoes with their juices, basil, garlic, capers (if using), olive oil, and black pepper. Cook over high heat until the ingredients are thoroughly heated, about 2 minutes. Correct the seasoning, adding salt or pepper to taste.

3. Transfer the pasta to bowls or soup plates, garnishing each with a sprig of basil. Serve the cheese on the side for sprinkling.   *Serves 4*

326 CALORIES PER SERVING; 11 G PROTEIN; 1 G FAT; 7 G SATURATED FAT; 54 G CARBOHYDRATE; 65 MG SODIUM; 2 MG CHOLESTEROL

ORECCHIETTE WITH BROCCOLI RABE AND ANCHOVIES

Orecchiette are one of Italy's most whimsically named pastas: literally, "little ears." With a little imagination, these tiny concave disks of dough do indeed look like tiny ears. Orecchiette are often paired with members of the cabbage family, such as cauliflower and broccoli rabe. The latter, also known as rapini and Italian broccoli, is a leafy cousin of broccoli. Look for it in the supermarket, or use regular broccoli.

PREPARATION TIME: 15 MINUTES   COOKING TIME: 15 MINUTES

1 pound broccoli rabe or 1 bunch broccoli
salt
2 cups dried orecchiette (about 8 ounces) or
    1 recipe fresh orecchiette (see page 71)
1½ tablespoons extra-virgin olive oil
1 to 2 cloves garlic, minced

2 to 4 anchovy fillets, rinsed, blotted dry, and
    finely chopped
2 tablespoons toasted fine dry bread crumbs
freshly ground black pepper
2 to 4 tablespoons grated Pecorino Romano
    cheese, or to taste

1. Holding the broccoli rabe by the stems, wash it in a deep bowl of cold water by plunging it up and down. Change the water, as necessary, until completely free of grit or sand. Trim any large tough stems from the broccoli rabe (save them for soup or stock).

2. Bring 4 quarts lightly salted water to a boil in a large pot. Cook the orecchiette until al dente, about 10 minutes for dried and 4 to 5 minutes for fresh. With a slotted spoon, transfer the orecchiette to a colander, rinse with cold water, and drain. Reserve the pasta cooking water.

3. Add the broccoli rabe to the boiling pasta water and cook until just tender, 2 to 4 minutes. Drain the broccoli rabe in a strainer or colander, refresh under cold water, and drain well. Blot the broccoli rabe dry and finely chop.

4. Just before serving, heat the olive oil in a large nonstick frying pan. Add the garlic and anchovies and cook over high heat until just beginning to brown, about 1 minute. Stir in the broccoli rabe and cook until thoroughly heated, about 2 minutes. Stir in the orecchiette and bread crumbs and cook until thoroughly heated, about 2 minutes. Add salt and pepper to taste. Serve the orecchiette at once, with the cheese on the side for sprinkling.

Serves 4

301 CALORIES PER SERVING; 12 G PROTEIN; 9 G FAT; 2 G SATURATED FAT; 45 G CARBOHYDRATE; 196 MG SODIUM; 53 MG CHOLESTEROL

"Corkscrews" with Cauliflower, Onions, and Pancetta

Cavatappi al Cavolfiore

This is a popular dish in Apulia, where it is traditionally made with orecchiette, tiny pasta "ears." You can certainly use fresh orecchiette (see page 71), but I also like making the recipe with cavatappi, dried ridged pasta tubes that are coiled just like their namesake, "corkscrews." Pancetta is Italian bacon—to rid it of the extra fat, I blanch it in boiling water. If unavailable or too fatty, you could use 1 to 2 ounces slivered prosciutto.

PREPARATION TIME: 15 MINUTES   COOKING TIME: 12 MINUTES

salt
1 small or ½ large head cauliflower
4 strips pancetta (Italian bacon) (about 2 ounces)
4 cups dried cavatappi (12 ounces) or other tube-shaped pasta, or orecchiette
1 tablespoon extra-virgin olive oil
1 medium onion, cut into thin wedges
1 to 2 cloves garlic, minced

¼ teaspoon hot pepper flakes
3 tablespoons fat free half-and-half, 2 percent, 1 percent, or skim milk or Basic Vegetable Broth (page 241) or Chicken Broth (page 239)
3 tablespoons finely chopped flat-leaf parsley
freshly ground black pepper
2 to 4 tablespoons freshly grated Pecorino Romano cheese, or to taste

1. Bring 2 quarts lightly salted water to a boil in a large pot. Stem the cauliflower and break it into florets. Boil the cauliflower until tender, about 5 minutes. Transfer the cauliflower with a slotted spoon to a colander to drain. (Reserve the cooking liquid.) Rinse with cold water and drain well. Cut each floret into ½-inch pieces.

2. Boil the pancetta in the cauliflower water for 2 minutes. Transfer to the colander and let cool. Cut the pancetta into ¼-inch slivers. (If using prosciutto, you don't need to blanch it.) Discard the water and bring 4 fresh quarts of water to a boil.

3. Cook the pasta in the boiling water until al dente, about 8 minutes. Drain the pasta in a colan-der, rinse with cold water, and drain again. The recipe can be prepared ahead to this stage.

4. Just before serving, heat the olive oil in a large nonstick frying pan. Add the pancetta, onion, garlic, and pepper flakes and cook over medium-high heat until fragrant but not brown, about 4 minutes. Stir in the cauliflower and cook until thoroughly heated, about 2 minutes. Stir in the pasta and half-and-half, milk, or broth and bring to a boil. Cook until the ingredients are thoroughly heated and most of the milk is evaporated, about 2 minutes. Add salt and pepper to taste. Stir in the parsley and 2 tablespoons cheese and cook for 30 seconds. Serve at once. Additional cheese can be served on the side.   *Serves 4*

422 CALORIES PER SERVING; 19 G PROTEIN; 10 G FAT; 3 G SATURATED FAT; 66 G CARBOHYDRATE; 218 MG SODIUM; 80 MG CHOLESTEROL

VARIATION:
"CORKSCREWS" WITH CAULIFLOWER, ONIONS, AND TOMATOES

Whenever I make a dish containing meat, I have to come up with a vegetarian version for my wife and daughter. In this recipe, fresh or dried tomatoes stand in for the pancetta.

Prepare the recipe above, replacing the pancetta with 1 large ripe tomato, cut into ½-inch dice, or 4 to 6 dried tomatoes, soaked in water until soft, then diced. You don't need to blanch the tomato, as you do the pancetta. Sauté the onion, garlic, and pepper flakes for 2 minutes before you add the tomato. Use vegetable broth or chicken broth instead of milk.

FUSILLI WITH FRESH ARTICHOKES

Italians love artichokes, and they've devised a quick, easy method for transforming the barbed, fibrous vegetable into tender, easy-to-eat morsels. One of the secrets is to divide and conquer: to cut the artichoke in quarters or sixths so that it's easy to trim off the tough parts. (Don't forget to rub the cut artichoke often with lemon to keep it from discoloring.) Canned and frozen artichokes are perfectly tasty (see Note), but they can't rival the sweet, licoricy flavor of the fresh ones. Don't be intimidated by either the artichokes or the length of this recipe—it's actually very simple. In fact, it's the sort of dish my wife and I would make on a busy weeknight.

PREPARATION TIME: 30 MINUTES   COOKING TIME: 10 MINUTES

salt
2 large artichokes, or 4 medium
1 lemon, cut in half (not needed if using canned artichokes)
1 to 1½ tablespoons extra-virgin olive oil
2 cloves garlic, crushed and peeled
1 medium onion, thinly sliced
3 tablespoons finely chopped flat-leaf parsley
1 large ripe tomato, seeded and cut into ¼-inch dice

2 tablespoons tomato paste
1 cup dry white wine
1½ cups Chicken Broth (page 239) or Basic Vegetable Broth (page 241), or tomato sauce (such as the Sugo di Pomodoro on page 59)
freshly ground black pepper
½ pound dried fusilli (spring-shaped pasta)
2 to 4 tablespoons Parmigiano-Reggiano, or to taste

1. Bring 2 quarts lightly salted water to a boil in a small pot and 4 quarts water in a large pot.

2. Trim the artichokes, rubbing often with cut lemon to prevent discoloring. First, cut off the top third of the artichoke and the bottom of the stem end. Cut the artichoke in quarters from top to bottom. Using a sharp paring knife, trim off any tough outside leaves and fibrous stem parts. Next, cut out the choke (the fibrous part inside). You should wind up with a piece that, viewed from the side, looks like a comma. As you finish trimming each piece, place it in a bowl of cold water with a squeeze of lemon juice. Breathe a sigh of relief. The hard part is over.

3. Cook the artichoke pieces in the smaller pot of boiling water until tender, about 5 minutes. Drain in a colander, refresh under cold water, and drain again. Thinly slice each artichoke quarter lengthwise. The recipe can be prepared several hours ahead to this stage. Store in the refrigerator for up to 4 hours.

4. Meanwhile, prepare the sauce. Heat the olive oil in a large nonstick frying pan over high heat. Add the garlic and cook until just beginning to brown, about 15 seconds. Reduce the heat to medium, add the onion and half the parsley, and cook until soft but not brown, about 3 minutes. Add the tomato and tomato paste and cook for 1 minute. Add the wine and boil until reduced by two-thirds. Add the broth and boil until the sauce is rich and thick, 3 to 5 minutes. Stir in the artichokes and salt and pepper to taste.

5. Meanwhile, cook the fusilli in the larger pot of boiling water until al dente, about 8 minutes. Drain in a colander. Stir the fusilli into the artichoke sauce and cook over medium heat, turning the pasta with tongs to coat with sauce. Sprinkle the remaining parsley on top and serve at once, with the cheese on the side for sprinkling on top.

Note: You can certainly make this recipe using canned or frozen artichokes. You'd need 1 14-ounce can of the former or 1½ 9-ounce packages of the latter. If using canned artichokes or artichoke hearts, rinse and drain well, cut in quarters, and blot dry. If using frozen artichokes, cook following the instructions on the package. Start the recipe at step 4.

Serves 4

355 CALORIES PER SERVING; 13 G PROTEIN; 8 G FAT; 2 G SATURATED FAT; 52 G CARBOHYDRATE; 570 MG SODIUM; 58 MG CHOLESTEROL

"PRIEST STRANGLERS" WITH CARAMELIZED ONIONS AND FAVA BEANS

This dish features one of my favorite pastas, a short, twisted noodle with the colorful name of strozzapreti—literally, "priest stranglers." Look for these noodles at Italian markets and gourmet shops or substitute gemelli (another twisted pasta whose name means "twins") or short fusilli. Fresh fava beans will give you the best results, if you have the time and patience to shuck them, but tasty results can be obtained from frozen or canned fava beans or lima beans. For a variation on this dish, use fresh peas or sugar snap peas.

PREPARATION TIME: 15 MINUTES   COOKING TIME: 20 MINUTES

3 pounds fresh fava beans or 1½ cups shelled,
    canned, or frozen fava beans
salt
1 cup dry white wine
¼ cup white wine vinegar
¼ cup honey
2 cups peeled baby onions or 1 large onion, peeled
    and cut into 16 thin wedges
2 cups Chicken Broth (page 239) or Basic
    Vegetable Broth (page 241)

1 teaspoon grated lemon zest
1 clove garlic, minced
½ cup chopped flat-leaf parsley
salt and freshly ground black pepper

8 ounces strozzapreti, gemelli, or other twisted
    dried pasta
2 to 4 tablespoons freshly grated Parmigiano-
    Reggiano cheese, or to taste

1. If using fresh fava beans, shuck them. Cook in boiling salted water until tender, about 3 minutes. Drain the fava beans, refresh under cold water, and peel off the papery skin. If using frozen favas, blanch in boiling water, drain, rinse, and peel. If using canned fava beans, rinse and drain.

2. Combine the wine, vinegar, and honey in a large nonstick frying pan and bring to a boil. Add the onions and boil until the onions are soft and the cooking liquid is reduced to a syrupy glaze, 10 to 12 minutes. (If the onions start to burn before they're cooked, add a little broth.) Bring 4 quarts water to a boil.

3. Stir the fava beans, broth, lemon zest, garlic, half the parsley, and salt and pepper into the onion mixture and simmer until the sauce is slightly thickened and well flavored.

4. Meanwhile, cook the pasta in the boiling water until al dente, about 8 minutes. Transfer to a colander and drain well. Stir the pasta into the sauce and simmer for 1 minute. Sprinkle the pasta with the remaining parsley and serve with the cheese on the side for sprinkling.   *Serves 4*

502 CALORIES PER SERVING; 27 G PROTEIN; 5 G FAT; 2 G SATURATED FAT; 109 G CARBOHYDRATE; 576 MG SODIUM; 61 MG CHOLESTEROL

BUCATINI WITH PEPPERS, PINE NUTS, AND CHICKPEAS

*Here's a colorful vegetarian pasta dish that's loaded with protein, thanks to the addition of almonds and chickpeas.
As for flavor, the raisins and orange add an unexpected sweetness. Bucatini look like thick hollow spaghetti.
You could also use perciatelli (another long, thick round noodle), long fusilli, or spaghetti.*

PREPARATION TIME: 20 MINUTES   COOKING TIME: 20 MINUTES

1½ tablespoons extra-virgin olive oil
3 tablespoons slivered almonds or pine nuts
1 onion, finely chopped
2 to 3 cloves garlic, minced
1 red or green bell pepper, cored, seeded, and cut into matchstick slivers
2 stalks celery, cut into ¼-inch dice
3 tablespoons raisins
3 tablespoons chopped flat-leaf parsley
½ cup cooked chickpeas

1 cup Basic Vegetable Broth (page 241) or chickpea cooking liquid
3 tablespoons fresh orange juice (or to taste)
½ teaspoon grated orange zest
salt and freshly ground black pepper

8 ounces bucatini or other long, thick pasta
1 to 2 ounces ricotta salata or Pecorino Romano cheese for grating (2 to 4 tablespoons—optional)

1. Heat the olive oil in a large, nonstick frying pan. Add the almonds and cook over medium heat until golden, about 2 minutes. Add the onion, garlic, pepper, celery, and raisins and half the parsley and cook until all the vegetables are soft but not brown, about 5 minutes.

2. Stir in the chickpeas, broth, orange juice, and orange zest and boil until reduced by half, about 5 minutes. Add salt and pepper to taste.

3. Meanwhile, cook the bucatini in 4 quarts boiling salted water until al dente, 8 to 10 minutes. Drain the pasta and stir it into the sauce. Simmer until the pasta is thoroughly heated and coated with sauce, about 2 minutes. Correct the seasoning, adding salt to taste. Sprinkle the pasta with the remaining parsley and serve with the cheese on the side for grating.

Serves 4

382 CALORIES PER SERVING; 12 G PROTEIN; 11 G FAT; 7 G SATURATED FAT; 61 G CARBOHYDRATE; 53 MG SODIUM; 49 MG CHOLESTEROL

QUICK SUMMER PASTA WITH TOMATOES AND ARUGULA

Here's a perfect pasta dish for the dog days of summer. All you need to cook are the noodles. The sauce—a coarse purée of fresh tomatoes and herbs—is "cooked" by the warm pasta. My favorite cheese for serving with this pasta is ricotta salata—a firm, snappy grating or shaving cheese made by pressing and aging ricotta.

PREPARATION TIME: 10 MINUTES   COOKING TIME: 10 MINUTES

3 cups ridged tube-shaped pasta, like penne rigati
salt
2 ripe tomatoes, peeled and very finely chopped
   (about 1½ cups)
1 to 2 cloves garlic, minced
1 tablespoon capers, drained
1½ tablespoons extra-virgin olive oil

1 tablespoon balsamic vinegar, or to taste
freshly ground black pepper
1 bunch arugula, washed, stemmed, and thinly
   slivered (see the box on page 43)
1 to 2 ounces ricotta salata or Pecorino Romano
   cheese

1. Cook the pasta in a large pot in at least 4 quarts rapidly boiling salted water until al dente, about 8 minutes. Meanwhile, combine the tomatoes, garlic, capers, oil, and vinegar in a large heatproof serving bowl. Add salt and pepper to taste.

2. When the pasta is cooked, drain well in a colander and stir it into the tomato mixture. Stir in the arugula. Correct the seasoning, adding salt or vinegar to taste. Serve at once, with shaved or grated ricotta salata on top.   *Serves 4*

199 CALORIES PER SERVING; 7 G PROTEIN; 8 G FAT; 1 G SATURATED FAT; 25 G CARBOHYDRATE; 119 MG SODIUM; 33 MG CHOLESTEROL

PENNE WITH SMOKED SALMON AND PEPPER VODKA

This dish sounds more Slavic than Italian, but I've seen it at trendy trattorie in Milano and elsewhere. It took some doing to create a low-fat version of a dish whose primary ingredients are butter, cream, and smoked salmon. My first step was to replace the butter and cream with stock and no-fat sour cream. (The latter certainly meshes with the Russian overtones of the dish.) The next step was to use kippered (baked) salmon instead of cold smoked salmon: both have a smoky flavor, but the kippered, which is hot smoked, contains a fraction of the fat. Please note that this is an extremely forgiving recipe. Sometimes, I finish the dish with pepper vodka, sometimes with dry white vermouth. Sometimes I use spinach for a green garnish, sometimes sugarsnap peas or asparagus. As for broth, at one point or another I've used fish broth, chicken broth, vegetable broth, and bottled clam broth—all with delectable results.

PREPARATION TIME: 5 MINUTES   COOKING TIME: 15 MINUTES

3 cups penne or other tube-shaped pasta
salt

FOR THE SAUCE:
1½ tablespoons extra-virgin olive oil
3 to 4 large shallots, minced (½ cup)
3 tablespoons dry white vermouth or white wine
1 cup fish broth, chicken broth, vegetable broth, or bottled clam broth

6 tablespoons no-fat sour cream
6 ounces kipper style (hot smoked) salmon, flaked
freshly ground black pepper
2 cups stemmed washed spinach leaves (see box on page 37) or 1 cup cooked sugarsnap peas or asparagus (cut into 2-inch pieces)
1 to 2 tablespoons pepper vodka or more vermouth

1. Cook the penne in 4 quarts rapidly boiling salted water until al dente, about 8 minutes. Drain in a colander, rinse well, and drain again.

2. Meanwhile, heat the olive oil in a nonstick frying pan. Add the shallots and cook over medium heat until soft but not brown, about 2 minutes. Add the vermouth and bring to a boil. Add the broth, sour cream, smoked salmon, and pepper and briskly simmer until the sauce is reduced, thick, and richly flavored, about 5 minutes. Stir in the spinach (or other vegetables) and cook until wilted. Remove the pan from the heat and stir in the vodka and salt and pepper to taste.

3. Stir the penne into the sauce and cook to warm. Serve at once.   *Serves 4*

449 CALORIES PER SERVING; 22 G PROTEIN; 8 G FAT; 1 G SATURATED FAT; 66 G CARBOHYDRATE; 454 MG SODIUM; 10 MG CHOLESTEROL

BAKED PASTA DISHES AND CRÊPES

CRÊPE FLORENTINE "CAKE"

This offbeat "cake" was inspired by a traditional Florentine dish that dates back to the age of Catherine de Médicis: crêpes filled with spinach and béchamel sauce. Rather than rolling the crêpes around the filling, as is traditionally done, I tried stacking and layering them with the sauce. The result was a colorful multilayer "cake" you can cut into wedges for serving. I've made the prosciutto optional to keep the peace with my vegetarian friends.

PREPARATION TIME: 30 MINUTES   COOKING TIME: 30 MINUTES

8 Lemon Herb Crêpes (½ recipe) (page 97)

FOR THE FILLING:
10 ounces fresh or frozen spinach
salt
1½ tablespoons extra-virgin olive oil
1 medium onion, minced
1 stalk celery, minced

1 ounce prosciutto, minced (optional)
2 tablespoons plus 1 teaspoon all-purpose
    unbleached white flour
1½ cups 2 percent, 1 percent, or skim milk
¼ cup freshly grated Parmigiano-Reggiano cheese
salt, freshly ground black pepper, and a little
    freshly grated nutmeg
2 egg whites

1. Prepare the crêpes, following the recipe on page 97. Preheat the oven to 375°F.

2. If using fresh spinach, stem and wash it (see box on page 37). Cook the spinach in ½ inch boiling salted water in a large saucepan until tender and much reduced in volume, about 2 minutes. If using frozen spinach, cook according to package directions. Transfer the spinach to a colander, rinse with cold water, and drain. Tightly squeeze the spinach between your fingers to wring out all the liquid, working in several batches. Finely chop the spinach with a knife.

3. Heat most of the olive oil in a saucepan, reserving 1 teaspoon for drizzling on top of the "cake." Add the onion and celery and cook over medium heat until soft and translucent but not brown, 3 to 4 minutes. Add the prosciutto (if using) after 2 minutes. Whisk in the flour and cook for 1 minute. Remove

the pan from the heat and whisk in the milk. Return the pan to the heat and bring the mixture to a simmer, whisking steadily. Reduce the heat and gently simmer the mixture until it is thick, and the raw-flour taste has been cooked out, about 3 minutes. Remove the pan from the heat and whisk 3 tablespoons cheese, the spinach, salt, pepper, and nutmeg: the mixture should be highly seasoned. Whisk in the egg whites.

4. Lay 1 crêpe, pale side down, in an attractive, low-sided, round baking dish. Spread 2 to 3 tablespoons spinach mixture on top. Place another crêpe, pale side down, on top and spread with more spinach mixture. Continue in this fashion until all the crêpes and spinach mixture are used up. The top layer should be crêpe. Lightly brush or drizzle the top crêpe with the remaining olive oil and sprinkle with the remaining 1 tablespoon Parmesan.

Crêpe Florentine "Cake"

91

5. Bake the crêpe florentine cake until the filling is thoroughly heated and set and the cake is slightly puffed, about 15 minutes. Let cool for 2 minutes, then cut into wedges for serving. There are several good possibilities for sauces, including the Sugo di Pomodoro on page 59 and the Roasted Vegetable Sauce on page 53.

Note: For an even lighter cake, you could beat the egg whites to stiff peaks and gently fold them into the spinach mixture. This would produce a soufflé cake.

Serves 6 as an appetizer, 4 as a light entrée

185 CALORIES PER APPETIZER SERVING;* 11 G PROTEIN; 8 G FAT; 3 G SATURATED FAT; 19 G CARBOHYDRATE; 370 MG SODIUM; 30 MG CHOLESTEROL

Analysis is based on 6 servings as an appetizer.

BARBARA'S SMOKED CHEESE LASAGNE

My wife and I saw a sign for smoked cheese lasagne on the blackboard menu of a trattoria in the Trastevere district of Rome. Unfortunately, we'd already eaten dinner, but we took the idea home with us. Barbara created her version, using a caramelized-onion tomato sauce and smoked mozzarella. As in other recipes, if your fat budget allows it, use low-fat, not no-fat, ricotta.

PREPARATION TIME: 40 MINUTES COOKING TIME: 1 HOUR

FOR THE TOMATO SAUCE:
2 tablespoons extra-virgin olive oil
1 large onion, finely chopped
3 shallots, finely chopped
4 cloves garlic, finely chopped
2 tablespoons balsamic vinegar
4 to 5 ripe tomatoes (2½ to 3 pounds), peeled and finely chopped, with their juices
5 tablespoons tomato paste
1 tablespoon dark brown sugar

½ teaspoon dried oregano
¼ teaspoon red pepper flakes
2 tablespoons finely chopped fresh basil
salt and freshly ground black pepper
12 dried lasagne noodles (3 × 13 inches)
2 cups low-fat or no-fat ricotta
2 egg whites
3 ounces smoked cheese, shredded

1 9 × 13-inch baking dish sprayed with spray oil

1. Heat the olive oil in a large nonstick frying pan. Add the onion and cook over medium heat for 5 minutes, or until a deep golden-brown. Reduce the heat slightly, add the shallots, and cook for 2 minutes, or until golden-brown. Add the garlic and cook for 1 minute.

2. Deglaze the pan with the balsamic vinegar. Add the tomatoes, tomato paste, sugar, oregano, pepper flakes, basil, salt, and pepper. Gently simmer the sauce until thick and richly flavored, about 10 minutes, scraping the sides of the pan often with a rubber spatula. Remove the pan from the heat and let stand for 30 minutes.

3. Cook the lasagne noodles in 4 quarts lightly salted boiling water until al dente, about 8 minutes. Drain in a colander, rinse with cold water, and let cool. When the noodles are cool enough to handle, drape them over the sides of the colander to keep them from sticking together.

4. Combine the ricotta and egg whites in a mixing bowl and stir to mix. Add salt and pepper to taste.

5. Assemble the lasagne. Spoon a little tomato sauce on the bottom of the baking dish. Arrange a layer of noodles on top. Spread a thin layer of the ricotta mixture on each noodle. Sprinkle on a little smoked cheese. Spoon on a little tomato sauce. Add another layer of pasta, followed by more ricotta, smoked cheese, tomato sauce, and a lasagna noodle. The last layer should be tomato sauce topped with a little smoked cheese.

6. Bake the lasagna, uncovered, in a 350°F. oven until thoroughly heated and the top is bubbling, 30 to 40 minutes. Serve at once.

Serves 6 to 8

336 CALORIES PER SERVING;* 19 G PROTEIN; 12 G FAT; 2 G SATURATED FAT; 39 G CARBOHYDRATE; 406 MG SODIUM; 7 MG CHOLESTEROL

Analysis is based on 6 servings.

CAVATELLI, CANNELLINI, AND MUSSELS

I first tasted this dish in a remarkable setting, a sixteenth-century wine cellar at a country estate in Apulia. The barrel-vaulted stone room was lit only by candles. A whole lamb spun on a turnspit in the fireplace. But what really captivated my taste buds was a stunning casserole of cavatelli (small pasta shaped like cowry shells), cannellini (white kidney beans), and mussels. Don't be frightened by the seemingly large number of ingredients. This dish is quite quick and easy to prepare.

PREPARATION TIME: 30 MINUTES　　COOKING TIME: 30 MINUTES

3 pounds mussels
1 cup dry white wine
1 small onion, peeled and quartered
2 bay leaves
1 cup cavatelli or small pasta shells
salt
1½ tablespoons extra-virgin olive oil
1 small onion, finely chopped (about ½ cup)
1 stalk celery, finely chopped
1 carrot, finely chopped

2 cloves garlic, minced
2 ripe tomatoes, peeled, seeded, and chopped
¼ cup finely chopped flat-leaf parsley
2 cups cooked cannellini beans
　(or other white beans)
about 1 cup mussel cooking liquid
　(reserved from above)
1 tablespoon tomato paste
¼ teaspoon chopped fresh rosemary, or to taste
salt and freshly ground black pepper

1. Scrub the mussels, discarding any that fail to close when tapped. Remove the cluster of strings at the hinge of each mussel shell. (This is most easily done with needlenose pliers.)

2. Bring the wine, quartered onion, and bay leaves to a boil in a large heavy pot. Add the mussels, tightly cover the pot, and cook over high heat—stirring the mussels occasionally, so that all cook evenly—until the shells open, about 8 minutes. (Discard any that do not open.) Transfer the mussels with a slotted spoon to a bowl to cool. Shell most of the mussels, leaving 12 in the shells for garnish. Strain the mussel cooking liquid through a strainer lined with cheesecloth and reserve.

3. Cook the cavatelli in a large pot in 4 quarts rapidly boiling salted water until al dente, about 8 minutes. Drain the cavatelli in a colander and rinse with cold water. Drain well.

4. Meanwhile, heat the oil in a large saucepan.

Cook the chopped onion, celery, carrot, and garlic over medium-low heat until lightly browned, stirring often, about 5 minutes. Stir in the tomatoes and half the parsley and continue cooking until the tomato has lost its rawness, about 2 minutes.

5. Stir in the beans, pasta, shelled mussels, mussel cooking liquid, tomato paste, rosemary, and salt and pepper to taste. Cook the mixture for a couple of minutes to blend the flavors. The casserole should be moist but not soupy. If too dry, stir in a little more mussel liquid. Correct the seasoning, adding salt, pepper, or rosemary to taste.

6. Transfer the mixture to an ovenproof dish. Preheat the oven to 400°F. Bake until thoroughly heated, 10 to 15 minutes. Garnish with whole mussels and sprinkle with the remaining parsley. Serve at once.

Serves 4 to 6

385 CALORIES PER SERVING;* 26 G PROTEIN; 8 G FAT; 0.9 G SATURATED FAT; 63 G CARBOHYDRATE; 349 MG SODIUM; 64 MG CHOLESTEROL

Analysis is based on 4 servings.

ROASTED GARLIC AND DRIED-TOMATO MANICOTTI

For me, manicotti are the ultimate comfort food: chamois-soft crêpes rolled around an airy ricotta filling.
(Many restaurateurs take a short cut, using pasta tubes instead of crêpes. But crêpes are the proper wrapper.)

PREPARATION TIME: 15 MINUTES (EXCLUDING PREPARATION OF CRÊPES)
COOKING TIME: 1 HOUR (INCLUDING THE TIME FOR ROASTING THE GARLIC)

8 crêpes (½ Lemon Herb Crêpes recipe, page 97)

FOR THE FILLING:
6 large cloves garlic (in the skins)
6 dried tomatoes (page 242)
2 cups low-fat or no-fat ricotta cheese
2 tablespoons freshly grated Parmigiano-Reggiano cheese (optional)

2 egg whites
½ teaspoon fresh or dried thyme
salt and freshly ground black pepper

spray oil or 1 teaspoon extra-virgin olive oil
1 cup of your favorite tomato sauce or any of the tomato sauces on pages 58–62

1. Prepare the crêpes as described on page 97. Roast the garlic cloves on a piece of foil in a 350°F. oven or toaster oven until soft and sweet, 30 to 40 minutes. Do not let them burn. Let the garlic cool, then cut off the ends and scrape the soft flesh out of the skins. Set aside. Pour boiling water over the dried tomatoes in a bowl and let stand for 20 minutes to soften. Blot the tomatoes dry, then cut into thin slivers.

2. In a mixing bowl, whisk together the ricotta, Parmesan, egg whites, thyme, roasted garlic, dried tomatoes, and salt and pepper to taste: the mixture should be highly seasoned. For a smooth filling, you can purée these ingredients in a food processor.

3. Place 3 to 4 tablespoons filling on the bottom third of each crêpe (the crêpe should be pale side up). Roll the crêpe into a tube. Arrange the tubes in a baking dish that's been lightly sprayed or brushed with oil. The recipe can be prepared ahead to this stage and stored in the refrigerator for 6 to 8 hours.

4. Preheat the oven to 400°F. Spoon the tomato sauce in a row down the center of the crêpes, leaving the ends exposed. Bake the manicotti until they are puffed and the filling is set, 15 to 20 minutes. Serve at once. *Makes 8 manicotti, enough to serve 8 as an appetizer, 4 as an entrée*

142 CALORIES PER PIECE OF MANICOTTI; 11 G PROTEIN; 3 G FAT; 0.2 G SATURATED FAT;
18 G CARBOHYDRATE; 525 MG SODIUM; 14 MG CHOLESTEROL

MUSHROOM MANICOTTI

The earthy flavor of mushrooms in these rich-tasting manicotti compensates for the reduced quantities of butter and cheese. For a special treat, use fresh porcini or other exotic mushrooms.

PREPARATION TIME: 15 MINUTES (EXCLUDING MAKING CRÊPES)   COOKING TIME: 30 MINUTES

8 crêpes (½ recipe Lemon Herb Crêpes, page 97)

FOR THE FILLING:
8 ounces fresh button mushrooms, porcini, cremini, shiitakes, or a mix of mushrooms
2 teaspoons fresh lemon juice
1 tablespoon extra-virgin olive oil
1 small onion, finely chopped
1 clove garlic, minced

2 tablespoons chopped flat-leaf parsley
salt, freshly ground black pepper, and a hint of freshly grated nutmeg
1¼ cups low-fat or no-fat ricotta cheese
1 egg white

1 cup Reduced-Fat Béchamel (page 54) or one of the tomato sauces on pages 58–62

1. Prepare the crêpes as described on page 97.
2. Wipe the mushrooms clean with a damp cloth and finely chop in a food processor with the lemon juice. (See Note. If using shiitakes, remove and discard the stems.) Heat the olive oil in a nonstick frying pan. Add the onion and garlic and cook over medium heat until soft but not brown, about 4 minutes.

3. Add the mushrooms and parsley to the onion mixture and increase the heat to high. Cook the mixture until all the mushroom liquid has evaporated. Add salt, pepper, and nutmeg to taste: the mixture should be highly seasoned. Transfer the mushroom mixture to a mixing bowl and let cool slightly. Stir in the ricotta and egg white.

3. Place 3 to 4 tablespoons filling on the bottom third of each crêpe (the crêpe should be pale side up). Roll the crêpe into a tube. Arrange the tubes in a baking dish that's been lightly sprayed or brushed with oil. The recipe can be prepared ahead to this stage and stored in the refrigerator for 6 hours.

4. Preheat the oven to 400°F. Spoon the béchamel or tomato sauce in a row down the center of the crepes, leaving the ends exposed. Bake the manicotti until they are puffed and the filling is set, 15 to 20 minutes. Serve at once.

Note: To chop mushrooms in a food processor, cut any large mushrooms in quarters, medium-size mushrooms in half. You can leave the small ones whole. Don't fill the processor bowl more than one-quarter of the way. Run the machine in brief bursts. Overcrowding the bowl or overprocessing the mushrooms will result in a watery mess.

Makes 8 manicotti, enough to serve 8 as an appetizer, 4 as an entrée

130 CALORIES PER PIECE OF MANICOTTI; 8 G PROTEIN; 4 G FAT; 0.6 G SATURATED FAT;

15 G CARBOHYDRATE; 275 MG SODIUM; 15 MG CHOLESTEROL

LEMON HERB CRÊPES

Crêpes are traditionally associated with French cuisine, but there's evidence (both linguistic and historic) that they originated in Italy. In any case, manicotti and crispelli alla fiorentina (crêpes florentine) would be sorry stuff without them. Thanks to the vibrant flavors of fresh herbs and lemon zest, you won't miss the butter and egg yolks found in traditional recipes.

PREPARATION TIME: 5 MINUTES   COOKING TIME: 10 TO 15 MINUTES

1 egg, plus 2 egg whites (or ½ cup egg substitute)
¾ cup skim milk
¾ cup water, or as needed
½ teaspoon salt, or to taste
½ teaspoon sugar
1 to 2 teaspoons extra-virgin olive oil

1 cup all-purpose unbleached white flour
1 teaspoon finely grated lemon zest
1 tablespoon finely chopped fresh herbs (including thyme, basil, oregano, and/or flat-leaf parsley)
spray oil (preferably olive)

1. Combine the egg and whites in a mixing bowl and whisk to mix. Whisk in the milk, water, salt, sugar, and oil. Sift in the flour and gently whisk just to mix. (Do not overwhisk, or the crêpes will be rubbery.) If the batter looks lumpy, strain it into another bowl. It should be the consistency of heavy cream. (If too thick, thin it with a little more water.) Whisk in the lemon zest and herbs.

2. Lightly spray one or more 6- or 7-inch crêpe pans with oil and heat over a medium flame. (When the pan is the proper temperature, a drop of water will evaporate off it in 2 to 3 seconds.) Off the heat, add 3 tablespoons crêpe batter to the pan in one fell swoop. Gently tilt and rotate the pan to coat the bottom with a thin layer of batter. (Pour back any excess—the crêpe should be as thin as possible.)

3. Cook the crêpe until lightly browned on both sides, 1 to 2 minutes per side, turning with a spatula. As the crêpes are done, stack them on a plate on top of one another. For the best results, spray the pans with oil between crêpes. The crêpes can be prepared up to 24 hours ahead to this stage.

Makes 16 to 18 crêpes

42 CALORIES PER CRÊPE; 2 G PROTEIN; 0.7 G FAT; 0.2 G SATURATED FAT; 0.7 G CARBOHYDRATE; 84 MG SODIUM; 14 MG CHOLESTEROL

A NEW MACARONI AND CHEESE

Macaroni and cheese, like spaghetti and meatballs, belongs to a family of comfort foods that are Italian in inspiration, but Italian-American in descent. The challenge of making a low-fat version of this perennially popular comfort dish lay in finding a way to provide a sufficiently rich cheese flavor without tipping the scales in fat grams. I first cut the fat by omitting the butter in the béchamel sauce. I then added puréed cottage cheese to the sauce—a trick I picked up from my friends at Eating Well magazine. Finally, I added just a little of two sharp-flavored cheeses, Cheddar and Pecorino Romano. Mustard is a nontraditional ingredient, but it helps reinforce the flavor of the cheese. For a festive touch, use multicolor macaroni. For a more sophisticated version of the dish, use a large tube-shaped noodle, like ziti rigati.

PREPARATION TIME: 20 MINUTES   COOKING TIME: 1 HOUR

salt
3 cups (10 ounces) elbow macaroni (preferably multicolor) or ziti rigati (with larger tube-shaped pasta, you'll need only 8 ounces)
1 cup 2 percent or 1 percent cottage cheese

FOR THE CHEESE SAUCE:
2½ tablespoons all-purpose unbleached white flour
1½ cups skim milk
2 teaspoons grainy mustard

¾ cup coarsely grated sharp white Cheddar cheese (about 2 ounces)
¼ cup freshly grated Pecorino Romano or Parmigiano-Reggiano cheese
freshly ground black pepper
freshly grated nutmeg
cayenne pepper

spray oil
2 to 3 tablespoons fine toasted bread crumbs

1. Bring 4 quarts lightly salted water to a rolling boil in a large pot. Cook the macaroni until al dente, about 8 minutes. Drain the macaroni in a colander, rinse with cold water to cool, and drain well. In a food processor, purée the cottage cheese until very smooth, scraping down the sides of the bowl with a rubber spatula. Preheat the oven to 400°F.

2. Have ready a large bowl of cold water. Place the flour in a 1-quart saucepan (preferably nonstick) over medium heat. Cook the flour, stirring with a whisk or wooden spoon, until it smells cooked, 3 to 5 minutes. (Quite suddenly, you'll notice a pronounced toasted smell.) Do not let the flour brown. Place the bottom of the saucepan in the bowl of cold water to stop the cooking. Set the pan aside until it and the flour are cool.

3. Add ¼ cup of the milk and whisk to a smooth paste. Gradually whisk in the remaining milk. Bring the mixture to a simmer over medium-high heat, whisking steadily. Simmer for 3 minutes. Remove the pan from the heat. Whisk in the cottage cheese, mustard, Cheddar, Romano, and salt, pepper, nutmeg, and cayenne to taste: the sauce should be highly seasoned.

4. Stir the macaroni into the sauce. Spoon the mixture into an attractive 8 × 12-inch baking dish you've lightly sprayed with oil. Sprinkle the top with the bread crumbs. Bake the macaroni and cheese until bubbling, crusty, and golden brown, 20 to 30 minutes.
Serves 4 to 6

521 CALORIES PER SERVING;* 30 G PROTEIN; 12 G FAT; 7 G SATURATED FAT; 72 G CARBOHYDRATE; 562 MG SODIUM; 36 MG CHOLESTEROL

Analysis is based on 4 servings.

GARLIC-ROASTED EGGPLANT "CANNELONI"

Canneloni traditionally refers to pasta or crêpe tubes baked with a ricotta filling. My low-fat version features a stuffing of garlic-roasted eggplant. For a smoky flavor, you could grill the eggplant instead of roasting it. (Studding the eggplant with garlic before roasting or grilling is a wonderful way to cook eggplant.) For a novel presentation I like to use smaller pasta tubes than canneloni— rigatoni or ziti, for example. But if you don't like working with a piping bag, you could certainly use larger pasta tubes.

PREPARATION TIME: 20 MINUTES   COOKING TIME: 1 TO 1¼ HOURS

FOR THE FILLING:
2 eggplants (1½ to 2 pounds), unpeeled
6 cloves garlic, peeled and cut in quarters
    lengthwise
spray olive oil
salt and freshly ground black pepper
1 tablespoon extra-virgin olive oil
2 tablespoons minced flat-leaf parsley
2 to 3 tablespoons fine dry bread crumbs (optional)

32 pasta tubes, such as rigatoni or ziti, each about
    ½ inch in diameter

2 cups of your favorite tomato sauce (for example,
    Neapolitan Tomato Sauce, page 60, or Roasted
    Vegetable Sauce, page 53)
3 to 4 tablespoons freshly grated Parmigiano-
    Reggiano cheese

1. Preheat the oven to 400°F. or preheat the barbecue grill to medium-high. Using the tip of a paring knife, make twelve ½-inch-deep slits in each eggplant and insert a sliver of garlic in each. Lightly spray (or brush) each eggplant with oil and season with salt and pepper. Roast the eggplants until very soft and cooked through, about 40 minutes, turning once or twice to ensure even cooking. Or for an even richer flavor, grill the eggplants until charred on all sides, about 20 minutes. Transfer the eggplants to a plate and let cool.

2. Cut each eggplant in half lengthwise and scoop out the flesh with a spoon. (Alternatively, you can peel the skin off with a paring knife.) Purée the eggplant with the garlic slivers in a food processor. Add the olive oil, parsley, and salt and pepper to taste: the filling should be highly seasoned. The mixture should be the consistency of soft ice cream: if too loose, add 2 or 3 tablespoons of bread crumbs.

3. Meanwhile, cook the rigatoni in 2 quarts boiling salted water until al dente, about 8 minutes. Rinse with cold water in a colander and drain well.

4. Using a piping bag fitted with a round tip, pipe the eggplant mixture into the rigatoni. Spoon a little tomato sauce into the bottom of a lightly oiled 12-inch baking dish. Arrange the rigatoni in rows in the dish, standing one end of each rigatoni on the end of the one next to it to create a rippled effect. The recipe can be prepared ahead to this stage and stored in the refrigerator.

5. Spoon the remaining tomato sauce over the filled pasta and sprinkle the Parmesan on top. Bake the canneloni until thoroughly heated and bubbling, 15 to 20 minutes. Serve at once.   *Serves 4*

275 CALORIES PER SERVING; 9 G PROTEIN; 9 G FAT; 2 G SATURATED FAT; 42 G CARBOHYDRATE; 242 MG SODIUM; 4 MG CHOLESTEROL

GNOCCHI AND DUMPLINGS

POTATO GNOCCHI

Gnocchi (pronounced "NYO-key") are small, soft dumplings that have the seemingly opposite virtues of being feather-light and pleasingly chewy. This is no small feat when you stop to consider that the two principal ingredients are potatoes (or another root vegetable) and flour. Bad gnocchi are simply starchy on the palate and leaden in the belly.

Here are some points to watch:

- *Use a dry, starchy potato, like an Idaho baking potato.*
- *Mash the potatoes by hand, or put them through a vegetable mill or ricer, or mash them in a mixer fitted with a dough hook. Never purée them in a food processor.*
- *It's best to add the flour to the potatoes when they are still warm.*
- *The gnocchi dough will be very soft, sticky, and hard to work with. It's supposed to be. Use plenty of flour for rolling it out.*

PREPARATION TIME: 30 MINUTES   COOKING TIME: 30 MINUTES (INCLUDING COOKING THE POTATOES)

---

2 pounds baking potatoes, scrubbed but not peeled
1 egg white (or egg yolk)
1 teaspoon salt or to taste

2½ to 3 cups all-purpose unbleached white flour, plus flour for rolling

1. Place the potatoes in a large pot with cold water to cover. Gradually bring to a boil. Briskly simmer the potatoes until soft (they'll be easy to pierce with a skewer), about 20 minutes. Drain and rinse them with cold water until cool enough to handle (but still hot), and drain again. Pull the skins off the potatoes with the help of a paring knife.

2. Purée the potatoes in a large mixing bowl with a potato masher, put them through a vegetable mill or ricer, or mash them in a mixer fitted with a dough hook. Stir in the egg white, salt, and flour. Add enough flour to obtain a soft dough—it should be the consistency of soft ice cream. The dough will be sticky, but it shouldn't be wet. Bring 4 quarts lightly salted water to a boil in a large pot.

3. Generously flour your work surface. Pinch off a 3-inch ball of dough and roll it out into a long, skinny, ½-inch-thick cylinder. Using a sharp paring knife, cut the cylinder on the diagonal into ½-inch pieces. These will be your gnocchi. Continue working until all the dough is rolled and cut. At this point the gnocchi can be frozen for future use. See Note.

4. Boil the gnocchi in the water until firm, about 5 minutes. Work in several batches, to avoid crowd-

Mixed Gnocchi

ing the pot. Transfer the gnocchi with a slotted spoon or wire skimmer to a colander to drain. The gnocchi can be served right away with your favorite sauce (see pages 53–63). Or you can layer them in a baking dish with sauce and cheese or sauce and vegetables to make a casserole that you can bake now or later.

Note: This recipe will make a rather large batch of gnocchi, which is how we make them in our house. Any excess can be frozen before cooking—they freeze well. Freeze them on a baking sheet, then transfer them to a plastic bag. To cook, add the frozen gnocchi directly to boiling water.

The roll-and-cut method described in step 3 is quick and easy and produces pleasingly rustic-looking gnocchi. For a fancier presentation, you can roll the individual gnocchi against the tines of a fork to make the traditional ridged oval shape.

Serves 8 to 10

254 CALORIES PER SERVING;* 7 G PROTEIN; 0.5 G FAT; 0 G SATURATED FAT; 55 G CARBOHYDRATE; 280 MG SODIUM; 0 MG CHOLESTEROL

Analysis is based on 8 servings.

SWEET POTATO GNOCCHI

I love the vivid orange color of these gnocchi and the rich, earthy flavor that comes from roasting the sweet potatoes in a hot oven.
For a particularly colorful presentation, serve sweet potato gnocchi with the basic potato gnocchi on page 101, the beet gnocchi
on page 104, and/or the wasabi gnocchi on page 105. There are lots of possibilities for sauces, including Enlightened
Pesto (page 57), the pumpkin sauce on page 77, and any of the tomato sauces on pages 58–62.

PREPARATION TIME: 30 MINUTES   COOKING TIME: 30 MINUTES (INCLUDING COOKING THE POTATOES)

1½ pounds sweet potatoes, unpeeled
1 egg white

1 scant teaspoon salt
1¾ to 2¼ cups all-purpose unbleached white flour

1. Preheat the oven to 400°F. Place the sweet potatoes in a nonstick roasting pan. Roast until very soft, 40 to 50 minutes. Transfer the sweet potatoes to a plate. When they are cool enough to handle, pull off the skin with the help of a paring knife.

2. Purée the potatoes in a large mixing bowl with a potato masher, put them through a vegetable mill or ricer, or mash them in a mixer fitted with a dough hook. Stir in the egg white, salt, and flour. Add enough flour to obtain a soft dough—it should be the consistency of soft ice cream. The dough will be a little drier than regular potato gnocchi dough. Bring 4 quarts lightly salted water to a boil in a large pot.

3. Generously flour your work surface. Pinch off a 3-inch ball of gnocchi dough and roll it out on a cutting board into a long, skinny ½-inch-thick cylinder.

Using a sharp paring knife, cut the cylinder on the diagonal into ½-inch pieces. These will be your gnocchi. Continue working until all the dough is rolled and cut. At this point the gnocchi can be frozen for future use. See Note on page 102.

4. Boil the gnocchi in the water until firm, about 5 minutes, working in several batches to avoid crowding the pot. Transfer the gnocchi with a slotted spoon or wire skimmer to a colander to drain. The gnocchi can be served right away with your favorite sauce (pages 53–63). Or you can layer them in a baking dish with sauce and cheese or sauce and vegetables to make a casserole that can be baked now or later. Store for 6 to 8 hours in the refrigerator.

Serves 6 to 8

288 CALORIES PER SERVING;* 6 G PROTEIN; 0.6 G FAT; 0.1 G SATURATED FAT; 69 G CARBOHYDRATE; 341 MG SODIUM; 0 MG CHOLESTEROL

*Analysis is based on 6 servings.

PINO'S BEET GNOCCHI

Puréed beets give these gnocchi a stunning rose color and earthy flavor that go beautifully with a variety of sauces.
Beet gnocchi are a specialty of my friend Pino Saverino, a chef from Chiavari, Italy, who now works in Miami.
For a more complete discussion of making gnocchi, see the basic recipe on page 101.

PREPARATION TIME: 30 MINUTES   COOKING TIME: 25 MINUTES

1 (16-ounce) can or jar of cooked beets, drained and blotted dry
2 eggs
2 pounds baking potatoes, unpeeled

2 teaspoons salt
2½ to 3 cups all-purpose unbleached white flour or as needed, plus flour for rolling the gnocchi
1 to 2 teaspoons vegetable oil (optional)

1. Purée the beets in a food processor or blender; add the eggs and blend until you have a smooth purée. Set the mixture aside.

2. Place the potatoes in a large pot with water to cover. Gradually bring to a boil. Boil the potatoes 20 to 30 minutes, until very tender (they'll be easy to pierce with a skewer). Drain the potatoes in a colander and let cool until you can comfortably handle them.

3. Pull the skin off the potatoes with the help of a paring knife and place them in a mixer fitted with a paddle or dough hook. Beat them until mashed. Alternatively, you can mash them with a pestle or purée them through a food mill. Do not purée in a food processor or the gnocchi will be gummy. Beat in the beet purée, the salt, and enough flour to obtain a soft, sticky dough.

4. Bring 4 quarts lightly salted water to a boil in a large pot.

5. Generously flour your work surface. Pinch off a 3-inch ball of dough and roll it into a long, skinny cylinder about ½ inch thick. Cut the cylinder on the diagonal into ½-inch pieces. These are the gnocchi. Continue rolling and cutting the dough until all is used up. Use plenty of flour on your hands and the cutting board to keep the gnocchi from sticking.

6. Boil the gnocchi in the water until firm, working in several batches to avoid crowding the pot. The cooking time will be 2 to 3 minutes once the water returns to a boil. The gnocchi should be light but firm. Transfer the cooked gnocchi with a wire skimmer or slotted spoon to a colander to drain. Rinse with cold water and drain again. Transfer the gnocchi to a roasting pan and toss with a little oil to prevent sticking. Continue cooking the gnocchi in this fashion until all the dough is used up.

The gnocchi can be served right away. There are a variety of great sauces for beet gnocchi, including the Enlightened Pesto on page 57 (the green and pink make a lovely combination), the pumpkin sauce on page 77, or the gorgonzola sauce on page 56. Tomato sauce would be too strong and too red. Ladle the hot sauce over the gnocchi and serve.

Another way to serve the gnocchi (this is especially good for a crowd) is to arrange them in a lightly oiled baking dish, top with sauce, and sprinkle with a little freshly grated Parmigiano Reggiano. Bake the gnocchi in a 400°F. oven until bubbling and beginning to brown, about 15 minutes.

Note: To freeze the gnocchi for future use, arrange the cooked gnocchi on a baking sheet in the freezer. When frozen hard, place them in resealable freezer bags. My wife and I like to freeze two-person portions, so we always have some on hand for dinner.

Serves 8 to 10

345 CALORIES PER SERVING;* 10 G PROTEIN; 2 G FAT; 0.5 G SATURATED FAT; 73 G CARBOHYDRATE; 717 MG SODIUM; 53 MG CHOLESTEROL

*Analysis is based on 8 servings.

WASABI GNOCCHI

I doubt anyone has ever made or served wasabi gnocchi in Italy. But I would be remiss in my familial if not writerly duties if I didn't include this recipe, for it comes from my stepson, Miami Beach chef Jake Klein. In keeping with his passion for Asian flavors (Jake and I opened a restaurant together in Hong Kong), Jake flavors the gnocchi with wasabi (Japanese horseradish). The green powder imparts a tangy flavor much in the spirit of high-flavor, low-fat cooking. I'm sure a progressive-minded Italian would approve.

PREPARATION TIME: 20 MINUTES   COOKING TIME: 15 MINUTES (INCLUDING COOKING THE POTATOES)

1½ pounds Idaho potatoes, peeled and cut into
  ½-inch dice
2 ounces fresh or frozen spinach (about 3
  tablespoons cooked)
1 egg

1 to 2 tablespoons wasabi powder
1 teaspoon salt
2 to 2½ cups all-purpose unbleached white flour,
  plus flour for rolling

1. Place the potatoes in a large pot with cold water to cover. Bring to a boil. Briskly simmer the potatoes until tender but not soft, 6 to 8 minutes. With a wire simmer, transfer the potatoes to a colander, drain well, and let cool slightly.

2. Boil the spinach in the potato water until cooked, about 2 minutes. Transfer the spinach to a blender with 2 or 3 tablespoons cooking liquid. Purée to a smooth paste.

3. Mash the potatoes in a large mixing bowl with a potato masher, put them through a vegetable mill or ricer, or mash them in a mixer fitted with a dough hook. Do not purée in a food processor or the gnocchi will be gummy. Stir in the puréed spinach and the egg, wasabi powder, salt, and flour. Add enough flour to obtain a soft dough—it should be the consistency of soft ice cream. The dough can be a little sticky, but it shouldn't be wet (add a little flour if necessary). Bring 4 quarts lightly salted water to a boil in a large pot.

4. Generously flour your work surface. Pinch off a 3-inch ball of gnocchi dough and roll it out into a long, skinny, ½-inch-thick cylinder. Using a sharp paring knife, cut the cylinder on the diagonal into ½-inch pieces. These will be your gnocchi. Continue working until all the dough is rolled and cut. At this point the gnocchi can be frozen for future use. (For instructions on how to freeze, see Note on page 102—basic gnocchi.)

5. Boil the gnocchi in the water until firm, about 5 minutes. Work in several batches, so you don't crowd the pan. Transfer the gnocchi with a slotted spoon or wire skimmer to a colander to drain. The gnocchi can be served right away with your favorite sauce. (Jake favors a nondairy tomato "cream" sauce made with silken tofu.) To prepare for later use, shock-chill the gnocchi by rinsing in ice water. Reheat them in water or the sauce.

Serves 6 to 8

279 CALORIES PER SERVING;* 8 G PROTEIN; 1 G FAT; 0.4 G SATURATED FAT; 58 G CARBOHYDRATE; 380 MG SODIUM; 36 MG CHOLESTEROL

Analysis is based on 6 servings.

ROMAN-STYLE SEMOLINA GNOCCHI

These dumplings are a cross between traditional flour-based gnocchi and polenta. If you live near an Italian market, you may be able to buy semolina (coarse-grained particles of durum wheat). Quick-cooking Cream of Wheat works well, too, and is available at any supermarket. The chicken broth isn't traditional, but it replaces some of the flavor traditionally provided by egg yolks and oceans of butter.

PREPARATION TIME: 15 MINUTES   COOKING TIME: 30 MINUTES, PLUS TIME TO CHILL THE GNOCCHI MIXTURE

2 cups skim, 1 percent, or 2 percent milk
2 cups chicken broth
1 cup semolina or quick-cooking Cream of Wheat
2 egg whites or ¼ cup egg substitute

½ cup freshly grated Parmigiano-Reggiano cheese
salt and freshly ground black pepper
spray oil
1½ tablespoons extra-virgin olive oil or butter

1. Bring the milk and broth to a simmer in a heavy saucepan. Add the semolina in a thin stream, whisking steadily. Simmer the mixture over medium heat until cooked and thick, 5 to 10 minutes, whisking to obtain a smooth consistency. Let the mixture cool to warm. Whisk in the egg whites, ¼ cup of the cheese, and salt and pepper to taste. Spread the semolina mixture on a nonstick baking sheet with a spatula (the layer should be about ¼ inch thick) and let cool until firm, about 1 hour.

2. Using a 2-inch cookie cutter, cut the semolina mixture into circles. Transfer the scraps to an attractive 10- to 12-inch by 6- to 8-inch baking dish you've lightly sprayed with oil. Press the scraps into a mostly smooth layer. Drizzle 2 teaspoons olive oil or butter over this layer and sprinkle with 1 tablespoon of the remaining cheese.

3. Arrange the gnocchi circles on top of the scraps, slightly overlapping each circle on the one before it. (The idea is to create an effect that looks like a tiled roof.) Drizzle the remaining oil or butter over this layer and sprinkle with the remaining cheese. The recipe can be made up to 48 hours ahead to this stage. Store in the refrigerator.

4. Preheat the oven to 425°F. Bake the gnocchi until thoroughly heated and lightly browned on top, 15 to 20 minutes. Serve at once.

Note: for a richer, more substantial dish, alternate the gnocchi layers with one of the tomato sauces on pages 58–62 and bake as described above.

Serves 6

213 CALORIES PER SERVING; 12 G PROTEIN; 7 G FAT; 2 G SATURATED FAT; 25 G CARBOHYDRATE; 546 MG SODIUM; 14 MG CHOLESTEROL

Tyrolean Dumplings (Canederli Tirolesi)

Most of us think of Italy as the epicenter of Mediterranean cooking. But majestically mountainous northern Italy shares the alpine soul—and cuisine—of its northern neighbors, Austria and Switzerland. Consider the following dumplings, which are reminiscent of Austria's Semelknoedeln (bread dumplings).

PREPARATION TIME: 10 MINUTES   COOKING TIME: 20 MINUTES

6 cups chicken broth
1 egg, plus 2 egg whites
⅔ cup 2 percent milk or skim milk
⅓ cup freshly grated Parmigiano-Reggiano cheese, plus 2 tablespoons for serving
1 ounce prosciutto, finely chopped

3 tablespoons finely chopped parsley
salt and freshly ground black pepper
6 cups finely diced stale crustless white bread
½ cup dried bread crumbs, plus ¾ cup for rolling the dumplings

1. Bring the stock to a simmer in a deep saucepan.
2. In a mixing bowl, whisk together the egg, egg whites, milk, cheese, prosciutto, parsley, salt, and pepper. Stir in the diced bread and enough bread crumbs to obtain a mixture you can mold into balls with your hands.
3. Wet your hands with cold water and roll the bread mixture into dumplings a little larger than walnuts. Transfer the finished dumplings to a sheet of waxed paper and chill for 30 minutes. Place the remaining bread crumbs in a shallow bowl.

4. Just before cooking, roll each dumpling in the remaining bread crumbs, shaking off the excess. Gently lower the dumplings into the simmering broth. Poach over medium-low heat until firm, 10 to 15 minutes. Be sure the dumplings remain covered by broth.
5. To serve, transfer the dumplings to soup bowls and ladle the broth over them. Sprinkle the remaining cheese on top and serve at once.

Makes 12 1½-inch dumplings,
enough to serve 4 to 6

307 CALORIES PER SERVING*; 19 G PROTEIN; 7 G FAT; 2.6 G SATURATED FAT; 41 G CARBOHYDRATE; 1,029 MG SODIUM; 45 MG CHOLESTEROL

Analysis is based on 6 servings.

POLENTA

POLENTA WITH TUSCAN MUSHROOM "HASH"

POLENTA DEL BOSCAIOLO

A boscaiolo is a woodcutter—just the sort of person whose long hours in the forest give him access to hidden clusters of porcini and other wild mushrooms. If you can find fresh porcini, you will have an absolutely sublime polenta, but delectable results can be obtained using shiitake mushrooms, portobellos, or even button mushrooms. (If using the latter, try to add ½ to 1 ounce dried porcini. Soak following instructions in the Note on page 110.)

PREPARATION TIME: 15 MINUTES   COOKING TIME: 40 MINUTES FOR THE POLENTA
(PLUS A FEW HOURS FOR CHILLING), 15 MINUTES FOR THE SAUCE

1 recipe Firm Polenta (page 112), prepared
   through step 3
spray oil or a little extra-virgin olive oil

FOR THE "HASH":
1 to 1½ tablespoons extra-virgin olive oil
1 medium onion, finely chopped
3 cloves garlic
1 pound fresh porcini mushrooms, shiitakes,
   portobellos, or button mushrooms, wiped clean,
   trimmed, and cut into ¼-inch slices (see Note)
1 large or 2 small ripe tomatoes, peeled and diced,

   with their juices
½ cup dry white wine
½ cup Chicken Broth (page 239) or Basic
   Vegetable Broth (page 241)
½ to 1 ounce dried porcini (optional) (see Note)
3 tablespoons chopped flat-leaf parsley
salt and freshly ground black pepper
3 to 4 tablespoons freshly grated Parmigiano-
   Reggiano cheese

1. Prepare the polenta following the recipe on page 112. Transfer it to a nonstick baking sheet to cool, then refrigerate until firm. Cut it into rectangles, squares, or other fanciful shapes and place the polenta shapes in a lightly oiled baking dish. Preheat the oven to 400°F.

2. Prepare the "hash": Heat the olive oil in a large nonstick frying pan. Add the onions and cook over medium heat for 2 minutes. Add the garlic and con-tinue cooking until the onions are just beginning to brown. Add the mushrooms to the onion mixture and cook over medium heat until soft, about 5 minutes.

3. Add the tomato(es) with their juices and cook until soft, about 5 minutes. Add the wine and boil until reduced to a glaze. Add the broth, soaked dried porcini (if using), and parsley. Briskly simmer the mixture until the sauce is thick and glazy, about 10

Polenta with Tuscan Mushroom "Hash"

minutes. Add salt and pepper to taste. The recipe can be prepared ahead to this stage.

4. Preheat the grill or broiler or the oven to 450°F.

5. Lightly brush the polenta pieces with oil. Grill, broil, or bake the polenta until thoroughly heated and lightly browned, 2 to 3 minutes per side. Reheat the mushroom hash and spoon it on top. Sprinkle with freshly grated Parmigiano-Reggiano cheese and serve at once.

Note: For an even richer mushroom flavor, add ½ to 1 ounce dried porcini to the sauce. Soak the porcini in the ½ cup broth (slightly warmed) until soft, about 30 minutes. Remove the porcini with your fingers, wringing the broth back into the bowl. Strain the broth into another bowl.

Transfer the porcini to a bowl of cold water. Agitate the porcini in the water with your fingers to wash out any grit. (The first soaking imbues the broth with porcini flavor; the second one is used to remove the grit.) Wring out the porcini and transfer to a cutting board. Trim off any gritty parts. The porcini are now ready for adding to the sauce. You don't add another ½ cup broth—just the porcini-soaking broth when you add the parsley and porcini.

Serves 6 to 8 as an appetizer, 4 as an entrée

234 CALORIES PER SERVING;* 7 G PROTEIN; 5 G FAT; 1 G SATURATED FAT; 39 G CARBOHYDRATE; 143 MG SODIUM; 4 MG CHOLESTEROL

Analysis is based on 6 servings as an appetizer.

BASIC POLENTA

Polenta has very ancient roots in Italy, although its primary ingredient—cornmeal—didn't arrive until the sixteenth century (after a Genoese sea captain named Columbus set sail for a shorter route to Asia and happened upon the Americas!). Polenta seems to have originated with the Etruscans as a sort of porridge called *puls* or *pulmentum*. Corn, like tomatoes, may have been a New World food, but it was adopted by northern Italians with gusto.

Following are two polenta recipes: one for a firm polenta you can cut into fanciful shapes for grilling, the other for a soft polenta you can eat like mashed potatoes. Over the years, I've found that the best way to prevent lumps is to make a slurry by dissolving the cornmeal in a few cups cold water, rather than adding it directly to boiling liquid. For extra flavor, you could cook the polenta in chicken or vegetable broth instead of water.

FIRM POLENTA

This polenta is prepared ahead of time, poured onto an oiled baking sheet to harden, and cut into fanciful shapes for baking, broiling, or grilling. There are lots of possibilities for sauces here, including Sugo di Pomodoro (page 59), Fresh Tomato Sauce with Capers and Olives (page 62), and Roasted Vegetable Sauce (page 53).

PREPARATION TIME: 10 MINUTES   COOKING TIME: 40 MINUTES,
PLUS 2 TO 3 HOURS FOR CHILLING, AND 5 TO 10 MINUTES FOR REHEATING

2 cups coarse yellow cornmeal, preferably stone-ground
7 cups water, Chicken Broth (page 239), or Basic Vegetable Broth (page 241)

salt and freshly ground black pepper
½ to 1 tablespoon extra-virgin olive oil or butter for cooking (optional)

1. In a mixing bowl, combine the cornmeal with 2 cups cold water and whisk to a smooth paste. Bring the remaining 5 cups water to a boil in a large heavy saucepan (preferably nonstick). Add the cornmeal mixture to the boiling water in a thin stream, whisking steadily. Boil the polenta over high heat, whisking steadily, until thick, 2 to 3 minutes. Add a little salt and pepper.

2. Reduce the heat to medium or medium-low and gently simmer the polenta until the mixture thickens enough to pull away from the sides of the pan. It should be the consistency of soft ice cream. It isn't necessary to whisk the polenta continuously, but you should give it a stir every 5 minutes or so. As the polenta thickens, switch from a whisk to a wooden spoon for stirring. The whole cooking process will take 30 to 40 minutes. Correct the seasoning, adding salt and pepper to taste: the polenta should be highly seasoned.

3. You can certainly eat the polenta at this stage and it will be delicious. But tradition calls for pouring it onto a baking sheet that's been lightly brushed or sprayed with oil, then covering it with plastic wrap and chilling it until firm, 2 to 3 hours. The polenta is then cut into strips, squares, rectangles, stars, or other shapes with a knife or cookie cutter.

4. To reheat the polenta for serving, bake it in a baking dish with a sauce on top, sauté it in a little olive oil or butter in a nonstick frying pan, or brush it with oil and grill it. I particularly like grilling, as the polenta picks up a smoky flavor.

Serves 6 to 8 as an appetizer, 4 as an entrée

147 CALORIES PER SERVING;* 3 G PROTEIN; 1.5 G FAT; 0 G SATURATED FAT; 31 G CARBOHYDRATE; 14 MG SODIUM; 0 MG CHOLESTEROL

Analysis is based on 6 servings as an appetizer.

SOFT POLENTA WITH GARLIC AND CHEESE

Here's a soft, creamy polenta you can eat like mashed potatoes. For extra richness, I cook the polenta in chicken or vegetable stock, adding milk at the end to make it creamy. One nice thing about this polenta is that you eat it the moment it comes off the stove.

PREPARATION TIME: 10 MINUTES   COOKING TIME: ABOUT 40 MINUTES

2 cups coarse yellow cornmeal, preferably stone-ground
6 cups Chicken Broth (page 239) or Basic Vegetable Broth (page 241), cold
1 clove garlic, minced
salt and freshly ground black pepper
1 to 2 cups skim, 1 percent, or 2 percent milk, or

low-fat half-and-half
3 to 4 tablespoons freshly grated Parmigiano-Reggiano cheese
1 tablespoon extra-virgin olive oil or butter (optional)

1. In a mixing bowl, combine the cornmeal with 2 cups of the cold broth and whisk to a smooth paste. Bring the remaining 4 cups broth to a boil in a large, heavy saucepan (preferably nonstick). Add the cornmeal mixture to the broth in a thin stream, whisking steadily. Boil the polenta over high heat for 2 minutes, whisking steadily. Add the garlic and a little salt and pepper.

2. Reduce the heat to medium or medium-low and gently simmer the polenta until the mixture thickens enough to pull away from the sides of the pan. After 20 minutes, stir in the milk or half-and-half. Continue cooking the polenta until soft and creamy, 10 to 20 minutes more. It should be the con-

sistency of fluffy mashed potatoes. Add milk as needed. It isn't necessary to whisk the polenta continuously while it is simmering, but you should give it a stir every 5 minutes or so. As the polenta thickens, switch from a whisk to a wooden spoon for stirring. The whole cooking process will take 35 to 40 minutes. Whisk in the cheese and correct the seasoning, adding salt and pepper to taste: the polenta should be highly seasoned.

3. Serve the polenta in soft mounds. If you're feeling extravagant, top each with a drizzle of olive oil or even a pat of butter.

Serves 6 to 8 as an appetizer, 4 as an entrée

210 CALORIES PER SERVING;* 8 G PROTEIN; 5 G FAT; 2 G SATURATED FAT; 36 G CARBOHYDRATE; 1,083 MG SODIUM; 21 MG CHOLESTEROL

Analysis is based on 6 servings as an appetizer.

CREAM OF WHEAT POLENTA

This dish was inspired by the semolina dumplings of Rome. Cream of Wheat may not be a traditional Italian ingredient (although it resembles semolina—see page 106), but it produces a lovely, light polenta. It has the added advantage over cornmeal-based polenta of requiring only 5 minutes' preparation time. Below are two variations on a theme of polenta. Sauce suggestions are listed below. You can use quick-cooking Cream of Wheat for this recipe, but do not use instant.

PREPARATION TIME: 10 MINUTES   COOKING TIME: 3 HOURS CHILLING TIME
(OPTIONAL), PLUS 6 MINUTES COOKING TIME

2 cups skim, 1 percent, or 2 percent milk, or low-fat half-and-half
½ cup quick-cooking Cream of Wheat
¼ cup freshly grated Parmigiano-Reggiano cheese

salt and freshly ground black pepper
spray oil
1 tablespoon extra-virgin olive oil or butter (optional)

1. Bring the milk to a simmer in a heavy saucepan. Add the Cream of Wheat in a thin stream, whisking steadily. Simmer the mixture over medium heat until cooked and thick, about 5 minutes, whisking steadily to obtain a smooth consistency. Whisk in the cheese and salt and pepper to taste.

2. Transfer the mixture to a pie pan lightly sprayed with oil. Let cool to room temperature, then cover with plastic wrap and chill for at least 3 hours.

3. To serve, cut the polenta into wedges. Heat the olive oil or butter in a nonstick frying pan. Pan-fry the polenta wedges until lightly browned on each side, 2 to 3 minutes per side. Alternatively, lightly brush the top of the polenta with the 1 tablespoon oil and broil until lightly browned. Alternatively, brush the polenta wedges on both sides with oil and lightly brown on a preheated grill.

Serves 4

148 CALORIES PER SERVING; 9 G PROTEIN; 2 G FAT; 1 G SATURATED FAT; 22 G CARBOHYDRATE; 235 MG SODIUM; 7 MG CHOLESTEROL

VARIATION: SOFT CREAM OF WHEAT POLENTA

Prepare the preceding recipe, using 6 tablespoons Cream of Wheat instead of ½ cup. If you like, add 1 minced clove garlic (when you bring the milk to a boil) or 1 tablespoon chopped fresh herbs (at the end). Serve the soft polenta the moment it comes off the stove.

POLENTA WITH CALABRIAN SAUSAGE SAUCE

This recipe takes me back to my restaurant-critic days in Boston—in particular, back to a homey, no-frills trattoria (long since gone) in Boston's "Little Italy," the North End. It was here that I first tasted polenta, and it was smothered with a red sauce sweet with fennel seed and aromatic with bell peppers. My low-fat version calls for turkey sausage, which is considerably leaner than pork. A vegetarian could substitute mushrooms or zucchini for the meat.

PREPARATION TIME: 15 MINUTES   COOKING TIME: 40 MINUTES FOR THE POLENTA (PLUS A FEW HOURS FOR CHILLING THE POLENTA), 20 MINUTES FOR COOKING THE SAUSAGE, 20 MINUTES FOR THE SAUCE

1 recipe Firm Polenta (page 112), prepared
   through step 3
spray oil or a few drops of extra-virgin olive oil
1 turkey sausage (6 to 8 ounces)
1 tablespoon extra-virgin olive oil
1 medium onion, finely chopped
3 cloves garlic
¼ to ½ teaspoon hot pepper flakes
1 green bell pepper, cored, seeded, and cut into
   2 × ½-inch strips

1 red bell pepper, cored, seeded, and cut into
   2 × ½-inch strips
1 28-ounce can imported peeled plum tomatoes,
   with their juices, finely chopped or coarsely
   puréed in the food processor or through a
   vegetable mill
½ teaspoon dried oregano
¼ teaspoon fennel seeds
3 tablespoons chopped flat-leaf parsley
salt and freshly ground black pepper

1. Prepare the polenta following the recipe on page 112. Transfer it to a nonstick baking sheet to cool, then refrigerate until firm. Cut it into rectangles or squares and place the polenta shapes in a lightly oiled baking dish.

2. Prick the sausage on all sides with a toothpick and cook it. You can do so either by baking it on a rack in a baking dish in a 400°F. oven for 20 minutes, or until no longer pink, or by poaching it in simmering water to cover for 10 minutes. Even better, you could grill the sausage. Blot off any excess fat with a paper towel, then cut the sausage on the diagonal into ¼-inch-thick slices.

3. Heat the 1 tablespoon olive oil in a large nonstick frying pan. Add the onions and cook over medium heat for 2 minutes. Add the garlic and pepper flakes and continue cooking until the onions are just beginning to brown.

4. Increase the heat to high. Add the peppers and cook until tender, about 5 minutes. Add the sausage, puréed tomatoes, oregano, fennel, and half the parsley. Reduce the heat to medium and gently simmer the sauce until thick and richly flavored, about 10 minutes. Correct the seasoning, adding salt and pepper to taste. Spoon the sauce over the polenta. The recipe can be made ahead to this stage. Let cool to room temperature, then cover with plastic wrap and refrigerate.

5. Preheat the oven to 400°F. Bake the dish until the polenta is thoroughly heated and the sauce is bubbling. Sprinkle with the remaining parsley and serve at once.

Serves 6 to 8 as a first course, 4 as an entrée

267 CALORIES PER SERVING;* 11 G PROTEIN; 6 G FAT; 1 G SATURATED FAT; 45 G CARBOHYDRATE; 471 MG SODIUM; 18 MG CHOLESTEROL

Analysis is based on 6 servings as a first course.

RISOTTI AND OTHER RICE DISHES

BASIC RISOTTO

As a rule, you don't stir rice when you cook it. Italy's famous rice dish, risotto, however, depends on diligent stirring to achieve its legendary creamy consistency. You don't need to stir continuously (especially if you use a nonstick pot), but stir often. Use a wooden spoon and stir well after each addition of broth. The broth must be very hot, and one batch of broth must be completely absorbed before you add the next. The entire process will take 18 to 20 minutes.

In addition to elbow grease, you'll need two other special ingredients: arborio rice and broth. The former is a starchy, pearly, short-grained rice from the Po Valley that has the unique ability to absorb up to five times its volume in liquid without becoming mushy. As it cooks, the rice starches thicken the broth into a smooth, creamy sauce, but the individual grains of rice will still be discernible. The broth is what gives the risotto its rich flavor, so I recommend using homemade broth.

PREPARATION TIME: 10 MINUTES   COOKING TIME: 25 MINUTES

1½ tablespoons extra-virgin olive oil
1 onion, finely chopped
1 clove garlic, minced
1½ cups arborio rice
½ cup dry white wine
5 to 6 cups Chicken Broth (page 239) or Basic
   Vegetable Broth (page 241), heated to
   simmering in another pot

salt and freshly ground black pepper
2 tablespoons chopped flat-leaf parsley
¼ to ½ cup freshly grated Parmigiano-Reggiano
   cheese

1. Heat the oil in a large heavy saucepan (preferably nonstick) over medium heat. Cook the onion and garlic until soft and translucent but not brown, about 4 minutes. Stir in the rice and cook for 1 minute, or until all the grains are shiny.

2. Add the wine and bring to a boil, stirring steadily. When most of the wine is absorbed, add ½ cup of the simmering broth. Cook the rice at a brisk simmer, stirring steadily. When most of the liquid is absorbed, add another ½ cup broth. Gradually add salt and pepper as you add the broth. Continue adding the broth, ½ cup at a time, until 5 cups are used up. If the rice is still hard, add ½ to 1 more cup broth. Stir in the parsley the last 3 minutes. You'll need about 18 minutes of cooking in all.

3. Remove the pan from the heat and stir in the cheese and salt and pepper to taste. Serve at once.

Serves 6 as a first course or side dish, 4 as an entrée

280 CALORIES PER SERVING;* 7 G PROTEIN; 7 G FAT; 2 G SATURATED FAT; 44 G CARBOHYDRATE; 905 MG SODIUM; 18 MG CHOLESTEROL

Analysis is based on 4 servings as a main course.

Lemon Parsley Risotto (recipe is on page 118)

LEMON PARSLEY RISOTTO

If I were to be banished to a desert island and could take only one condiment with me, I would choose lemon. I love the perfumed fragrance of the zest (oil-rich outer rind) of the lemon as much as I love the refreshing, mouth-puckering tartness of the juice. Lemon Parsley Risotto makes a lovely, refreshingly light entrée for summertime.

PREPARATION TIME: 10 MINUTES   COOKING TIME: 25 MINUTES

1½ tablespoons extra-virgin olive oil
½ red onion, finely chopped (about ¾ cup)
1½ cups arborio rice
½ cup dry white wine
5 to 6 cups Basic Vegetable Broth (page 241) or Chicken Broth (page 239), heated to simmering in another pot

1½ teaspoons finely grated lemon zest
salt and freshly ground black pepper
¼ cup fresh lemon juice
½ cup finely chopped flat-leaf parsley
¼ to ½ cup freshly grated Parmigiano-Reggiano cheese

1. Heat the oil in a large heavy saucepan (preferably nonstick) over medium heat. Cook the onions until soft and translucent but not brown, about 2 minutes. Stir in the rice and cook for 1 minute, or until all the grains are shiny.

2. Add the wine and bring to a boil, stirring often. When most of the wine is absorbed, add ½ cup broth and the lemon zest. Cook the rice at a brisk simmer, stirring steadily. When most of the liquid is absorbed, add another ½ cup broth. Gradually add salt and pepper as you add the broth. Continue adding the broth, ½ cup at a time, until 5 cups are used up. If the rice is still hard, add ½ to 1 more cup broth. Stir in the lemon juice and parsley the last 3 minutes. You'll need about 18 minutes of cooking in all.

3. Remove the pan from the heat and stir in the cheese and salt and pepper to taste. Serve at once.

Serves 6 as a first course or side dish, 4 as an entrée

280 CALORIES PER SERVING;* 10 G PROTEIN; 5 G FAT; 1 G SATURATED FAT; 44 G CARBOHYDRATE; 421 MG SODIUM; 3 MG CHOLESTEROL

Analysis is based on 6 servings as a first course.

RISOTTO WITH SAFFRON AND SQUASH BLOSSOMS

Risotto originated in the Po Valley in northern Italy, where its invention, so legend goes, is associated with a stained-glass window maker named Valarius. The master craftsman achieved exceptionally brilliant colors by adding saffron to his paints. One day, at the wedding of Valarius's daughter, one of his apprentices persuaded the cook to add saffron to the rice. Soon the guests were eating a first for the region, a mountain of saffron-colored rice. Valarius pronounced the dish "risus optimus," Latin for "excellent rice." The words were eventually shorted to risotto. To this day, saffron-flavored risotto remains a Milanese specialty.

In addition to saffron, traditional risotto alla milanese contains poached marrow, an admittedly tasty ingredient that is off the charts in terms of fat and cholesterol. I've replaced the marrow with another popular northern Italian risotto ingredient: zucchini blossoms. These are available in Italian markets and greengrocers in early summer. But don't worry if you can't find zucchini blossoms: saffron risotto is plenty delicious by itself.

PREPARATION TIME: 10 MINUTES COOKING TIME: 25 MINUTES

½ teaspoon saffron threads
1½ tablespoons extra-virgin olive oil
1 medium onion, finely chopped (1 cup)
1 clove garlic, minced
1½ cups arborio rice
½ cup dry white wine
5 to 6 cups Chicken Broth (page 239) or Basic
    Vegetable Broth (page 241), heated to
    simmering in another pot

8 to 10 zucchini or squash blossoms, washed,
    patted dry, and cut crosswise into ½-inch slices
¼ to ½ cup freshly grated Parmigiano-Reggiano
    cheese
salt and freshly ground black pepper

1. Place the saffron threads in a small bowl and pulverize them with the end of a wooden spoon. Add 1 tablespoon hot water and let stand for 10 minutes.

2. Meanwhile, heat the olive oil in a large, heavy saucepan (preferably nonstick) over medium heat. Cook the onion and garlic until soft and translucent but not brown, about 4 minutes. Stir in the rice, and cook for 1 minute, or until all the grains are shiny.

3. Add the wine and bring to a boil, stirring constantly. Add the saffron. When most of the wine is absorbed, add the first ½ cup broth. Cook the rice at a brisk simmer, stirring steadily. When most of the

liquid is absorbed, add another ½ cup broth. Gradually add salt and pepper as you add the broth. Continue adding the broth, ½ cup at a time, until 5 cups are used up. Stir in the zucchini blossoms after 12 minutes of cooking. If the rice is still hard, add ½ to 1 more cup broth. When ready, the risotto will have a creamy sauce, but the individual grains of rice will still be discernible. Remove the pan from the heat. You'll need about 18 minutes of cooking in all.

4. Stir in the cheese, and salt and pepper to taste. Serve at once. *Serves 6 as a first course or side dish, 4 as an entrée*

281 CALORIES PER SERVING;* 7 G PROTEIN; 7 G FAT; 2 G SATURATED FAT; 43 G CARBOHYDRATE; 909 MG SODIUM; 18 MG CHOLESTEROL

Analysis is based on 6 servings as a first course.

SEAFOOD RISOTTO

Black mussels, white squid, and pink shrimp make this one of the prettiest risottos in Italy.
For a more extravagant risotto, you could add clams, scallops, and/or lobster tails.

PREPARATION TIME: 20 MINUTES   COOKING TIME: 30 MINUTES

1½ pounds mussels
1 pound cleaned squid (calamari) (see box on page 158)
1 pound large shrimp
2 medium onions, finely chopped
4 cloves garlic, minced
½ cup finely chopped flat-leaf parsley

1½ cups dry white wine
5 to 6 cups Fish Broth (page 240), Chicken Broth (page 239), or bottled clam broth (juice)
½ teaspoon saffron threads
1½ tablespoons extra-virgin olive oil
1½ cups arborio rice
salt and freshly ground black pepper

1. Scrub the mussels, discarding any with cracked shells or shells that fail to close when tapped. Remove any threads that may cluster at the hinge of the mussel shells (pull them out with needlenose pliers). Cut the squid bodies crosswise into ¼-inch rings. Leave the heads (tentacle sections) whole. Peel and devein the shrimp, reserving the shells.

2. Place 1 chopped onion, 2 garlic cloves, and 3 tablespoons parsley in a large saucepan with the shrimp shells and wine. Bring to a boil. Add the mussels and tightly cover the pan. Cook the mussels over high heat until the shells are open and the mussels are cooked: about 8 minutes. Stir the mussels once or twice to allow the shells on the bottom to open. Transfer the mussels with a slotted spoon to a colander over a bowl to drain and cool.

3. When the mussels are cool, take ½ of them out of the shells, discard the shells, and place with the squid and shrimp. Leave the remaining mussels in the shell for garnish. Strain the mussel cooking liquid through a strainer lined with cheesecloth or a paper towel into a large measuring cup. Add enough fish broth to obtain 6 cups liquid. Place this liquid in a pot and bring to a simmer. Place the saffron threads in a small bowl and pulverize them with the end of a wooden spoon. Add 1 tablespoon hot broth and let stand for 10 minutes.

4. Heat the olive oil in a large heavy saucepan (preferably nonstick) over medium heat. Cook the remaining onion, 2 cloves garlic, and 3 tablespoons parsley until soft and translucent but not brown, about 4 minutes. Stir in the rice and cook for 1 minute, or until all the grains are shiny.

5. Add ½ cup mussel broth mixture and the saffron and bring to a boil, stirring steadily. When most of the liquid is absorbed, add another ½ cup broth. Gradually add salt and pepper as you add the broth. Cook the rice at a brisk simmer. Continue adding the broth, ½ cup at a time, until 5 cups are used up. If the rice is still hard, add ½ to 1 more cup broth. When ready, the risotto will have a creamy sauce, but the individual grains of rice should still be discernible. You'll need about 18 minutes of cooking in all.

6. The last 5 minutes, stir in the shrimp. The last 3 minutes, stir in the squid. When both are cooked, stir in the shelled mussels and salt and pepper to taste. Warm the mussels in the shells in any remaining broth. Transfer the risotto to plates or a platter and garnish with the mussels in the shells. Sprinkle with the remaining 2 tablespoons parsley and serve at once.

Serves 6 as a first course
or side dish, 4 as an entrée

440 CALORIES PER SERVING;* 34 G PROTEIN; 6 G FAT; 1 G SATURATED FAT; 69 G CARBOHYDRATE; 268 MG SODIUM; 311 MG CHOLESTEROL

Analysis is based on 6 servings as a first course.

BARLEY MUSHROOM RISOTTO

The thing I like best about Italian cuisine is the way ordinary dishes can astonish you. I had the following barley risotto at an Umbrian restaurant called Villa Roncalli. It was probably the most plebeian-sounding and plain-looking dish on the menu, but the flavors were so deep, so rich, so soulful and satisfying, I wouldn't have traded it for all the truffles in Piedmont. (Well, maybe for all the truffles in Piedmont.)

There are several options for mushrooms here. Villa Roncalli chef Maria Luisa Leocastre uses fresh porcini. Dried porcini work well and are more readily available. Or for an Asian touch, you could use fresh shiitakes or dried Chinese black mushrooms.

PREPARATION TIME: 20 MINUTES ACTUAL PREPARATION, BUT THE BARLEY AND PORCINI MUST BE PRESOAKED SEVERAL HOURS AHEAD   COOKING TIME: ABOUT 1 HOUR

1 cup pearl barley
salt
1 ounce dried porcini mushrooms or 4 ounces
    fresh
4 to 5 cups veal broth (page 239), Chicken Broth
    (page 239), or Basic Vegetable Broth (page 241)
1½ tablespoons extra-virgin olive oil

1 medium onion, finely chopped
3 tablespoons finely chopped flat-leaf parsley
½ cup dry white wine
freshly ground pepper
¼ to ½ cup freshly grated Parmigiano-Reggiano
    cheese

1. Soak the barley in 8 cups cold water for at least 4 hours or overnight. Drain the barley.

2. Boil the barley in 3 quarts lightly salted water until al dente, about 20 minutes. Drain the barley, rinse under cold water, and drain well again. The recipe can be prepared up to 24 hours ahead to this stage. Store in refrigerator.

3. If using dried porcini, soak them in a bowl in 1 cup hot broth for 30 minutes or until soft. Remove the porcini from the broth with your fingers, reserving the broth, and wring dry. Transfer the porcini to a mixing bowl with cold water to cover. Agitate the mushrooms with your fingers to wash away any sand. (The first soaking extracts the flavor of the porcini; the second soaking rinses away any grit.) If using fresh porcini, trim off the sandy ends of the stems, wipe clean with a damp cloth, and thinly slice. If using dried Chinese black mushrooms, soak and stem them, but do not wash. If using fresh shiitakes, stem and thinly slice.

4. Strain the porcini soaking liquid into a sauce-pan and add the remaining broth. (Simply place all the broth in a saucepan if using fresh porcini.) Bring to a gentle simmer.

5. Heat the oil in a large, heavy saucepan. Cook the onion and half the parsley over medium heat until lightly browned, about 5 minutes. If using fresh porcini, add them at this stage as well. Add the barley, dried porcini (if using), and wine and bring to a boil. When most of the wine is absorbed, add ½ cup broth. Gradually add salt and pepper as you add the broth. Cook the barley at a gentle boil. Continue adding the broth, ½ cup at a time, until all is used up. When ready, the risotto will have a loose, creamy sauce and will be richly flavored. The individual grains of rice will still be discernible. You'll need 20 to 30 minutes of cooking time in all.

6. Stir in the Parmesan and correct the seasoning, adding salt and pepper to taste. Sprinkle the remaining 1½ tablespoons parsley over the risotto and serve at once.

Serves 4

327 CALORIES PER SERVING; 11 G PROTEIN; 9 G FAT; 2 G SATURATED FAT; 48 G CARBOHYDRATE; 949 MG SODIUM; 5 MG CHOLESTEROL

MILANESE RISOTTO PIE

We had just landed in Milan, and tired as I was after a night of flying, I couldn't dream of going straight to our hotel room.
So I found a bar where huge wedges of risotto pie were being sold as a snack. Risotto pie is easy to make
(not to mention a great way to use up leftovers) and makes a fine dish for a brunch or buffet.

PREPARATION TIME: 30 MINUTES   COOKING TIME: 20 TO 30 MINUTES

1 recipe Basic Risotto (page 117)
1 to 2 ounces prosciutto, trimmed of all fat and
   thinly slivered
½ cup cooked peas
1 roasted red bell pepper, cored, seeded, and diced,
   or ½ cup diced pimiento
1 egg, plus 2 egg whites, lightly beaten (or ½ cup
   egg substitute)

¼ cup finely chopped flat-leaf parsley
salt and freshly ground black pepper
spray olive oil
2 to 3 tablespoons toasted bread crumbs (page
   247)

1. Preheat the oven to 400°F. Prepare the risotto. Into it stir the prosciutto, peas, bell pepper, eggs, whites, and parsley. Add salt and pepper to taste.

2. Spray a 12-inch nonstick frying pan with spray oil and line it with bread crumbs, shaking out the excess. Add the risotto, smoothing the top with the back of a spoon. Spray the top of the risotto with oil.

3. Bake the risotto pie until set, 20 to 30 minutes. The sides should be crusty and brown. Remove the pan from the heat and let cool for 5 minutes. Invert the pie onto a platter, taking care not to burn your arm on the handle. Risotto pie can be served hot or at room temperature. Cut into wedges for serving.

Serves 6

333 CALORIES PER SERVING;* 12 G PROTEIN; 8.6 G FAT; 2.6 G SATURATED FAT; 50 G CARBOHYDRATE; 1,045 MG SODIUM; 57 MG CHOLESTEROL

Analysis is based on 6 servings.

🐚

ARANCINE (SICILIAN STUFFED RICE "FRITTERS")

Arancine means "little oranges." With a little imagination, these round, golden brown rice fritters from Sicily do, indeed, resemble tiny citrus fruits. My low-fat verrsion features a filling of sautéed vegetables instead of the traditional ground beef. (For a virtually no-fat version of the dish, you could roast or grill the vegetables instead of sautéing them.) There are two ways to cook the arancine: sautéed in a little olive oil or "bake-fried" in a hot oven. If your fat budget allows it, go for the former, which produces crisper, more succulent fritters. But bake-frying makes tasty arancine, as well. This dish is a great way to use up leftover risotto.

PREPARATION TIME: 20 MINUTES (PLUS 20 MINUTES FOR MAKING THE RISOTTO)
COOKING TIME: 10 TO 15 MINUTES

1 batch basic risotto (page 117)

FOR THE FILLING:
2 to 3 teaspoons extra-virgin olive oil
½ small onion, minced
1 clove garlic, minced
½ red bell pepper, cut into the finest imaginable dice
½ yellow bell pepper, cut into the finest imaginable dice
2 teaspoons drained chopped capers

1 tablespoon tomato paste
salt and freshly ground black pepper

TO FINISH THE ARANCINE:
1 egg plus 4 egg whites (or ¾ cup egg substitute), lightly beaten with a fork
approximately 1 cup toasted bread crumbs
1 to 2 tablespoons extra-virgin olive oil (if sautéing the fritters) or
spray olive oil (if baking)

1. Prepare the risotto and let cool completely. Prepare the filling. Heat the olive oil in a nonstick frying pan. Add the onion, garlic, and bell peppers. Cook over medium heat until peppers are tender and most of the juices have evaporated, about 5 minutes. Add the capers and tomato paste and cook for 2 minutes. Add salt and pepper to taste. Let the mixture cool to room temperature.

2. Pinch off a walnut-size piece of risotto mixture and roll it into a ball between the palms of your hands. (Wet your hands with a little water to prevent sticking.) Make a deep depression in one side of the ball with your thumb. Place a tiny spoonful of filling in the depression. Pinch the hole shut and roll the rice back into a round ball. Repeat until all the risotto and filling are used up. The recipe can be prepared ahead to this stage. Place the beaten egg mixture in one shallow bowl, the bread crumbs in another.

3a. If pan-frying the arancine, flatten each ball between the palms of your hands into a thick pancake.

(OK, this is no longer an orange shape, but it facilitates pan-frying.) Dip each fritter first in egg mixture, then in crumbs, shaking off the excess. Heat 1 tablespoon olive oil in a nonstick frying pan. Cook the arancine over medium-high heat until crusty and golden brown on both sides, 2 to 4 minutes per side, turning with a spatula. Work in several batches to avoid crowding the pan, adding oil as needed. Drain the arancine on paper towels, sprinkle with a little more salt and pepper, and serve at once.

3b. If bake-frying the arancine, preheat the oven to 425°F. Dip the arancine in egg, then in crumbs, as described above, shaking off the excess. Bake-fried arancine can be left as balls. Arrange them on a nonstick baking sheet sprayed with oil. Generously spray or brush the sides and tops of the arancine with oil. Bake the arancine until sizzling hot and lightly browned, 10 to 15 minutes. Transfer to a platter and serve at once.

Makes 28 to 30 arancine, which will serve 8 to 10.

249 CALORIES PER SERVING; 10 G PROTEIN; 6 G FAT; 1 G SATURATED FAT; 36 G CARBOHYDRATE; 395 MG SODIUM; 23 MG CHOLESTEROL

BREADS

GRISSINI

BREAD STICKS

*Grissini are associated with the Piedmont city of Turin, but variations on the theme of audibly crisp bread sticks
turn up the breadth and length of Italy. What you may not know is how easy bread sticks
are to make at home. Here's a basic recipe, plus several regional variations.*

PREPARATION TIME: 20 MINUTES   COOKING TIME: 20 MINUTES, PLUS 2 TO 3 HOURS RISING TIME

1 envelope (2½ teaspoons) dry yeast
1 tablespoon sugar
2 tablespoons warm water, plus 1¼ cups water at
  room temperature
3 cups all-purpose unbleached white flour
1 cup whole-wheat flour (or more white flour)
2 teaspoons salt
1 tablespoon extra-virgin olive oil

FOR THE TOPPING:
1 egg white, beaten with a pinch of salt for glaze
1 tablespoon fennel seeds, sesame seeds, poppy
  seeds, cracked black peppercorns, and/or coarse
  salt

1. Combine the yeast with the sugar and 2 tablespoons warm water (110° to 115°F.) in a small bowl and let stand until foamy, 5 to 10 minutes.

2. Place the flours and salt in the bowl of a food processor fitted with a dough blade. With the machine running, add the yeast mixture, remaining water, and oil. Process for 1 minute, or until the dough comes together into a smooth ball. (If the dough is too dry, add a little more water.) Knead the dough until smooth and springy, 3 to 4 minutes in the processor, running the machine in spurts.

2a. To make the dough in a mixer, place the yeast mixture, water, oil, sugar, and salt in the mixing bowl. Using the dough hook, incorporate the flour, mixing at low speed to obtain a stiff dough. Knead the dough in the mixer until pliable and smooth, 8 to 10 minutes.

2b. To make the dough by hand, place the yeast mixture, water, oil, sugar, and salt in a large heavy mixing bowl. Stir in the flour with a wooden spoon to obtain a stiff dough. Turn the mixture out onto a work surface and knead until pliable and smooth, 6 to 8 minutes. For kneading instructions see Hand Method, step 2, page 65.

3. Place the dough in a lightly oiled bowl and cover with plastic wrap. Let rise in a warm, draft-free spot until doubled in bulk, 1 to 2 hours.

4. Punch the dough down and cut it in half. Roll each half into a rectangle 14 to 16 inches long and 10 inches wide. Cut each rectangle crosswise into ½-

Bread Sticks

inch strips. Stretch these strips to the desired length (16 to 18 inches) by taking an end in each hand and gently pulling and twirling. Arrange the grissini on nonstick or lightly oiled baking sheets, 1 inch apart. Loosely cover with plastic wrap and a dish towel and let rise until doubled in height, 30 to 60 minutes. Preheat the oven to 400°F.

5. Lightly brush the tops of the grissini with the egg-white mixture, taking care not to drip any on the baking sheet. Sprinkle the bread sticks with seeds, pepper, and/or coarse salt.

6. Bake the grissini until crisp and golden-brown, about 20 minutes. Transfer to wire racks to cool.

Makes 36 to 40 grissini

55 CALORIES PER BREAD STICK; 2 G PROTEIN; 0.6 G FAT; 0 G SATURATED FAT; 11 G CARBOHYDRATE; 121 MG SODIUM; 0 MG CHOLESTEROL.

ALMOND GRISSINI

These bread sticks make a stunning, unexpected centerpiece for a dinner table or buffet table,
yet they're easy to make, consisting of a strip of bread stick dough knotted around an almond.

PREPARATION TIME: 20 MINUTES   COOKING TIME: 20 MINUTES, PLUS 2 TO 3 HOURS RISING TIME

1 recipe Grissini (page 125), prepared through step 3

about 40 unskinned almonds
1 egg white, beaten with a pinch of salt, for glaze

Proceed with step 4 but stretch the bread sticks out to 20 inches long. Knot the top of each breadstick around an almond as pictured on page 124. Arrange the bread sticks on nonstick or lightly oiled baking sheets, 1 inch apart. Loosely cover with plastic wrap and a dish towel and let rise until doubled in height, 30 to 60 minutes. Preheat the oven to 400°F. Proceed to step 5.   *Makes about 36 to 40 grissini*

60 CALORIES PER BREAD STICK; 2 G PROTEIN; 1 G FAT; 0.1 G SATURATED FAT; 10 G CARBOHYDRATE; 115 MG SODIUM; 0 MG CHOLESTEROL.

TAPERED BREAD STICKS IN THE STYLE OF SANTA MARGHERITA

*The bread sticks made in the Ligurian seaside town of Santa Margherita come with
pointed ends and are brushed with olive oil instead of egg-white glaze.*

PREPARATION TIME: 20 MINUTES   COOKING TIME: 20 MINUTES, PLUS 2 TO 3 HOURS RISING TIME

**1 recipe Grissini (page 125), prepared through
step 3**

1. Tear off 1½-inch balls of the grissini dough and
roll them between the palms of your hands or on the
work surface to make sticks about 6 inches long and
⅓ inch in diameter. Roll the ends so that they taper
to sharp points.

2. Arrange the grissini on nonstick or lightly oiled
baking sheets, 1 inch apart. Loosely cover with plas-

**1 tablespoon extra-virgin olive oil
coarse sea salt for sprinkling**

tic wrap and a dish towel and let rise until doubled in
bulk, 30 to 60 minutes. Preheat the oven to 400°F.

3. Lightly brush the tops of the grissini with olive
oil and sprinkle with sea salt. Bake the grissini until
crisp and golden-brown, 15 to 20 minutes. Transfer
to wire racks to cool.

Makes 36 to 40 grissini

52 CALORIES PER BREAD STICK; 1 G PROTEIN; 0.8 G FAT; 0.1 G SATURATED FAT; 10 G CARBOHYDRATE; 114 MG SODIUM; 0 MG CHOLESTEROL.

PEPENESE (SESAME BREAD STICKS)

Pepenese are short, stubby, sesame seed–dotted bread sticks from Portofino.

PREPARATION TIME: 20 MINUTES   COOKING TIME: 20 MINUTES, PLUS 2 TO 3 HOURS RISING TIME

1 recipe grissini (page 125), made using all white flour (4 cups) and prepared through step 3

1 egg white, lightly beaten with a pinch of salt
2 to 3 tablespoons sesame seeds

1. Tear off 1½-inch balls of the grissini dough and roll them between the palms of your hands or on the work surface to make short, stubby bread sticks, each about 3 inches long and ½ inch in diameter.

2. Arrange the *pepenese* on nonstick or lightly oiled baking sheets, 1 inch apart. Loosely cover with plastic wrap and a dish towel and let rise until dou-bled in bulk, 30 to 60 minutes. Preheat the oven to 400°F.

3. Lightly brush the tops of the *pepenese* with the egg-white mixture and sprinkle with sesame seeds. Bake the *pepenese* until crisp and golden brown, 15 to 20 minutes. Transfer to wire racks to cool.

Makes 36 to 40 pepenese

50 CALORIES PER BREAD STICK; 2 G PROTEIN; 0.4 G FAT; 0 G SATURATED FAT; 10 G CARBOHYDRATE; 115 MG SODIUM; 0 MG CHOLESTEROL.

TARALLI

(SPICED RING-SHAPED BISCUITS)

I first tasted these ring-shaped biscuits in Boston's "Little Italy," the North End. They looked like tiny bagels and they were sold ten to a bunch on a string. The analogy is apt: like bagels, traditional taralli *are boiled first, then baked. This produces a hard, jaw-breakingly crisp pastry that's often dipped in wine to soften it before eating.*

Taralli are a specialty of southern Italy, where bakeries sell both sweet and hot versions— *the former flavored with fennel seed, the latter fired with cracked black pepper.*

For an even easier way to make taralli, *see Note.*

PREPARATION TIME: 30 MINUTES   COOKING TIME: 30 MINUTES, PLUS 30 MINUTES FOR RISING

1 package (2½ teaspoons) dry yeast
1 teaspoon sugar
2 tablespoons warm water (110° to 115°F.)
6 tablespoons extra-virgin olive oil, plus oil for the baking sheet
¾ cup dry white wine

1½ teaspoons sea salt, plus salt for the water
2 teaspoons fennel seeds or cracked black peppercorns
about 3 cups all-purpose unbleached white flour, plus flour for rolling

1. Combine the yeast, sugar, and water in a small bowl and let stand until foamy, 5 to 10 minutes. Transfer the mixture to the bowl of a mixer or a large mixing bowl. Stir in the 6 tablespoons olive oil and the wine, salt, and fennel. Using a dough hook, add enough flour to obtain a firm but pliable dough. (If working by hand, stir the flour in with a wooden spoon.) Knead until smooth, about 10 minutes in a mixer, 5 minutes by hand. For kneading instructions, see Hand Method, step 2, page 65.

2. Transfer the dough to a lightly oiled bowl, turn once or twice to oil the top, then cover with plastic wrap and a dish towel. Let the dough rest for 30 minutes. Bring 3 quarts salted water to a boil in a large pot. Preheat the oven to 375°F.

3. Pinch off a fist-sized piece of dough and roll it into a tube ¼ inch thick. Cut the tube into 5-inch lengths. Bring the ends together and pinch to form a ring. Shape the remaining *taralli* the same way.

4. Gently lower the *taralli*, a few at a time, into the boiling water. Cook until they rise to the surface again. Transfer them to a wire rack on a baking sheet to drain. Boil all the *taralli* in this fashion.

5. Transfer the *taralli* to lightly oiled nonstick baking sheets. Bake until lightly browned, about 30 to 40 minutes. Transfer the *taralli* to a rack to cool. You can serve them the same day or let them harden for a few days. For a novel gift, tie the *taralli* in bunches with string.

Note: for a delectable if nontraditional variation, omit boiling the *taralli* in step 4. Arrange the rings on a baking sheet, cover with plastic wrap, and let rise until doubled in bulk, about 1 hour. Bake the *taralli* until lightly browned, 15 to 20 minutes. This produces a bread-stick-like *taralle*.

Makes 4 to 4½ dozen taralli

47 CALORIES PER PIECE; 1 G PROTEIN; 2 G FAT; 0.2 G SATURATED FAT; 6 G CARBOHYDRATE; 67 MG SODIUM; 0 MG CHOLESTEROL

CARAMELIZED ONION FOCACCIA

Focaccia is one of Italy's most successful exports—a flat bread that's thicker than pizza but thinner than a conventional loaf of bread. The preparation varies from bakery to bakery and town to town, some versions being firm and crisp, others being soft and chewy. Focaccia seems to take its name from the Latin word focus, *meaning "hearth."*

PREPARATION TIME: 30 MINUTES   COOKING TIME: 20 MINUTES, PLUS ABOUT 2 HOURS FOR RISING

1 envelope (2½ teaspoons) dry yeast
1 teaspoon sugar
1½ cups warm water (110°to 115°F.)
4 to 4½ cups unbleached all-purpose white flour
2½ teaspoons coarse salt, plus salt for sprinkling
1 tablespoon extra-virgin olive oil (optional)
¼ cup fine yellow cornmeal (optional)

FOR THE TOPPING:
1½ tablespoons extra-virgin olive oil
1 large or 2 medium onions, thinly sliced
salt and freshly ground black pepper
spray olive oil (optional)

1. Combine the yeast, sugar, and 2 tablespoons of the warm water in a small bowl and let stand until foamy, 5 to 10 minutes.

2. Place the flour and salt in the bowl of a food processor fitted with a dough blade. With the machine running, add the yeast mixture, the remaining water, and the oil (if using). Process for 1 minute or until the dough comes together into a smooth ball. (If the dough is too dry, add a little more water.) Knead the dough in the processor until smooth and springy, 3 to 4 minutes, running the machine in spurts.

2a. To make the dough in a mixer, place the yeast mixture, the remaining water, the oil (if using), and the salt in the mixing bowl. Using the dough hook, incorporate the flour, mixing at low speed to obtain a stiff dough. Knead the dough in the mixer until pliable and smooth, 8 to 10 minutes.

2b. To make the dough by hand, place the yeast mixture, the remaining water, the oil, and the salt in a large heavy mixing bowl. Stir in the flour with a wooden spoon to obtain a stiff dough. Turn the mixture out onto a work surface and knead until pliable and smooth, 6 to 8 minutes. For kneading instructions, see Hand Method, step 2, page 65.

3. Place the dough in an oiled bowl, turn to coat with oil, cover with plastic wrap and a dish towel, and let rise in a warm place until doubled in bulk, 1 to 2 hours.

4. Meanwhile, prepare the topping: Heat the olive oil in a large nonstick frying pan. Add the onions and cook, stirring often, until nicely caramelized (a deep golden-brown). Start over a medium-high flame and gradually reduce the heat to low to prevent the onions from burning. The whole process will take 15 to 20 minutes. Season the onion mixture with salt and pepper to taste.

5. Punch the dough down and roll it out into a large rectangle about ½ inch thick. Transfer it to a nonstick baking sheet that's been lightly sprayed or brushed with olive oil. (Alternatively, transfer the focaccia to a baker's peel liberally sprinkled with cornmeal.) Cover the focaccia with plastic wrap and a clean cloth and let rise until doubled in height, 30 to 60 minutes. Place a baking stone or sheet pan in the oven on the middle shelf and preheat the oven to 375°F.

6. Poke your fingers over the surface of the focaccia to decoratively dimple the surface. Arrange the caramelized onions on top. Sprinkle with a little more salt and/or pepper.

7. Bake the focaccia until puffed and golden brown, 20 to 30 minutes. (If using the peel, slide the

focaccia onto the preheated baking stone or baking sheet.) Let cool slightly before serving. Cut the fo- caccia into rectangles and serve at once.

Serves 8

262 CALORIES PER SERVING; 7 G PROTEIN; 3 G FAT; 0.4 G SATURATED FAT; 50 G CARBOHYDRATE; 668 MG SODIUM; 0 MG CHOLESTEROL

FIRM FOCACCIA WITH ROSEMARY

Here's a thinner, firmer, denser focaccia of the sort you find at Italian bars and sandwich shops.
One novel way to serve it is to cut the focaccia into long thin strips, like bread sticks.

PREPARATION TIME: 30 MINUTES   COOKING TIME: 20 MINUTES, PLUS 1½ TO 2 HOURS FOR RISING

1¼ cups warm water (110°to 115°F.)
1½ envelopes (4 teaspoons) dry yeast
1 tablespoon sugar
2 tablespoons extra-virgin olive oil

2½ teaspoons coarse salt, plus salt for sprinkling
3½ to 4 cups all-purpose unbleached white flour,
  plus flour for sprinkling
1 tablespoon fresh or dried rosemary leaves

1. In the bowl of a heavy-duty mixer, combine the water, yeast, and sugar with a dough hook. Mix at low speed for 5 minutes to dissolve the sugar and yeast. Let stand until foamy, 5 to 10 minutes.

2. Running the mixer on low speed, add 1 tablespoon of the olive oil, 2½ teaspoons salt, and enough flour to obtain a soft, pliable dough. Add flour as needed: the dough should be soft but not sticky. Knead the dough in the mixer until smooth, about 10 minutes. Transfer the dough to an oiled bowl, turn to coat with oil, and cover with plastic wrap. Let the dough rise in a warm, draft-free spot until doubled in bulk, 1 to 2 hours.

2a. To prepare the dough by hand, mix the ingredients in step 1 in a large mixing bowl. Stir in the salt and flour with a wooden spoon. Turn the dough onto a floured work surface and knead until smooth by hand. Let the dough rise as described above.

2b. To prepare the dough in a food processor (use a plastic dough blade), mix the ingredients in step 1 in the processor bowl. Add the salt and enough flour to obtain a soft, pliable dough. (You'll need a little more flour than if working in a mixer or by hand.) Run the machine in bursts to knead the dough, about 5 minutes. Let the dough rise as described above.

3. Turn the dough out onto a lightly floured work surface and gather it into a ball. Using a rolling pin, roll it out to form an oval rectangle about ¼ inch thick. Brush the top with a little of the remaining olive oil and invert it onto a nonstick baking sheet. Cover the focaccia with a clean dish towel and let rise until doubled in height, 30 to 60 minutes. Preheat the oven to 400°F.

4. Lightly flour your fingertips and use them to poke a series of holes in the top of the raised focaccia. The holes should be spaced about 1 inch apart. Drizzle the top of the focaccia with the remaining olive oil. Sprinkle with rosemary and salt.

5. Bake the focaccia until crusty and nicely browned on top, about 20 minutes. Transfer it to a wire rack to cool for 5 minutes. Cut the focaccia into squares, wedges, or 1-inch strips for serving.

Serves 8

239 CALORIES PER SERVING; 6 G PROTEIN; 4 G FAT; 0.5 G SATURATED FAT; 44 G CARBOHYDRATE; 667 MG SODIUM; 0 MG CHOLESTEROL

APULIAN POTATO BREAD

This bread was inspired by the restaurant Angelo Ricci in the town of Caglie in Apulia. Like many great Italian restaurants, it looked utterly unpretentious on the outside and seemed to be located in the middle of nowhere. The food was extraordinary, but what I really remember are the breads, which were baked in a wood-burning stone oven out back.

PREPARATION TIME: 20 MINUTES   COOKING TIME: 2 TO 3 HOURS FOR RISING, PLUS ABOUT 40 MINUTES FOR BAKING

1 pound red-skinned potatoes, peeled and quartered
2 teaspoons sea salt for cooking the potatoes, plus 1 tablespoon salt for the dough
1½ envelopes (4 teaspoons) dry yeast

1 teaspoon sugar
2 tablespoons extra-virgin olive oil, plus oil for brushing
6 to 7 cups flour
½ cup cornmeal for sprinkling

1. Place the potatoes in a large pot with 2 quarts water and 2 teaspoons salt. Bring the potatoes to a boil, reduce the heat to medium, and gently simmer the potatoes until very soft, about 15 minutes. Drain the potatoes in a colander over a bowl, reserving the potato liquid. Let both cool until tepid.

2. In the bowl of a mixer fitted with a dough hook, dissolve the yeast and sugar in ¼ cup warm potato water (about 110° to 115°F.). Let stand until foamy, 5 to 10 minutes. Mash the potatoes with a potato masher or purée through a ricer or vegetable mill. (Do not purée the potatoes in a food processor, or the mixture will be gummy.) Add the olive oil, mashed potatoes, and 1½ cups potato cooking liquid to the yeast mixture. Mix at low speed to blend.

3. Running the mixer on low speed, add the 1 tablespoon salt and enough flour to obtain a pliable dough. It should be soft but not sticky. Add flour as needed. Knead the dough in the mixer until smooth, about 10 minutes. Transfer the dough to an oiled bowl and cover with plastic wrap. Let the dough rise in a warm, draft-free spot until doubled in bulk, 1 to 2 hours.

4. Turn the dough out onto a lightly floured work surface and cut it in half. Roll each half into a round or oblong loaf.

5. Place the loaves on a baker's peel or the back of a baking sheet that you've generously sprinkled with cornmeal. Cover with a clean dish towel and let rise until doubled in bulk, about 1 hour. Preheat the oven

to 450°F. If you have a baker's stone, preheat it in the oven. If not, preheat a baking sheet.

6. Spray the loaves with water. Make 2 or 3 shallow slashes in the top with a razor blade and immediately slide the loaves onto the baking stone or baking sheet. Spray the loaves 2 more times with water, once w baking, again after 10 minutes. Turn the heat down to 375° after 20 minutes. Bake the loaves until crusty and brown, about 40 minutes in all. (When done, the breads will sound hollow when tapped on the bottom.) Transfer the breads to a wire rack to cool. Serve warm or at room temperature.

Note: To prepare the dough by hand, mix the ingredients in step 2 in a large mixing bowl. Stir in the salt and flour with a wooden spoon. Turn the dough out onto a floured work surface and knead until smooth by hand. (For kneading instructions, see Hand Method, step 2, page 65.) Let the dough rise as described above.

To prepare the dough in a food processor (use a plastic dough blade), mix the ingredients in step 2 in the processor bowl. Add the salt and enough flour to obtain a soft, pliable dough. (You'll need a little more flour than if working in a mixer or by hand.) Run the machine in bursts to knead the dough, about 5 minutes. Let the dough rise as described above.

Makes 2 loaves

150 CALORIES PER SLICE; 4 G PROTEIN; 2 G FAT; 0.2 G SATURATED FAT; 30 G CARBOHYDRATE; 551 MG SODIUM; 0 MG CHOLESTEROL

CIBATTA

Cibatta (pronounced "chee-BA-ta") means "slipper" in Italian. If you use your imagination, these long, flat, crusty breads do, indeed, look like slippers. The dough is wetter than most bread doughs and contains a lot more yeast, which is what makes cibatta so light and moist inside. (The yeast has another advantage: The dough can be made, leavened, and baked in less than 2 hours.) Here's how my friend Pino Saverino, a chef from Chiavari, makes this traditional bread.

PREPARATION TIME: 20 MINUTES   COOKING TIME: 1 HOUR FOR RISING TIME, PLUS 20 MINUTES FOR BAKING

1 cup warm water (110° to 115°F.)
2 tablespoons yeast (preferably cake yeast, which is available from bakeries, but dry yeast will work as well)
1 tablespoon sugar
2 tablespoons extra-virgin olive oil, plus oil for the bowl

2 teaspoons salt
3½ to 4 cups all-purpose unbleached white flour, plus flour for sprinkling
¼ cup fine cornmeal or more flour

1. In the bowl of a heavy-duty mixer fitted with a dough hook, combine the water, yeast, sugar, and olive oil. Mix at low speed for 5 minutes to dissolve the sugar and yeast. Let stand until foamy, 5 to 10 minutes.

2. Running the mixer on low speed, add the salt and enough flour to obtain a soft, pliable dough. It should be very soft but not too sticky. Add flour as needed. Knead the dough in the mixer until smooth, about 10 minutes. Transfer the dough to an oiled bowl and cover with plastic wrap. Let the dough rise in a warm, draft-free spot until doubled in bulk, 30 to 60 minutes.

3. Turn the dough out onto a lightly floured work surface and roll it into an oblong shape. Using a pastry cutter, cut the oblong shape crosswise on the diagonal into 8 equal-size pieces. Take one end of each piece in each hand and gently stretch the dough into a slipper shape 6 to 8 inches long, 2½ inches wide, and ¾ inch thick. Sprinkle one or two nonstick baking sheets with cornmeal. Arrange the *cibatte* on the baking sheets, leaving 2 inches between each. Lightly dust the tops with flour and cover with a clean dish towel. Let the *cibatte* rise until doubled in bulk, about 20 minutes. Preheat the oven to 400°F.

4. Bake the *cibatte* until crusty and golden brown, about 20 minutes. Transfer to a wire rack to cool. Serve as soon as possible.

Note: To prepare the dough by hand, mix the ingredients in step 1 in a large mixing bowl. Stir in the salt and flour with a wooden spoon. Turn the dough out onto a floured work surface and knead by hand until smooth. Let the dough rise as described above.

To prepare the dough in a food processor (use a plastic dough blade), mix the ingredients in step 1 in the processor bowl. Add the salt and enough flour to obtain a soft, pliable dough. (You'll need a little more flour than if working in a mixer or by hand.) Run the machine in bursts to knead the dough, about 5 minutes. Let the dough rise as described above.

Makes 8 cibatte

257 CALORIES PER PIECE; 7 G PROTEIN; 4 G FAT; 0.6 G SATURATED FAT; 67 G CARBOHYDRATE; 535 MG SODIUM; 0 MG CHOLESTEROL

PIZZAS

BASIC NEAPOLITAN PIZZA DOUGH

My first pizza in Naples came as something of a shock. Where were the olives, the pepperoni, the gooey carpet of cheese? For a true Neapolitan pizza is a paragon of understatement, a slab or circle of moist, puffy dough, smokily browned in a wood-fired oven.. The topping—when the pizza comes topped at all—is limited to a whisper of tomato sauce and perhaps a few atoms of cheese. The crust is the focal point, and the toppings are kept sparse to keep it that way. Here's the basic dough recipe: topping ideas begin on page 139. Italian flour is softer than American flour. The cake flour in the following recipe has a softening effect on the dough.

PREPARATION TIME: 10 TO 15 MINUTES, PLUS 2 TO 3 HOURS RISING TIME　　COOKING TIME: 6 TO 8 MINUTES

2 packages (5 teaspoons) dried yeast
1 teaspoon sugar
1⅓ cups warm water (110° to 115°F.)
2½ cups all-purpose unbleached white flour, plus
　flour for rolling and stretching the dough

1 cup cake flour
2½ teaspoons salt
spray oil
¼ cup cornmeal for sprinkling (optional)
2 to 3 teaspoons extra-virgin olive oil

1. Dissolve the yeast and sugar in 3 tablespoons of the warm water in a small bowl. Let stand until foamy, 5 to 10 minutes.

2. Combine the flours and salt in a large mixing bowl and whisk well to mix. Make a well in the center and add the yeast mixture and remaining water. Working with your fingertips, gradually mix in the flour mixture. Add flour as necessary to obtain a very soft, pliable, but not quite sticky dough. Turn the dough out onto a lightly floured work surface and knead until smooth, 8 to 10 minutes. For kneading instructions, see Hand Method, step 2, page 65.

2a. If making the dough in a mixer, dissolve the yeast and sugar in the water in the mixing bowl. When foamy, add the remaining water, flours, and salt. Using a dough hook, mix the dough at low speed until it comes away from the sides of the bowl in a

smooth, soft pliable ball. (Add a little flour if necessary.) This will take about 10 minutes.

2b. If using a food processor, add the flours and salt and mix with a plastic dough blade. Work in the yeast mixture and remaining 1 cup water, running the machine in bursts until the dough comes away from the sides of the processor bowl in a smooth, soft, pliable ball. When making the dough in a machine, you should still turn it onto a floured work surface and knead it a little by hand.

3. Place the dough in a large bowl lightly sprayed with oil and cover with plastic. Let the dough rise until doubled in bulk, 1 to 2 hours. Preheat the oven to 500°F. If you have a baking stone, preheat it as well. If you don't, preheat a heavy baking sheet or cookie pan.

4. Punch the dough down and cut it in half (to

make two 12-inch pizzas) or quarters (to make four 6-inch pizzas). Lightly sprinkle your work surface with flour and roll, pat, or stretch each ball to form a circle. Gently stretch each circle with the palms of your hands or over your fists (pulling your fists apart in the manner of a pizzamaker), to make a 12-inch circle (or a 6-inch circle if making a small pizza) with a slightly raised rim. Transfer the pizzas to a peel (baker's paddle) or flat cookie sheet generously sprinkled with cornmeal. Garnish the pizzas with one of the toppings on pages 139 through 142. Brush the edges of the crusts with olive oil.

5. Slide the pizzas onto the baking stone or baking sheet in the preheated oven. (The hotter the better.) Bake until the crust is puffed and nicely browned, 6 to 10 minutes, turning as needed to ensure even baking.

Note: You're probably not used to baking at 500°F., but this high heat is necessary to produce a crust that's puffy, moist, and light, yet crisp. Also, to simulate the floor of a wood-fired or commercial pizza oven, I like to bake the pizza on a preheated baking stone (available at cookware shops). If you don't have a baking stone, bake the pizza on the back of a preheated baking sheet. The only disadvantage of this method is the tendency for any stray cornmeal to burn, filling your oven with smoke. Put on the exhaust fan and don't worry: your pizza isn't burning. The inconvenience is well worth producing a proper crust.

Makes two 12-inch pizzas, enough to serve 4

449 CALORIES PER SERVING; 13 G PROTEIN; 4 G FAT; 1 G SATURATED FAT; 90 G CARBOHYDRATE; 1,337 MG SODIUM; 0 MG CHOLESTEROL

WHITE PIZZA

This is the simplest of all pizzas and one of the most satisfying. For the best flavor, use coarse sea salt.
(I like to bite into the crunchy crystals of salt.) The pepper isn't strictly traditional, but I like its flavor.

PREPARATION TIME: 5 MINUTES (ONCE YOU HAVE THE DOUGH)　　　COOKING TIME: 6 TO 8 MINUTES

1 recipe Basic Neapolitan Pizza Dough (page 137) or milk dough (page 143), prepared through step 3
1 to 1½ tablespoons extra-virgin olive oil
12 sage leaves, thinly slivered

coarse sea salt
freshly grated black pepper (optional)
¼ to ½ cup freshly grated Parmigiano-Reggiano or Pecorino Romano cheese

1. Preheat the oven with a baking stone or baking sheet to 500°F. Prepare, raise, and stretch out the pizza dough as described in step 4 on page 137 to make two 12-inch crusts.

2. Drizzle the tops of the pizzas with olive oil and sprinkle with the sage, salt, pepper, and cheese. Brush the edges of the crust with oil.

3. Slide the pizzas onto the baking stone or preheated baking sheet. Bake until the crust is puffed and nicely browned, 6 to 10 minutes, turning as needed to ensure even baking.

Makes two 12-inch pizzas, enough to serve 4

506 CALORIES PER SERVING; 16 G PROTEIN; 8 G FAT; 2 G SATURATED FAT; 91 G CARBOHYDRATE; 1,953 MG SODIUM; 5 MG CHOLESTEROL

PIZZA MARINARA (MARINER'S STYLE)

This is a favorite in pizzerias in Italy, a thin crust topped with oregano-scented
tomato sauce and a gutsy garnish of anchovies, capers, and olives.

PREPARATION TIME: 5 MINUTES (ONCE YOU HAVE THE DOUGH)   COOKING TIME: 6 TO 8 MINUTES

1 recipe Basic Neapolitan Pizza Dough (page 137) or milk dough (page 143), prepared through step 3
1 cup homemade Neapolitan Tomato Sauce (page 67) or a good commercial brand
10 fresh oregano leaves or ½ teaspoon dried oregano

2 to 6 anchovy fillets, drained, rinsed, blotted dry, and cut into ½-inch pieces
1 to 2 tablespoons drained capers
8 black olives, pitted
coarse sea salt
1 tablespoon extra-virgin olive oil (optional)

1. Preheat the oven with a baking stone or baking sheet to 500°F. Prepare, raise, and roll or stretch out the pizza dough as described in step 4 on page 137 to make two 12-inch crusts.

2. Spread the tomato sauce on top of the crust in a thin layer and sprinkle with the oregano. Arrange the anchovy pieces, capers, and olives on top. Sprinkle the pizza with coarse salt. If using the olive oil, drizzle some oil over the pizza and brush the edges with oil.

3. Slide the pizzas onto the baking stone or preheated baking sheet. Bake until the crust is puffed and nicely browned, 6 to 10 minutes, turning as needed to ensure even baking.

Makes two 12-inch pizzas, enough to serve 4

485 CALORIES PER SERVING; 14 G PROTEIN; 6 G FAT; 0.8 G SATURATED FAT; 94 G CARBOHYDRATE; 1,611 MG SODIUM; 2 MG CHOLESTEROL

PIZZA MARGHERITA

This pizza is named for Queen Margherita di Savoia. One day, so the story goes, the owner of the Brandi Pizzeria in Naples (founded in 1780 and still in existence) was asked to cater a banquet for the queen. In a patriotic gesture, he decorated the pizza with red tomato sauce, green basil leaves, and white mozzarella—the colors of what was to become the Italian flag. The traditional topping for a margherita is puréed San Marzano plum tomatoes. For a truly exceptional pizza margherita, use fresh mozzarella (the sort that comes packed in water), rather than the rubbery vacuum-packed supermarket variety. For extra flavor, you could use smoked mozzarella.

PREPARATION TIME: 5 MINUTES (ONCE YOU HAVE THE DOUGH)   COOKING TIME: 6 TO 8 MINUTES

1 recipe Basic Neapolitan Pizza Dough (page 137) or milk dough (page 143), prepared through step 3

1 28-ounce can plum tomatoes, drained and puréed in the food processor (you'll need about 1 cup purée—save the remaining purée and can juices for soups or other sauces)

4 ounces thinly sliced fresh mozzarella cheese

24 fresh basil leaves

1 tablespoon extra-virgin olive oil (optional)

1. Preheat the oven with a baking stone or baking sheet to 500°F. Prepare, raise, and roll or stretch out the pizza dough as described in step 4 on page 145 to make two 12-inch pizzas.

2. Spread the puréed tomatoes on top of the crust in a thin layer. Arrange the mozzarella and basil leaves on top of the tomato layer. If using the olive oil, drizzle some over the pizza and brush the edges of the crust with oil.

3. Slide the pizzas onto the baking stone or preheated baking sheet. Bake until the crust is puffed and nicely browned and the cheese is melted, 6 to 10 minutes, turning as needed to ensure even baking.

Makes two 12-inch pizzas, enough to serve 4

565 CALORIES PER SERVING; 21 G PROTEIN; 9 G FAT; 4 G SATURATED FAT; 100 G CARBOHYDRATE; 1,766 MG SODIUM; 22 MG CHOLESTEROL

Four Seasons Pizza

The four seasons pizza is the Italian version of "the works," and it says a lot about the simplicity and purity of flavors characteristic of Italian cooking. In North America, the toppings would be piled together in a cacophonous jumble. In Italy, the various ingredients are arranged singly on the pizza in quadrants—whence the name four seasons—*so you can taste each without distraction.*

PREPARATION TIME: 5 MINUTES (ONCE YOU HAVE THE DOUGH)   COOKING TIME: 10 TO 15 MINUTES

1 recipe Basic Neapolitan Pizza Dough (page 137) or milk dough (page 143), prepared through step 3
1 recipe tomato sauce (such as Sugo di Pomodoro, page 59, or Neapolitan Tomato Sauce, page 60)
2 ounces very thinly sliced prosciutto
4 ounces button mushrooms, wiped clean with a damp cloth and trimmed

2 cooked fresh artichokes (see Note on page 84) or 1 13-ounce can artichoke hearts, rinsed and drained
2 roasted red peppers (page 10)
coarse sea salt
1 tablespoon extra-virgin olive oil (optional)

1. Preheat the oven with a baking stone or baking sheet to 500°F. Prepare, raise, roll or stretch out the pizza dough as described in step 4 on page 137 to make two 12-inch pizzas. Cover the pizzas with a clean dish towel and let rise until soft and slightly puffed, 10 to 20 minutes.

2. Spread the tomato sauce on top of the crust in a thin layer. Arrange prosciutto slices on one quarter of each pizza. Thinly slice the mushrooms and arrange them on a second quarter of each pizza. Thinly slice the artichokes and arrange them on a third quarter of

each pizza. Cut the peppers into thin strips and arrange them on the fourth quarter of each pizza. Sprinkle the mushroom, artichoke, and pepper quadrants with salt. If using the olive oil, drizzle some over the pizza and brush the edges of the crust with oil.

3. Slide the pizzas onto the baking stone or preheated baking sheet. Bake until the crust is puffed and nicely browned, 6 to 10 minutes, turning as needed to ensure even baking.

Makes two 12-inch pizzas, enough to serve 4

581 CALORIES PER SERVING; 23 G PROTEIN; 6 G FAT; 2 G SATURATED FAT; 115 G CARBOHYDRATE; 1,986 MG SODIUM; 12 MG CHOLESTEROL

MILK-BASED PIZZA DOUGH FROM SORRENTO

Readers of High-Flavor, Low-Fat Vegetarian Cooking *may remember Amadeo Cinque, the amiable pizzaiolo (pizzamaker) of the Vela Bianca (White Sail) restaurant in Sorrento. Signor Cinque makes his pizza dough with milk—an innovation that produces an exceptionally sweet, moist dough. I've streamlined his recipe from the first book, but the results are still impressive.*

PREPARATION TIME: 10 TO 15 MINUTES, PLUS 2 TO 3 HOURS FOR RISING   COOKING TIME: 6 TO 8 MINUTES

1½ packages (4 teaspoons) dried yeast
1 teaspoon sugar
2½ cups all-purpose unbleached white flour, plus flour for rolling and stretching the dough
1 cup cake flour

1½ teaspoons salt
1 cup 2 percent, 1 percent, or skim milk
spray oil
¼ cup cornmeal for sprinkling

1. Dissolve the yeast and sugar in 3 tablespoons warm water (110° to 115°F.) in a small bowl. Let stand until foamy, 5 to 10 minutes.

2. Combine the flours and salt in a large mixing bowl and whisk well to mix. Make a well in the center and add the yeast mixture and milk. Working with your fingertips, gradually mix the flour mixture into the milk mixture. Add flour as necessary to obtain a soft, pliable, but not sticky dough. Turn the dough out onto a lightly floured work surface and knead until smooth, 8 to 10 minutes.

2a. If making the dough in a mixer, dissolve the yeast and sugar in the water in the mixing bowl. When foamy, add the milk, flours, and salt. Using a dough hook, mix the dough at low speed until it comes away from the sides of the bowl in a smooth, soft, pliable ball. (Add a little flour if necessary.) This will take about 10 minutes.

2b. If using a food processor, add the flours and salt and mix with a plastic dough blade. Work in the yeast mixture and milk, running the machine in bursts until the dough comes away from the sides of the processor bowl in a smooth, soft, pliable ball. When making the dough in a machine, you should still turn it onto a floured work surface and knead it a little by hand.

3. Place the dough in a large bowl lightly sprayed with oil and cover with plastic. Let the dough rise until doubled in bulk, 1½ to 2 hours.

4. Punch the dough down, cut it in half, and roll each half into a ball. Place the balls on a lightly floured work surface and cover with plastic wrap or a slightly damp dish towel. Let the dough rise until doubled in bulk again, 30 to 60 minutes.

5. Preheat the oven to 500°F. If you have a baking stone, preheat it as well. If you don't, preheat a heavy baking sheet or cookie sheet.

6. Lightly sprinkle your work surface with flour and roll, pat, or stretch each ball to form a circle. Gently stretch each circle with the palms of your hands or over your fists (pulling your fists apart in the manner of a pizzamaker), to make a 12-inch circle (or a 6-inch circle if making a small pizza) with a slightly raised rim. Transfer the pizzas to a peel (baker's paddle) or flat cookie sheet generously sprinkled with cornmeal. Garnish the pizzas with one of the toppings on pages 139 through 142.

7. Slide the pizzas onto the baking stone or preheated baking sheet. Bake until the crust is puffed and nicely browned, 6 to 10 minutes, turning as needed to ensure even baking.

Makes two 12-inch pizzas, enough to serve 4

456 CALORIES PER SERVING; 14 G PROTEIN; 3 G FAT; 1 G SATURATED FAT; 92 G CARBOHYDRATE; 835 MG SODIUM; 5 MG CHOLESTEROL

FISH SOUPS AND STEWS

FISHERMAN'S STEW

ZUPPA DEL PESCATORE

Here's a stunning fish stew for people who find making bouillabaisse too complicated and time-consuming. Quite literally, you can make it from start to finish in 30 minutes. You don't even need fish broth (although using it will make a tastier zuppa). The more types of seafood you use, of course, the better the stew will be, but I've made this recipe using only one or two types of fish as a one-pot family supper on weeknights and the results were still delicious. Feel free to use all or some of the seafoods called for below or make substitutions, based on what's freshest and best in your area or at your fish market.

PREPARATION TIME: 10 MINUTES   COOKING TIME: 20 TO 30 MINUTES

1½ tablespoons olive oil
1 medium onion, finely chopped
2 cloves garlic, thinly sliced
1 large red ripe tomato, finely chopped, with its
  juices
1 large or 2 medium baking potatoes
  (about 1 pound)
1 quart water, or fish broth for a richer stew
3 tablespoons finely chopped flat-leaf parsley
1 bay leaf

½ teaspoon dried oregano
salt and freshly ground black pepper

FOR THE SEAFOOD:
12 littleneck clams, scrubbed
12 mussels, scrubbed, threads at the hinge of the
  shell removed with needlenose pliers.
12 shrimp or prawns, peeled and deveined
1 pound fish fillets (possibilities include snapper,
  mahi-mahi, cod, bass, and swordfish)

1. Heat the olive oil in a large sauté pan (preferably nonstick). Add the onion and cook over medium heat for 2 minutes. Add the garlic and cook until the onion and garlic are soft and translucent but not brown, about 2 minutes more. Add the tomato and cook until soft, about 2 minutes.

2. Add the potatoes, the water, half the parsley, the bay leaf, the oregano, and salt and pepper and bring to a boil. Reduce the heat to medium and gently simmer the potatoes, uncovered, until half-cooked, about 10 minutes.

3. Add the clams and mussels, cover the pan, and cook until the shells just begin to open, about 5 minutes. Discard any clams and mussels that do not open. Add the shrimp and fish and continue simmering until all the seafood is cooked and the potatoes are soft, about 3 minutes. Correct the seasoning, adding salt and pepper to taste. Remove and discard

Fisherman's Stew

the bay leaf. Serve fisherman's stew in shallow bowls, with extra bowls for holding the empty clam and mussel shells. Garnish with the remaining parsley.

Serves 4

350 CALORIES PER SERVING; 36 G PROTEIN; 8 G FAT; 1 G SATURATED FAT; 33 G CARBOHYDRATE; 174 MG SODIUM; 95 MG CHOLESTEROL

GENOESE FISH SOUP

BURRIDA

Burrida belongs to an extended family of fish soups and stews that includes Spain's zarzuela and France's bouillabaisse. Every city on the Ligurian coast has a version: this one comes from the picturesque port town of Camoglie. The traditional way to prepare the soup is to purée the vegetables through a vegetable mill, poaching the seafood in the resulting broth. But sometimes I like to serve the fish and vegetables together as a stew. Let freshness be your guide when choosing seafood: if some of the items called for in the recipe aren't available or fresh, use others.

PREPARATION TIME: 30 MINUTES   COOKING TIME: 15 MINUTES

½ teaspoon saffron threads
1 tablespoon extra-virgin olive oil
1 medium onion, finely chopped
2 cloves garlic, minced
1 stalk celery minced
1 small or ½ large bulb fennel, cut into ½-inch
  dice (about 1 cup)
¼ cup finely chopped flat-leaf parsley
salt and freshly ground black pepper
1 tablespoon tomato paste
4 ripe tomatoes, peeled, seeded, and diced
  (about 3 cups)
1 large or 2 small potatoes, peeled and cut into
  ½-inch dice

6 cups Fish Broth (page 240) or 4 cups bottled clam
  juice plus 2 cups water, or 6 cups water
1 herb bundle made by tying together a bay leaf, a
  sprig of thyme, and a sprig of rosemary

FOR THE SEAFOOD:
1 (1½-pound) lobster or 1 or 2 crabs
18 mussels
18 littleneck or cherrystone clams (the smallest
  you can find)
1½ pounds fish fillets, cut into 2-inch diamonds
18 shrimp
6 squid, cleaned, bodies cut into rings, tentacles
  left whole

1. Place the saffron in a bowl and grind it to a powder with the end of a wooden spoon. Add 2 tablespoons hot water and let stand for 10 minutes.

2. Meanwhile, heat the olive oil in a large pot. Add the onion, garlic, celery, and fennel and half the parsley. Add salt and pepper to taste and cook over medium heat until soft but not brown, about 5 minutes. Add the tomato paste and cook for 1 minute.

3. Increase the heat to high, add the tomatoes, and cook until the tomato juices have evaporated, about 2 minutes. Add the potatoes, fish broth, and herb bundle and bring to a boil. Reduce the heat and simmer the mixture until the potatoes are very soft, about 20 minutes. Season the soup with a little more salt and pepper and discard the herb bundle.

4. Force the soup through a vegetable mill or ricer into a wide shallow pot. (Alternatively, strain the soup into a pot, purée the vegetables in a food processor, and add the purée to the pot.)

5. If using lobster, cook it in 2 inches boiling water in another pot until the shell turns red, about 3 minutes. Drain the lobster in a colander and let cool. When cool enough to handle, break off and crack the claws. Cut the tail section into 1-inch medallions. If using crab, cook, clean, and cut into sections.

6. Just before serving, bring the soup to a boil. Add the mussels, clams, and lobster and cook just until the clam and mussel shells open, about 8 minutes. Discard any clams and mussels that do not open. Add the fish the last 4 minutes; the shrimp and squid, the

last 2 minutes. Cook until all the shellfish is done. Correct the seasoning of the soup, adding salt and pepper. Sprinkle the remaining parsley on the top and serve at once.

Note: There are many possibilities for fish. The Genoese would use an assortment of bony but flavorful Mediterranean sea creatures, such as *scorfano* (rascasse or wraisse), *gallinella* (sea hen), and conger eel. In this country, you could use monkfish, snapper, halibut, cusk, sea bass, and/or swordfish.

Serves 6 as a first course, 4 as an entrée

526 CALORIES PER SERVING;* 83 G PROTEIN; 9 G FAT; 2 G SATURATED FAT; 23 G CARBOHYDRATE; 495 MG SODIUM; 508 MG CHOLESTEROL

Analysis is based on 6 servings as a first course.

SQUID AND SWISS CHARD SOUP

Zimino is a stew of Swiss chard and cuttlefish that originated in Genoa and was traditionally served on Friday.
I first tasted it at the restaurant Cesarina in Santa Margherita, where it was made with seppiolini, cuttlefish fish so
tiny a half dozen would fit in a tablespoon. I know you can't buy seppiolini in this country or probably even seppie
(cuttlefish). I also know that squid has a significantly different texture and flavor. Nevertheless, the combination
of Swiss chard and squid makes a delicious seafood soup with distinctly Ligurian overtones.

PREPARATION TIME: 20 MINUTES   COOKING TIME: 40 MINUTES

1 pound cleaned squid (see box on page 158)
1½ tablespoons extra-virgin olive oil
1 onion, finely chopped
2 stalks celery, finely chopped
1 small or ½ large bulb fennel, finely chopped
2 cloves garlic, finely chopped
¼ cup finely chopped flat-leaf parsley
1 bay leaf
5 to 6 cups Fish Broth (page 240), mussel broth,
   Chicken Broth (page 239), or bottled clam juice

salt and freshly ground black pepper
1 bunch Swiss chard, stemmed, washed, and thinly
   sliced crosswise
1 teaspoon fresh lemon juice or red wine vinegar
   (optional)
3 tablespoons toasted pine nuts

1. Cut the squid bodies into thin rings. Leave the tentacle section whole. Heat the olive oil in a large saucepan. Add the onion, celery, fennel, and garlic and cook until lightly browned, about 6 minutes, stirring often. Add half the parsley, the bay leaf, the fish broth, the squid, and a little salt and pepper.

2. Simmer the soup, covered, until the squid are very tender, about 40 minutes. Stir in the Swiss chard the last 10 minutes of cooking. Discard the bay leaf. If a sharper-tasting broth is desired, add a little lemon juice or vinegar. Correct the seasoning, adding salt and pepper to taste. Sprinkle the remaining parsley and the pine nuts over the stew and serve at once.

Note: Sometimes I make *zimino* with spinach instead of Swiss chard. You'd need a 10-ounce package of fresh spinach or 5 ounces frozen spinach.

Makes 5 to 6 cups, enough to serve 4

231 CALORIES PER SERVING; 22 G PROTEIN; 11 G FAT; 2 G SATURATED FAT; 12 G CARBOHYDRATE; 99 MG SODIUM; 264 MG CHOLESTEROL

VENETIAN SHELLFISH SOUP

Variations of this soup turn up all along the Italian coast. The shellfish and seasonings change from region to region: one cook might use vongole *(tiny clams with brown-striped shells); another,* fasolari *(pink clams); a third,* cannolicchi *(tiny razor clams). Here's a Venetian version, made with both clams and mussels.*

PREPARATION TIME: 10 MINUTES   COOKING TIME: 8 MINUTES

1 pound of the smallest mussels you can find
   (20 to 24 mussels)
12 to 16 of the tiniest clams you can find
1 cup dry white wine
3 cups Fish Broth (page 240) or bottled clam juice
1 small onion, finely chopped
1 clove garlic, minced

1 tomato, peeled, seeded, and finely chopped
1 stalk celery, finely diced
¼ teaspoon hot pepper flakes (optional)
¼ cup finely chopped flat-leaf parsley
salt and freshly ground black pepper

1. Scrub the mussels and clams, discarding any with cracked shells or open shells that fail to close when tapped. Using tweezers or needlenose pliers, pull out any tufts of black threads clumped at the hinge of the mussels.

2. Bring the wine to a boil. Add the fish broth, onion, garlic, tomato, celery, pepper flakes, and half the parsley and bring to a boil. Add the mussels and clams, cover the pan tightly, and cook over high heat until the mussel and clam shells just open, about 8 minutes. Stir the soup once or twice to give the shellfish on the bottom room to open. Discard any mussels or clams that do not open. Add salt and pepper to taste.

3. With a slotted spoon or wire skimmer, transfer the mussels, clams, and vegetables to a tureen or 4 soup bowls. Strain the broth through a strainer lined with a cheesecloth or paper towels over the shellfish. Or, if you're in a hurry, ladle the broth over the shellfish, leaving the last ½ inch (the part where the grit gathers) in the pot. Sprinkle the remaining 2 tablespoons parsley on top and serve at once, with crusty bread for dunking.   *Serves 4*

117 CALORIES PER SERVING; 10 G PROTEIN; 1 G FAT; 0 G SATURATED FAT; 6 G CARBOHYDRATE; 227 MG SODIUM; 27 MG CHOLESTEROL

UMBRIAN CLAM "CHOWDER"

The Villa Roncalli occupies a former seventeenth-century hunting lodge on the outskirts of the city of Foligno in Umbria. To call its young chef, Maria Luisa Leocastre, gifted would be an understatement. Maria Luisa has mastered that quintessential Italian art of extracting stunning flavors from just a few simple ingredients. Consider the following clam "chowder," which is made with cannellini beans instead of potatoes. The only thing less than wonderful about this soup is the color. The parsley helps, but try to concentrate on the flavor, not the appearance.

PREPARATION TIME: 15 MINUTES   COOKING TIME: 15 MINUTES

32 littleneck clams, 24 cherrystone clams, or
   12 ounces canned clams with juices (see Note)
1½ cups dry white wine
2½ to 3 cups Fish Broth (page 240), chicken
   broth (page 239), Basic Vegetable Broth (page
   241), or bottled clam juice
1 tablespoon extra-virgin olive oil

1 onion, finely chopped
2 cloves garlic, finely chopped
2 stalks celery, finely chopped
¼ cup finely chopped flat-leaf parsley
1½ cups cooked cannellini beans (14-ounce can)
salt and freshly ground black pepper

1. If using fresh clams, scrub the shells, discarding any with cracked shells or open shells that fail to close when tapped. Bring the wine to a boil. Add the clams, cover the pot tightly, and cook over high heat until the clams just open, about 8 minutes. Stir the clams once or twice to give the shellfish on the bottom room to open.

2. Transfer the clams to a bowl with a slotted spoon to cool so you can shell them. Shell all but 4 of the clams and set aside. Strain the clam cooking liquid through a strainer lined with a cheesecloth or paper towels into a large measuring cup. Add enough fish broth to obtain 4 cups liquid. If using canned clams, you'll need to add 2 cups broth.

3. Heat the olive oil in a large saucepan. Add the onion, garlic, celery, and half the parsley. Cook until the vegetables are soft but not brown, about 4 minutes. Stir in the beans, shelled clams, and clam broth and simmer until richly flavored, about 5 minutes. Purée the soup in a blender and return it to the pot. Correct the seasoning, adding salt and pepper to taste.

4. To serve, ladle the soup into bowls. Sprinkle each with parsley and float a clam in the center. Alternatively, you can garnish each bowl of soup with a few croutons.

Note: You can make a 5-minute version of this soup by using canned clams and beans. Try to buy canned baby clams (you'll need 10 to 12 ounces).   *Serves 4*

264 CALORIES PER SERVING; 17 G PROTEIN; 5 G FAT; 0.6 G SATURATED FAT; 24 G CARBOHYDRATE; 70 MG SODIUM; 24 MG CHOLESTEROL

Shellfish

Shrimp with Cherry Tomatoes

La Vela Bianca (The White Sail) in Sorrento is the sort of Italian trattoria that lives in our collective imaginations: down-to-earth, homey, with red-checkered curtains and tablecloths and wide windows overlooking the water. What it lacks in glitz, it makes up for in good, simple, honest food. La Vela Bianca uses fish broth to make the sauce for the following shrimp. A slightly different but equally delectable dish can be made using white wine, which is more readily available in many American homes than fish broth. Use the smallest, ripest cherry tomatoes you can find.

PREPARATION TIME: 10 MINUTES   COOKING TIME: 5 MINUTES

1½ pounds shrimp
1 tablespoon extra-virgin olive oil
3 cloves garlic, peeled and flattened with the side
   of a cleaver

¼ teaspoon hot pepper flakes, or to taste
8 large or 12 small cherry tomatoes, cut in half
½ cup Fish Broth (page 240) or dry white wine
3 tablespoons chopped flat-leaf parsley

1. Peel and devein the shrimp. Heat the olive oil in a large nonstick frying pan. Add the garlic and sizzle in the oil over high heat until it just begins to brown, about 1 minute. Add the pepper flakes and cook for 10 seconds.

2. Add the shrimp and tomatoes and cook over high heat for 1 minute. Add the fish broth and bring to a boil. Continue cooking at a boil until the shrimp are done, 1 to 2 minutes more. Stir in the parsley and serve at once.   *Serves 4*

175 CALORIES PER SERVING; 29 G PROTEIN; 5 G FAT; 0.9 G SATURATED FAT; 2 G CARBOHYDRATE; 301 MG SODIUM; 262 MG CHOLESTEROL

Shrimp with Cherry Tomatoes

SHRIMP WITH BEANS AND ROSEMARY

I often muse on why Italian cuisine is so universally popular. I believe there are three reasons: its simplicity and directness, its emphasis on great raw materials, and the speed with which so many dishes can be prepared. All three factors come into play in this Tuscan dish—a favorite at our house when dinnertime arrives and no one has made any special plans for cooking. Note the optional use of fish, chicken, or clam broth to replace some of the oil in the traditional recipe, reducing the fat but maintaining the flavor.

PREPARATION TIME: 10 MINUTES   COOKING TIME: 5 MINUTES

1½ tablespoons extra-virgin olive oil
1 clove garlic, minced
3 tablespoons chopped flat-leaf parsley
2 teaspoons chopped fresh rosemary or sage
1 pound shrimp, peeled and deveined

2 cups cooked cannellini beans
salt and freshly ground black pepper
½ cup Fish Broth (page 240), Chicken Broth (page 239), or bottled clam broth (juice) (optional)

1. Heat 1 tablespoon of the olive oil in a large nonstick skillet. Add the garlic, 2 tablespoons of the parsley, and the rosemary and cook over medium heat until fragrant but not brown, about 1 minute. Stir in the shrimp, beans, salt, and pepper and cook for 1 minute. Add the fish broth and simmer until the shrimp are firm, pink, and cooked, 2 to 3 minutes more. Correct the seasoning, adding salt and pepper to taste.

2. Drizzle the remaining ½ tablespoon olive oil over the shrimp and beans, sprinkle with the remaining tablespoon parsley, and serve at once.

Serves 4

261 CALORIES PER SERVING; 27 G PROTEIN; 6 G FAT; 1 G SATURATED FAT; 23 G CARBOHYDRATE; 205 MG SODIUM; 175 MG CHOLESTEROL

CLAMS IN GREEN SAUCE

Camoglie is one of the best-kept secrets on the Ligurian coast, a thoroughly Italian seaside community on a curved pebble beach ringed with tall, pastel-colored, green-shuttered nineteenth-century apartment buildings. A spacious promenade runs from one end of the half-mile-long cove to the other, and best of all, there are no cars. This dish turns up at the homey trattorie that line the promenade. For the best results, use the smallest clams you can find, because they're the sweetest and most tender. Mussels or shrimp could be cooked the same way.

PREPARATION TIME: 10 MINUTES   COOKING TIME: 8 MINUTES

48 littleneck clams or 40 cherrystone clams
1½ tablespoons extra-virgin olive oil
2 cloves garlic, flattened with the side of a cleaver and peeled
½ teaspoon hot pepper flakes

1 bunch flat-leaf parsley, stemmed and finely chopped (about 1 cup)
1½ cups dry white wine
freshly ground black pepper

1. Scrub the clams with a brush under cold running water. Discard any clams with cracked shells or shells that fail to close when tapped.

2. Heat the olive oil in a large, heavy saucepan. Add the garlic and cook over medium heat until fragrant, about 1 minute. Add the pepper flakes and most of the parsley and cook for 30 seconds. Add the wine and bring to a boil. Add the clams, tightly cover the pan, and cook over high heat until the clam shells open wide, about 8 minutes. Stir the clams once or twice to give the shells on the bottom space to open. Discard any clams that do not open.

3. Serve the clams in bowls with the broth ladled on top. Sprinkle with the remaining parsley. Serve with crusty bread for dipping and bowls for the empty shells.   *Serves 4*

193 CALORIES PER SERVING; 14 G PROTEIN; 6 G FAT; 0.8 G SATURATED FAT; 5 G CARBOHYDRATE; 73 MG SODIUM; 36 MG CHOLESTEROL

MUSSELS STEAMED WITH ROSEMARY AND ROASTED PEPPERS

One of the most appealing aspects of Italian cuisine is its reliance on a few bold, simple flavors. I was recently thumbing through a Sri Lankan cookbook and was struck by the difference in approach the two countries take to mussels. The Sri Lankan version contains over a dozen spices and seasonings, and the resulting dish is magnificent. Then I remembered the steamed-mussel dish I tasted in Santa Margherita on the Ligurian coast. It contained only two primary flavorings and it was magnificent, too, perhaps even more magnificent in its simplicity. Instructions for roasting and grilling peppers are found on page 10. If you're in a hurry, you could use bottled or canned pimientos.

PREPARATION TIME: 10 MINUTES   COOKING TIME: 10 MINUTES

4 pounds mussels
2 cups dry white wine
1 onion, finely chopped

1 roasted or grilled red bell pepper, cut into ¼-inch strips
2 branches fresh rosemary, or 1 tablespoon dried

1. Scrub the mussels, discarding any with cracked shells or shells that fail to close when tapped. Use needlenose pliers to remove any black threads attached to the hinge end. Bring the wine, onion, roasted pepper, and rosemary to boil in a large, heavy pot. Add the mussels and cover the pot tightly.

2. Cook the mussels until the shells open wide, about 8 minutes, stirring once or twice to give the mussels on the bottom room to open. Discard any mussels that do not open. Transfer the cooked mussels and vegetables with a slotted spoon to serving bowls. Ladle the broth on top, taking care to leave the grit in the bottom of the pot. Serve the mussels with crusty bread for dipping and bowls for holding the empty shells.   *Serves 4*

161 CALORIES PER SERVING; 20 G PROTEIN; 3 G FAT; 0 G SATURATED FAT; 11 G CARBOHYDRATE; 379 MG SODIUM; 74 MG CHOLESTEROL

LOBSTER FRA DIAVOLO

I've never seen lobster fra diavolo on a menu in Italy, but when I was growing up in Baltimore, no dish seemed more quintessentially Italian. Here's an updated version of this childhood favorite. A professional chef would probably cut up the lobsters alive. This can be disconcerting to home cooks, so I've called for the lobster to be parboiled before cutting. I've also given instructions for making shrimp fra diavolo (see below), for people who are squeamish about cooking lobster.

PREPARATION TIME: 30 MINUTES   COOKING TIME: 15 MINUTES

2 2- to 2½-pound Maine or Florida lobsters (or 4 1¼-pound lobsters)
1½ tablespoons extra-virgin olive oil
½ to 1 teaspoon hot pepper flakes, or to taste
1 large onion, finely chopped
4 cloves garlic, minced
1 green bell pepper, cored, seeded, and finely chopped
2 red ripe tomatoes, peeled, seeded, and finely chopped

3 tablespoons good-quality brandy or grappa
½ cup dry white wine
about 1 tablespoon balsamic vinegar
3 tablespoons tomato paste
2 bay leaves
¼ cup finely chopped flat-leaf parsley
1½ cups reserved lobster cooking liquid (or chicken, fish, or vegetable broth)
salt and freshly ground black pepper

1. Place the lobsters in a large pot with 2 inches of cold water (at least 2 cups). Cover the pot tightly and bring to a boil. Cook the lobsters until they begin to turn red, about 3 minutes. Transfer the lobsters to a colander and let cool, reserving the cooking liquid. When the lobsters have cooled, break off the claws, break into 2 sections, and crack each. Twist the tail and body in separate directions to remove the tail. Using a large knife or cleaver, cut the lobster tails in half lengthwise. Remove the vein running the length of the tail.

2. Heat the olive oil in a large sauté pan. Add the pepper flakes, onion, garlic, and green pepper. Cook the mixture over medium heat until it begins to brown, about 6 minutes, stirring often.

3. Increase the heat to high and stir in the tomatoes. Cook until the tomato liquid begins to evaporate, about 1 minute. Stir in the brandy and bring to a boil. Stir in the wine and vinegar and bring to a boil. Stir in the tomato paste, the bay leaves, half the parsley, 1½ cups of the lobster cooking liquid, salt, and pepper. Simmer this mixture until thick and richly flavored, about 10 minutes.

4. Add the lobster pieces. Gently simmer until the lobster is cooked (the meat will be firm and white), about 5 minutes. Season the sauce to taste, adding salt, vinegar, or pepper flakes. The mixture should be highly seasoned. Sprinkle the remaining 2 tablespoons parsley on top and serve at once. I like to serve lobster fra diavolo over cooked linguine or spaghetti.

Note: To make shrimp fra diavolo, start at step 2. Instead of adding lobster cooking liquid in step 3, add 1½ cups chicken, fish, or vegetable broth. Add 1½ pounds shrimp in place of the lobster in step 4.

Serves 4

540 CALORIES PER SERVING; 89 G PROTEIN; 8 G FAT; 1 G SATURATED FAT; 18 G CARBOHYDRATE; 1,719 MG SODIUM; 305 MG CHOLESTEROL

VENETIAN-STYLE SQUID IN BLACK INK SAUCE

Baby squid simmered in a dark, rich ink sauce is a classic dish of Venice. The ink adds not only color, but a pleasing briny flavor that gives this dish a unique taste. Once you know how to clean squid (see below), the dish is a cinch to make. You could ask your fishmonger to clean the squid for you, saving the silvery ink sacs.

PREPARATION TIME: 15 MINUTES   COOKING TIME: 20 MINUTES

2 pounds small, uncleaned squid (or 1½ pounds cleaned squid, with ink sacs reserved)
1½ tablespoons olive oil
1 to 2 cloves garlic, minced
1 small onion, finely chopped

¼ cup chopped flat-leaf parsley
1 red ripe tomato, peeled, seeded, and finely chopped, with its juices
1 cup dry white wine
salt and freshly ground black pepper

1. Clean the squid, following the directions below. Cut the body crosswise into ½-inch rings. Cut the tentacles into 1-inch sections. Reserve the ink sacs.

2. Heat the olive oil in a nonstick skillet. Add the garlic, onion, and half the parsley and cook over medium heat until golden-brown, about 6 minutes. Add the tomatoes and cook until most of the juices have boiled away, about 3 minutes.

3. Stir in the squid and sauté for 1 minute. Add the wine, salt, and pepper and simmer until the squid are very tender, 20 to 30 minutes. Halfway through, squeeze the squid ink from sacs into the sauce. Correct the seasoning, adding salt and pepper to taste. Sprinkle the remaining parsley over the squid and serve at once.   *Serves 4*

310 CALORIES PER SERVING; 36 G PROTEIN; 8 G FAT; 1 G SATURATED FAT; 1 G CARBOHYDRATE; 108 MG SODIUM; 528 MG CHOLESTEROL

How to Clean Squid

Here's a simple way to clean squid. First, cut off the tentacles just above the eyes. Squeeze the base of the tentacles to remove the "beak," the squid's mouth, which looks like a celluloid chickpea. Discard it.

Next, hold the body by the tail and scrape it lengthwise toward the head with the back of a knife. Turn the squid over and scrape again. This loosens the entrails, which will come out when you pull out the head. Any entrails that remain can be scraped out with a small spoon.

The ink is found in a small, elongated, silvery sac amid the entrails. Gently cut it away with a paring knife and squeeze it into a sauce or stew. (Soap and water will wash off any ink that gets on your fingers.) Better still, wear rubber gloves when handling squid ink.

Finally, stab the "pen" (the transparent quill) that protrudes from the head end with the knife. Pull the body away, and the quill should slip right out. Discard it. Pull off any reddish skin on the body or tentacles with your fingers. (The skin is edible, but many people find it unaesthetic.) Rinse the body inside and out: it is now ready for stuffing or cutting into rings.

A QUICK CALAMARI SAUTÉ

As a foodie who came of age in Boston in the 1970s, I remember with fondness a postage-stamp-sized eatery called the Daily Catch. Located in the heart of Boston's "Little Italy," the North End, the Daily Catch specialized in calamari (squid) and almost single-handedly popularized this tentacled sea fare to Boston's non-Italian community. The Daily Catch remains a no-frills eatery where the chef serves his food right in the skillet in which it was cooked. This quick calamari sauté is a great way to get people to try squid—even if they think they don't like it.

PREPARATION TIME: 10 MINUTES   COOKING TIME: 6 MINUTES

1½ pounds cleaned calamari
salt and freshly ground black pepper
1½ tablespoons all-purpose unbleached white flour
1 tablespoon extra-virgin olive oil
1 clove garlic, minced
¼ teaspoon hot pepper flakes

¾ cup dry white wine
2 tablespoons toasted pine nuts
2 tablespoons drained capers
1 teaspoon grated lemon zest
3 tablespoons chopped flat-leaf parsley

1. Wash the calamari and blot dry. Cut the bodies crosswise into ½-inch rings. Leave the heads whole, but cut any long tentacles into 1-inch pieces. Season the calamari with salt and pepper and lightly dust with flour.

2. Heat the olive oil in a large nonstick frying pan. Add the garlic and pepper flakes and cook over high heat until fragrant, about 30 seconds. Add the calamari and sauté for 1 minute. Add the wine, pine nuts, capers, lemon zest, and half the parsley and sim-mer until the calamari are cooked and the sauce is reduced, thickened, and richly flavored, 2 to 3 minutes. Do not overcook, or the calamari will become tough.

3. Correct the seasoning, adding salt or pepper to taste: the mixture should be highly seasoned. Serve at once. The Daily Catch used to serve this dish over linguine.

Note: Instructions on cleaning calamari can be found on page 158. *Serves 4*

259 CALORIES PER SERVING; 28 G PROTEIN; 8 G FAT; 1 G SATURATED FAT; 0 G CARBOHYDRATE; 236 MG SODIUM; 396 MG CHOLESTEROL

FISH DISHES

FISH IN A FOIL BAG

BRANZINO IN CARTUCCIO

Here's a high-tech Italian version of fish en papillote, the specialty of a wonderful open-air seafood restaurant called Rosa, high on a cliff overlooking the town of Camoglie. The chef had prepared a large whole sea bass in cartuccio, and it was served to a party of eight. It certainly makes a festive party dish—one that can be prepared for unexpected company in 10 to 15 minutes. But you can also make the fish in cartuccio in individual portions, which my wife and I often do for a casual midweek supper. I've written the following recipe for individual portions: preparation of one large fish is explained below. Once again, there are lots of possibilities for fish: sea bass, black bass, snapper, or fillets or steaks of mahi-mahi, swordfish, or cod—to name just a few.

PREPARATION TIME: 10 MINUTES   COOKING TIME: 20 TO 25 MINUTES

2 medium potatoes (about 12 ounces), peeled and
    very thinly sliced
1½ tablespoons extra-virgin olive oil
salt and freshly ground black pepper
4 4- to 6-ounce portions of boneless fish fillets

1 tomato, cut into ¼-inch dice
4 sprigs fresh thyme, or 1 teaspoon dried
4 sprigs fresh basil, or 1 teaspoon dried
4 bay leaves
½ cup dry white wine

1. Preheat the oven to 400°F. Arrange a large (12 × 20 inches) rectangle of heavy-duty foil on a work surface, shiny side down. In the center, spread out one-quarter of the sliced potatoes. Drizzle with a little oil and season with salt and pepper. Place a piece of fish on top and season with salt and pepper. Arrange one-quarter of the diced tomatoes, a sprig each of thyme and basil, and a bay leaf on top. Drizzle with a little more oil and a final sprinkling of salt and pepper.

2. Bring together the short edges of the foil rectangle high over the fish without sealing. Crimp or pleat the sides to form an airtight seal. Add 2 tablespoons wine in the top, then crimp or seal the top edges to form an airtight seal. Prepare the remaining packages the same way.

3. Place the *cartucci* on a baking sheet. Bake until the foil is puffed and the fish inside is cooked, 20 to 25 minutes. (To test for doneness, you can open one of the packets, but 20 minutes of baking should do the trick.) Serve the *cartucci* on plates or a platter. Have each person open the packet and slide the fish, vegetables, and juices onto his plate.

Note: To make one large *cartuccio*, you'll need a whole fish weighing 3 to 4 pounds. Trim the fins off the fish (or have your fishmonger do it). Wash it thoroughly inside and out and pat dry. Season the fish

Fish in a Foil Bag (Branzino in Cartuccio)

inside and out with salt and pepper. You'll also need to make a much larger foil rectangle. To do so, attach several sheets together, folding joining edges over several times to make a tight seal. Assemble as described above, but use only 2 bay leaves. You'll need to bake a large fish for 40 to 60 minutes.   *Serves 4*

258 CALORIES PER SERVING; 22 G PROTEIN; 8 G FAT; 1 G SATURATED FAT; 19 G CARBOHYDRATE; 87 MG SODIUM; 91 MG CHOLESTEROL

SNAPPER IN THE STYLE OF LIVORNO

WITH CAPERS, OLIVES, AND TOMATOES

Livorno (Leghorn in English) is a port city on the Tuscan coast famed for its seafood. While precise definitions of Livornese-style fish vary, the preparation generally includes a colorful assortment of capers, tomatoes, and black olives. There are lots of possibilities for fish. The locals would use branzino (sea bass). Here in Florida, we like snapper. But you could also use striped bass, sea bass, cod, grouper—almost any delicate white fish.

PREPARATION TIME: 20 MINUTES   COOKING TIME: 10 MINUTES

1½ pounds snapper fillets
salt and freshly ground black pepper
3 to 4 tablespoons all-purpose unbleached white
    flour
1½ tablespoons extra-virgin olive oil
1 small onion, thinly sliced

3 cloves garlic, thinly sliced
1 ripe tomato, peeled, seeded, and diced
12 black olives
2 tablespoons drained capers
3 tablespoons chopped flat-leaf parsley
1 cup dry white wine

1. Wash and dry the fish fillets. Run your fingers over the fillets, feeling for bones. Pull out any bones you find with tweezers or pliers. Season the fish with salt and pepper and dust with flour, shaking off the excess. I do this on a paper towel.

2. Heat half the oil in a nonstick frying pan over high heat. Add the fish fillets and quickly brown on both sides, about 1 minute per side. Transfer the fish to a plate. Add the remaining oil, the onion, and the garlic and cook over medium heat until the vegetables are soft but not brown, about 4 minutes. Add the tomato, olives, and capers and half the parsley and cook until most of the tomato juices boil away, about 3 minutes.

3. Return the fish to the pan, add the wine, and bring to a boil. Briskly simmer the fish until cooked, about 3 minutes per side. Most of the wine should evaporate and the sauce should thicken. If the fish cooks before the sauce thickens, transfer the fish to plates or a platter and boil down the sauce. Stir in the remaining parsley and correct the seasoning, adding salt and pepper to taste. Spoon the sauce over the fish and serve at once.

Note: To test for doneness, press the fish with your finger: it should flake easily. Another test is to insert a slender metal skewer into the thickest part of the fish. When the fish is ready, the skewer will be very hot to the touch. *Serves 4*

310 CALORIES PER SERVING; 37 G PROTEIN; 12 G FAT; 2 G SATURATED FAT; 5 G CARBOHYDRATE; 298 MG SODIUM; 62 MG CHOLESTEROL

SWORDFISH BRAISED AND GLAZED WITH BALSAMIC VINEGAR

When I was growing up, few people had ever heard of balsamic vinegar. Today, we can't seem to cook without it! This sweet-sour condiment from the province of Emilia-Romagna has captured our culinary fancy, turning up in dishes all over the world. Not bad for an ingredient that, until recently, was made by hand in tiny batches in farmhouse attics and virtually unknown outside its birthplace, Modena. The following recipe is also delicious with salmon.

PREPARATION TIME: 15 MINUTES   COOKING TIME: 20 MINUTES

4 6-ounce pieces of swordfish steak
    (each about ¾ inch thick)
salt and freshly ground black pepper
3 tablespoons all-purpose unbleached white flour
1 tablespoon extra-virgin olive oil
3 to 4 tablespoons balsamic vinegar

3 tablespoons dry white wine
1 cup Fish Broth (page 240) or bottled clam broth
2 sprigs fresh rosemary, or 2 teaspoons dried
1 clove garlic, minced
2 tablespoons finely chopped flat-leaf parsley

1. Preheat the oven to 400°F. Season the fish steaks on both sides with salt and pepper. Dust the fish with flour, shaking off the excess. (I like to do this on a paper towel.)

2. Heat the olive oil in a large, nonstick frying pan. Lightly brown the swordfish steaks on both sides over high heat, 1 to 2 minutes per side. Add 3 tablespoons vinegar and the wine and bring to a boil. Add the fish broth, rosemary, and garlic and bring to a gentle simmer.

3. Place the pan in the oven and bake until the swordfish is cooked, 15 to 20 minutes. Alternatively, you can cook the fish on the stove, 4 to 5 minutes per side. (When the fish is cooked, it will flake easily when pressed with your finger. Another test is to insert a slender metal skewer into the thickest part of the fish. When the fish is ready, the skewer will be very hot to the touch.)

4. Transfer the fish to a platter or plates. Boil the pan juices until about ½ cup liquid remains. Correct the seasoning, adding salt and pepper to taste. If a more lively balsamic vinegar flavor is desired, add ½ to 1 tablespoon vinegar, but be sure to bring the sauce to a boil to mellow its sharpness. Strain or spoon the sauce over the fish. Sprinkle with the parsley and serve at once.   *Serves 4*

283 CALORIES PER SERVING; 35 G PROTEIN; 10 G FAT; 2 G SATURATED FAT; 8 G CARBOHYDRATE; 157 MG SODIUM; 67 MG CHOLESTEROL

SWORDFISH "FIG PICKERS"
(SICILIAN SWORDFISH ROULADES)

This dish, a specialty of Sicily, has a curious name and history. Beccafico (literally "fig picker") refers to a thrush or other tiny game bird. Throughout Italy, small roulades of meat or seafood are called beccafico on account of their resemblance to trussed, roasted game birds. The traditional fish for this recipe is fresh sardine—a quintessential Mediterranean fish that is almost impossible to find fresh in this country. For this reason, I call for another popular Sicilian fish—swordfish—but you could also use boneless fillets of snapper, mahi-mahi, or sole. (If using sole, you don't need to slice it on the diagonal.)

PREPARATION TIME: 25 MINUTES   COOKING TIME: 20 MINUTES

1½ pounds skinless swordfish (cut in a rather thick steak); or large boneless fillets of snapper, mahi-mahi, or sole; or fresh scaled and cleaned sardines (gutted and heads removed)

FOR THE STUFFING:
1½ tablespoons extra-virgin olive oil, plus a little oil or spray oil for the pan
1 medium onion, finely chopped
1 stalk celery, finely chopped (about 3 tablespoons)

2 tablespoons currants or chopped raisins
2 tablespoons toasted pine nuts
1 cup toasted bread crumbs
3 tablespoons minced flat-leaf parsley
½ teaspoon grated fresh lemon zest, plus 1 tablespoon fresh lemon juice, plus lemon wedges for serving
2 tablespoons Parmigiano-Reggiano cheese
salt and freshly ground black pepper

1. Cut the fish sharply on the diagonal into ¼-inch-thick slices. Each slice should be about 2 inches wide and 2½ inches long. You should have 20 to 24 slices in all. Place each piece of fish between 2 sheets of plastic wrap and gently flatten with the side of a cleaver. The new pieces should be about 2½ to 3 inches wide and 3½ to 4 inches long. (Don't worry if the pieces come out a little larger or smaller. The important thing is to obtain pieces of uniform size.)

2. Prepare the stuffing: Heat 1 tablespoon oil in a nonstick frying pan. Add the onion, celery, currants, and pine nuts and cook over medium heat until the onion is soft but not brown, about 4 minutes. Add the bread crumbs, parsley, lemon zest, and Parmesan and cook until toasted and flavorful, about 5 minutes. Stir in salt and pepper to taste.

3. Preheat the oven to 400°F. Arrange one of the fish slices on the work surface, narrow edge toward you. Spread a spoonful of stuffing on top of the fish.

Starting at the edge closest to you, roll it up to form a compact roll. Place the roll, seam side down, in an attractive, lightly oiled, 8 × 12-inch baking dish. Continue rolling and stuffing the fish slices until all are used up.

4. Drizzle the lemon juice and remaining ½ tablespoon oil over the roulades. Sprinkle any remaining stuffing on top. Season with salt and pepper. Bake the roulades until fish is cooked through, 15 to 20 minutes. (One way to test for doneness is to press a roulade with your finger. When cooked, it will break into flakes. Another test is to insert a metal skewer. When the roulades are cooked, the skewer will come out very hot to the touch.) Serve the roulades with lemon wedges for squeezing. If a sauce is desired, consider one of the tomato sauces on pages 58–62.

Note: If you're lucky enough to live in a city where fresh sardines are available, by all means use them.

Bone them and spread the filling over the fish. Roll
each sardine up widthwise (the long way), so that the
tails stick up over the roulades.

*Makes 20 to 24 rolls, enough to
serve 6 as a first course, 4 as an entrée*

279 CALORIES PER SERVING;* 27 G PROTEIN; 11 G FAT; 3 G SATURATED FAT; 17 G CARBOHYDRATE; 303 MG SODIUM; 96 MG CHOLESTEROL

Analysis is based on 6 servings as a first course.

GRILLED SWORDFISH WITH RED ONION "JAM"

Here's a contemporary Italian dish with a Californian twist. The "jam" is a sort of chutney—made by glazing sliced red onions in balsamic vinegar and honey.

PREPARATION TIME: 20 MINUTES   COOKING TIME: 1 HOUR

FOR THE ONION JAM:
2 teaspoons extra-virgin olive oil
2 medium red onions, thinly sliced
⅔ cup balsamic vinegar
⅓ cup dry red wine
1 to 2 tablespoons honey

salt and freshly ground black pepper
1½ pounds swordfish, cut into ½-inch-thick steaks
2 teaspoons extra-virgin olive oil
1 tablespoon fresh lemon juice
4 sprigs flat-leaf parsley

1. Prepare the onion jam: Heat the 2 teaspoons oil in a nonstick skillet. Add the onions and cook over high heat for 2 minutes. Add the vinegar, wine, and honey and bring to a boil. Reduce the heat and gently simmer the onions until reduced to a jamlike consistency; the vinegar and wine should be completely absorbed. This will take 30 to 45 minutes. Correct the seasoning, adding honey for sweetness and salt and pepper to taste: the jam should be tart, a little sweet, and highly seasoned. The jam can be prepared several days ahead of time and stored in the refrigerator.

2. Brush the swordfish slices with the 2 teaspoons olive oil and season with salt and pepper. Arrange the fish on a plate and squeeze the lemon juice on top. Marinate the fish for 15 minutes. Preheat the grill to high.

3. Grill the swordfish until cooked, 2 to 3 minutes per side, turning each steak 45 degrees after 30 seconds of grilling to create an attractive crosshatch of grill marks. Transfer the steaks to plates or a platter and place a heaping spoonful of onion jam on top. Garnish each with a parsley sprig and serve at once.

Serves 4

348 CALORIES PER SERVING; 35 G PROTEIN; 11 G FAT; 2 G SATURATED FAT; 21 G CARBOHYDRATE; 175 MG SODIUM; 67 MG CHOLESTEROL

Monkfish "Splendido"

Baked with Pine Nuts, Olives, and Sage

I'm of the school that holds that fish tastes best when eaten in sight of water. Few sites are more apt or lovely than the Splendido Hotel in Portofino, which has a terrace restaurant that offers bird's-eye views of the boat-studded harbor and the craggy cliffs around it. Like so many Italian recipes, this one uses a few simple flavors to reinforce the primal taste of the fish. There's one unexpected ingredient—Worcestershire sauce—perhaps a throwback to the days when Portofino was almost exclusively an English resort. There are lots of possibilities for fish here: the Splendido normally uses sea bass. I've crafted the recipe for monkfish; good choices would include mahi-mahi, cod, salmon, and tilefish.

PREPARATION TIME: 10 MINUTES   COOKING TIME: 15 MINUTES

1½ pounds monkfish, washed, patted dry, and cut into ½-inch-thick medallions
salt and freshly ground black pepper
2 to 3 tablespoons all-purpose unbleached white flour
1 tablespoon extra-virgin olive oil
8 fresh sage leaves or basil leaves
1 bay leaf
1 tablespoon toasted pine nuts
8 black olives
1 cup dry white wine
1 tablespoon Worcestershire sauce

1. Preheat the oven to 400°F. Season the fish with salt and pepper and dust with flour, shaking off the excess. (I do this on a paper towel.)

2. Heat the oil in a nonstick frying pan over a high flame. Add the fish pieces and lightly brown on both sides, about 1 minute per side. Place the sage leaves, bay leaf, pine nuts, and olives on top of the fish. Add the wine, Worcestershire sauce, and additional salt and pepper to the pan and bring to a boil.

3. Transfer the pan to the oven and bake, uncovered, until the fish is tender, 12 to 15 minutes. (When done, it will flake easily when pressed with your finger. Another test is to insert a slender metal skewer into the thickest part of the fish. When the fish is ready, the skewer will be very hot to the touch.)

4. Transfer the fish to plates or a platter. Boil the pan juices down to a syrupy glaze. Spoon this over the fish and serve at once.   *Serves 4*

212 CALORIES PER SERVING; 25 G PROTEIN; 5 G FAT; 0 G SATURATED FAT; 6 G CARBOHYDRATE; 109 MG SODIUM; 41 MG CHOLESTEROL

BLUEFISH PUTTANESCA

Puttanesca traditionally refers to a Roman pasta dish, a lively sauté of tomatoes, olives, capers, hot peppers, and anchovies tossed with spaghetti. The preparation is said to have originated in a former Red Light district called the Trastevere. As you probably know, the dish takes its name from puttana, *prostitute, although whether that's because it's hot and spicy or because it can be made in a matter of minutes remains a matter of debate. One day, when I was presented with some gorgeous bluefish by a fisherman friend, it struck me that the flavorings in spaghetti puttanesca would be perfect for full-flavored seafood. The result is this bluefish puttanesca, which would be delectable with any rich fish, from mackerel to salmon to tuna.*

PREPARATION TIME: 20 MINUTES   COOKING TIME: 25 MINUTES

1½ pounds boneless, skinless bluefish or salmon
  fillets
salt and freshly ground black pepper
1½ tablespoons extra-virgin olive oil
1 to 2 cloves garlic, minced
8 anchovy fillets, cut into ¼-inch pieces
½ teaspoon hot pepper flakes, or to taste

2 tablespoons drained capers
8 chopped pitted black olives
1 pound ripe tomatoes, peeled, seeded, and
  coarsely chopped
3 tablespoons chopped flat-leaf parsley
spray olive oil

1. Run your fingers over the fish, feeling for bones, and remove any you find with pliers or tweezers. Sprinkle the fillets with salt and pepper. Preheat the oven to 400°F.

2. Heat the olive oil in a large nonstick frying pan. Add the garlic, anchovy fillets, and pepper flakes and cook over medium heat for 20 seconds. Add the capers, olives, and tomatoes, increase the heat to high, and cook until most of the tomato liquid evaporates, 3 to 5 minutes. Stir in half the parsley and salt and pepper to taste.

3. Lightly spray a baking dish with oil. Spoon one-third of the mixture into the baking dish and arrange the fish pieces on top. Spoon the remaining puttanesca mixture over the fish. The recipe can be prepared ahead to this stage and be refrigerated for a few hours. (If you do prepare it ahead, let the sauce cool to room temperature before putting it over the fish.)

4. Bake the fish until the sauce is bubbling and the bluefish is cooked, 15 to 20 minutes. (When done, it will flake easily when pressed with your finger. Another test is to insert a slender metal skewer into the thickest part of the fish. When the fish is ready, the skewer will be very hot to the touch.) Sprinkle the remaining parsley on top and serve at once.   *Serves 4*

294 CALORIES PER SERVING; 38 G PROTEIN; 13 G FAT; 2 G SATURATED FAT; 6 G CARBOHYDRATE; 604 MG SODIUM; 107 MG CHOLESTEROL

TUNA WITH SICILIAN MINTED TOMATO SAUCE

This is one of the most popular Sicilian ways of preparing tuna. Traditionally, it would be made with a tuna "roast" (a fist-thick steak weighing a couple of pounds). But 1-inch tuna steaks, which are more readily available in the United States, work well, too. Mint is popular in Sicily and Apulia, perhaps a legacy of the Moors. Of course you'll try to use fresh mint for this recipe. But lacking fresh mint, I've raided mint tea bags and still produced fine results.

PREPARATION TIME: 25 MINUTES   COOKING TIME: 30 MINUTES

1½ pounds fresh tuna in 1 large, thick (2-inch) chunk, or 2 to 4 steaks, each 1 inch thick

FOR THE STUFFING:
⅓ cup washed, stemmed, finely chopped fresh mint leaves, or 4 teaspoons dried mint
3 cloves garlic, minced
salt and freshly ground black pepper

FOR THE SAUCE:
1 tablespoon extra-virgin olive oil
1 large onion, finely chopped

¼ to ½ teaspoon hot pepper flakes (optional)
2 tablespoons tomato paste
½ cup dry white wine
1 28-ounce can imported peeled plum tomatoes, with their juices, puréed in a food processor or put through a vegetable mill
½ teaspoon ground coriander, or to taste
½ teaspoon sugar (optional)

1. Using the tip of a paring knife, make ½-inch-deep holes in the tuna on both sides, spaced 1 inch apart. Combine half the mint with the garlic, salt, and pepper. Mash these ingredients together in a bowl with the back of a spoon to form a coarse paste. Stuff this paste into the holes you've made in the tuna. Season the outside of the tuna with salt and pepper.

2. Prepare the sauce: Heat the olive oil in a large nonstick frying pan. Add the onion and pepper flakes (if using) and cook over medium heat until the onion is soft and translucent but not brown. Add the tomato paste and sauté for 2 minutes. Add the wine and bring to a boil, stirring to dissolve the tomato paste. Add the puréed tomatoes, the coriander, the sugar (if using), the remaining 2½ tablespoons fresh mint, and a little salt and pepper. Simmer the sauce until thickened and richly flavored, about 10 minutes. Correct the seasoning, adding salt, sugar, or mint to taste.

3. Place the tuna in the pan, spooning the sauce over it. There are two ways to cook the fish. You can gently simmer it on top of the stove over medium-low heat, turning once with a large spatula. In this case, you'll need about 10 to 15 minutes per side. Or you can bake the tuna under the sauce in a preheated 350°F. oven for about 30 minutes. Unlike Asian and many North American preparations of tuna, Sicilian-style tuna is served fully cooked, not rare in the center. Serve at once with the sauce spooned over the fish.

Serves 4

299 CALORIES PER SERVING; 41 G PROTEIN; 4 G FAT; 1 G SATURATED FAT; 16 G CARBOHYDRATE; 147 MG SODIUM; 74 MG CHOLESTEROL

BASIL-GRILLED TUNA WITH BITTER GREENS

This quick, attractive dish combines the fish and salad course. I've called for the most readily available
bitter greens: arugula, radicchio, and Belgian endive. You could certainly augment the blend with other greens.

PREPARATION TIME: 15 MINUTES, PLUS 20 MINUTES MARINATING TIME   COOKING TIME: 5 MINUTES

1½ pounds fresh tuna, cut into ½-inch-thick
   steaks
2 cloves garlic, peeled
12 fresh basil leaves
salt
4 tablespoons fresh lemon juice, plus 1 lemon cut
   in slices or wedges for garnish

1½ tablespoons extra-virgin olive oil
freshly ground black pepper
1 bunch arugula, washed and stemmed
1 small bunch radicchio, broken into leaves
2 Belgian endives, broken into leaves

1. Trim any bloody spots or sinews off the tuna. Arrange the fish steaks in a glass baking dish. In a mortar and pestle, combine the garlic, basil, and salt and pound to a smooth paste. Work in 3 tablespoons lemon juice, ½ tablespoon olive oil, and the pepper. (If you don't have a mortar and pestle, purée the ingredients for the marinade in a blender or even finely chop them and stir to mix.) Pour the mixture over the fish and marinate for 20 to 30 minutes, turning the tuna steaks two or three times.

2. Slice all the bitter greens crosswise into ¼-inch strips. Place the greens in a bowl with the remaining 1 tablespoon olive oil, 1 tablespoon lemon juice, and salt and pepper, but do not toss. Preheat the grill to high.

3. Grill the tuna steaks until cooked to taste, about 1 minute per side for medium-rare, basting with marinade. (Alternatively, the fish can be cooked in a ridged skillet or under the broiler.) Just before serving, toss the bitter greens with the dressing, adding salt and pepper to taste. Arrange the tuna on a platter or plates and top with the bitter greens. Garnish with lemon slices or wedges and serve at once.

Serves 4

246 CALORIES PER SERVING; 40 G PROTEIN; 7 G FAT; 1 G SATURATED FAT; 4 G CARBOHYDRATE; 70 MG SODIUM; 74 MG CHOLESTEROL

WHOLE FISH BAKED IN A SALT CRUST

Rarely does the confluence of so few ingredients result in such a dramatic dining showpiece. This dish contains only two ingredients—fish and salt—but it never fails to dazzle guests at home or in restaurants. The theory is that the salt crust seals in the moisture and freshness of the fish. One common choice for fish in Italy is branzino (sea bass). But the species of fish is really less important than its freshness. Because of the simplicity of the presentation, there is nothing to mask the flavor of fish that is less than impeccably fresh. Here in Florida, I prepare the recipe with snapper. Elsewhere in the country, you could use porgies, scups, black bass, small striped bass, or even trout.

PREPARATION TIME: 10 MINUTES   COOKING TIME: 25 TO 40 MINUTES

1 large whole fish (2½ to 3 pounds) or 4 small fish (1½ pounds each)

10 to 12 cups coarse sea salt or kosher salt
Salsa Verde (page 173)

1. Preheat the oven to 450°F. Trim the fins off the fish, wash it, and pat it dry. Spread half the salt in an attractive baking dish or baking sheet just large enough to hold the fish. Place the fish on top, pressing it into the salt. Spread the remaining salt over the fish to completely envelop it. Compact the salt by patting it.

2. Bake the fish until cooked, 25 to 40 minutes or as needed. (To test for doneness, insert a slender metal skewer into the thickest part of the fish. When the fish is cooked, it will come out very hot to the touch.)

3. To serve, present the fish to your guests at the table. Using 2 large spoons, remove the top of the salt crust. Brush off any excess salt with a pastry brush. Transfer the fish to a platter and remove the skin. (This eliminates all the excess sodium from the fish.) Fillet the fish and serve it on plates with Salsa Verde on the side.   *Serves 4*

340 CALORIES PER 4 SERVING; 53 G PROTEIN; 12 G FAT; 2 G SATURATED FAT; 1 G CARBOHYDRATE; 784 MG SODIUM; 118 MG CHOLESTEROL

SALSA VERDE

GREEN SAUCE

Italians serve this simple sauce with some of their simplest but most cherished preparations, such as fish baked in a salt crust or bollito misto (boiled meats). I've replaced some of the oil in the traditional recipe with vegetable broth.

¼ cup minced flat-leaf parsley
2 teaspoons drained capers, finely chopped
1 to 2 cloves garlic, minced
1 teaspoon grated fresh lemon zest
2 tablespoons fresh lemon juice

2 tablespoons extra-virgin olive oil
3 tablespoons Basic Vegetable Broth (page 241), Chicken Broth (page 239), or water
salt and freshly ground black pepper

Combine all the ingredients for the sauce in mixing bowl and whisk to mix, adding salt and pepper to taste.   *Serves 4*

CHICKEN DISHES

CHICKEN ALLA DIAVOLA

Sightly, succulent, and mercifully simple is this flattened, marinated grilled chicken—a dish with a parentage claimed by both the Florentines and the Romans. The traditional recipe calls for a whole chicken to be spatchcocked (cut down the backbone and opened like a book). If your fat budget allows, use the whole bird. Because chicken skin and dark meat are high in fat, I call for boneless, skinless chicken breasts below. I've also turned up the heat a few notches by adding mustard and hot pepper flakes to the traditional marinade. After all, alla diavola means "in the style of the devil"!

PREPARATION TIME: 10 MINUTES, PLUS 30 MINUTES FOR MARINATING   COOKING TIME: 10 MINUTES

4 half chicken breasts (6 ounces each)

FOR THE MARINADE:
¼ cup fresh lemon juice
2 teaspoons dry mustard

1 tablespoon extra-virgin olive oil
2 teaspoons cracked black peppercorns, or to taste
½ teaspoon hot pepper flakes
coarse sea salt

1. Trim any fat or sinews off the chicken breasts. Gently flatten each breast between 2 sheets of plastic wrap to achieve a uniform thickness, using a scallopine pounder or the side of a cleaver. Arrange the chicken breasts in a nonreactive baking dish.

2. Combine the lemon juice and mustard in a mixing bowl and whisk to mix. Whisk in the oil, peppercorns, and pepper flakes. Pour the marinade over the chicken, turning the breasts once or twice. Mari-nate the chicken, refrigerated, for at least 30 minutes or as long as 2 hours.

3. Preheat the grill to high. Oil the grate. Grill the chicken breasts until cooked, 2 to 3 minutes per side, seasoning with salt and basting with any extra marinade. I like to serve chicken alla diavola with the arugula salad on page 43.   *Serves 4*

320 CALORIES PER SERVING; 53 G PROTEIN; 9 G FAT; 2 G SATURATED FAT; 2 G CARBOHYDRATE; 159 MG SODIUM; 144 MG CHOLESTEROL

Chicken alla Diavola

CHICKEN VERDICCHIO

When I lived in Boston, this simple sauté was a favorite at the family restaurants in the North End (Boston's "Little Italy"). Verdicchio is a pungent, crisp white wine from central Italy. It goes particularly well with the earthy flavor of artichokes. Naturally, the dish will be best if made with fresh artichokes. (Complete instructions on trimming and cooking artichokes are found on page 84.) But canned or frozen artichokes will produce a perfectly tasty version of this dish, too. (Skip step 1 and add them 5 minutes before the chicken is done.) I've written the recipe for boneless, skinless chicken breasts, but if your fat budget allows it, make it with a cut-up whole chicken for an even richer flavor.

PREPARATION TIME: 15 MINUTES   COOKING TIME: 20 MINUTES

1 pound boneless skinless chicken breasts,
    cut into 2-inch diamond-shaped pieces, or
    1 chicken, cut into 8 even pieces
salt and freshly ground black pepper
2 tablespoons all-purpose unbleached white flour
1½ tablespoons extra-virgin olive oil
1 onion, finely chopped
1 clove garlic, minced
3 tablespoons chopped flat-leaf parsley
2 to 3 cups Verdicchio or other dry white Italian
    wine

½ pound baby red potatoes (8 potatoes), scrubbed
    and cut in halves or quarters to obtain 1-inch
    pieces)
3 large or 4 medium artichokes, trimmed,
    quartered, and cooked (see steps 2 and 3, page
    84), or 1 14-ounce can artichoke hearts, rinsed
    and drained
8 black olives (optional)

1. In a mixing bowl, toss the chicken with salt and pepper and the flour. Heat half the olive oil in a non-stick frying pan. Brown the chicken pieces over a high flame, 1 to 2 minutes per side. Transfer the chicken to a plate lined with paper towels to drain.

2. Add the remaining oil to the pan and heat. Add the onion, the garlic, and half the parsley and cook over medium heat until soft and translucent but not brown, about 4 minutes.

3. Return the chicken to the pan with 2 cups wine and the potatoes and bring to a boil. Reduce the heat and simmer until the chicken and potatoes are cooked and the sauce reduced and flavorful, 15 to 20 minutes. (If the chicken starts to dry out, add a little more wine: the dish should be quite saucy.) Add the cooked artichokes and olives the last 5 minutes. Correct the seasoning, adding salt or pepper to taste. Garnish with the remaining parsley and serve.

Serves 4

439 CALORIES PER SERVING; 40 G PROTEIN; 10 G FAT; 2 G SATURATED FAT; 27.5 G CARBOHYDRATE; 183.6 MG SODIUM; 96 MG CHOLESTEROL

CHICKEN CACCIATORE

When I was growing up, chicken cacciatore was probably the best-known Italian dish. For that matter, it was the only Italian dish many Americans had ever heard of. This was long before the pasta revolution, before our discovery of regional Italian cooking, before the explosive proliferation of Italian restaurants in this country. Today, cacciatore sounds dated if not clichéd, and I bet it's been a good long time since you've sampled this soulful dish—chicken "in the style of a hunter." I've written the following recipe for boneless, skinless chicken breasts, but if your fat budget allows it, make it with a cut-up whole chicken: the bones will produce an even richer flavor.

PREPARATION TIME: 15 MINUTES   COOKING TIME: 20 TO 30 MINUTES

1½ pounds boneless, skinless chicken breasts
salt and freshly ground black pepper
1½ tablespoons olive oil
½ teaspoon hot pepper flakes, or to taste
1 medium onion, finely chopped
1 stalk celery, finely chopped
1 green bell pepper, cored, seeded, and cut into
　¼-inch dice
5 ounces thinly sliced porcini, shiitake, or
　portobello mushrooms, or regular button
　mushrooms

½ cup dry white wine
1 28-ounce can imported peeled plum tomatoes
　with their juices
1 bay leaf
3 tablespoons finely chopped flat-leaf parsley
2 to 3 teaspoons red wine vinegar

1. Rinse and dry the chicken breasts and cut into 2-inch pieces. Season with salt and pepper. Heat half the oil in a large nonstick frying pan over high heat. Add the chicken pieces and brown on both sides, about 1 minute per side. Transfer the chicken to a plate with a slotted spoon.

2. Heat the remaining oil in the pan. Add the pepper flakes, onion, celery, and bell pepper and cook over medium heat until the vegetables are soft and translucent, about 5 minutes. Add the mushrooms and cook until tender and most of the mushroom liquid has evaporated, about 3 minutes. Stir in the chicken and the white wine and bring to a boil.

3. Purée the tomatoes with their juices in a food processor or through a vegetable mill. Add them to the chicken with the bay leaf and half the parsley. Gently simmer the cacciatore over medium heat until the chicken is cooked and the sauce is thick and richly flavored, about 20 minutes. Add vinegar to taste the last 5 minutes. Remove and discard the bay leaf. Correct the seasoning, adding salt and pepper to taste. Sprinkle the remaining parsley on top and serve at once.   *Serves 4*

347 CALORIES PER SERVING; 42 G PROTEIN; 10 G FAT; 2 G SATURATED FAT; 17 G CARBOHYDRATE; 429 MG SODIUM; 104 MG CHOLESTEROL

CHICKEN BREASTS STUFFED WITH SPINACH AND CHEESE

This quick, easy dish was inspired by the famous cima *(stuffed veal breast) of Parma.*
For the best results, use fresh tender young leaf spinach (the sort sold in bunches).

PREPARATION TIME: 20 MINUTES   COOKING TIME: 35 MINUTES

2 large boneless skinless chicken breasts
  (4 halves—about 1½ pounds)
4 slices country-style white bread, crusts removed
½ cup skim milk
3 ounces stemmed, washed fresh spinach or
  ¼ package frozen

salt
8 fresh basil leaves, thinly slivered (optional)
¼ cup freshly grated Parmigiano-Reggiano cheese
freshly ground black pepper
1 tablespoon extra-virgin olive oil or spray olive oil
¾ cup toasted bread crumbs

1. Preheat the oven to 400°F. Wash and dry the chicken breasts. Remove the "tenderloins" (the long, cylindrical strips of meat on the inside of the breasts) and reserve for another recipe. Cut each breast into halves. Lay one of the half breasts lengthwise on a cutting board at the edge of the board. Cut a deep horizontal pocket in the breast, taking care not to pierce the top, bottom, or far side. It helps to hold the breast flat with your free hand while cutting the pocket. Cut pockets in the remaining breasts the same way.

2. Prepare the stuffing: Place the bread in a shallow bowl and pour the milk over it. Let stand for 10 minutes. Cook the spinach in ½ inch boiling salted water until tender, about 1 minute. Drain well and let cool. Squeeze the spinach between your fingers to wring out all the water. Finely chop the spinach and transfer to a mixing bowl. Squeeze the bread between your fingers to wring out the milk. Add it to the mix-

ing bowl with the basil and cheese and add salt and pepper to taste. Mix well.

3. Place a spoonful of stuffing mixture in the pocket of each chicken breast. Pin the pockets shut with lightly oiled toothpicks. Brush the chicken breasts on both sides with half the olive oil and dredge in bread crumbs, shaking off the excess. Transfer the chicken breasts to a lightly oiled nonstick baking dish. Drizzle the remaining oil over the chicken breasts.

4. Bake the chicken breasts until cooked, 20 to 25 minutes. (To test for doneness, press breasts with your finger—they should be firm, yet a little yielding. Another way to test for doneness is to insert a metal skewer: it should come out very hot to the touch.) There are three ways to serve chicken breasts: whole, cut in half, or sliced with a sharp knife or electric knife and fanned out. *Serves 4*

429 CALORIES PER SERVING; 12 G PROTEIN; 12 G FAT; 3 G SATURATED FAT; 30 G CARBOHYDRATE; 559 MG SODIUM; 109 MG CHOLESTEROL

CHICKEN ROLLATINI IN RED, WHITE, AND GREEN

Italians love meats that are stuffed and rolled. This one produces colorful pinwheels of red prosciutto, white fontina cheese, and bright-green escarole leaves. (It's important to use imported Italian fontina, which has an intense, robust flavor.) If escarole is unavailable, you could substitute twelve fresh spinach leaves.

PREPARATION TIME: 25 MINUTES   COOKING TIME: 20 MINUTES

2 large chicken breasts (4 halves—about
   1½ pounds in all)
salt and freshly ground black pepper
4 escarole leaves, washed
2 very thin slices prosciutto, cut in half crosswise

1½ ounces fontina cheese, thinly sliced
1 cup all-purpose unbleached white flour for
   dredging (in a shallow bowl)
1 tablespoon extra-virgin olive oil

1. Preheat the oven to 400°F. If using whole (double) chicken breasts, cut them in half. Remove the "tenderloin" (the finger-shaped muscle running the length of each breast) and reserve for another recipe. Place each half breast between two large pieces of plastic wrap. Using a scaloppini pounder or the flat side of a heavy cleaver, pound the breast into a large (at least 4 × 6 inches) rectangle ⅛ to 3/16 inch thick. Pound gently but firmly, taking care not to tear the breast. Pound all the chicken breasts in this fashion. Lightly season the breasts with salt and pepper.

2. Cook the escarole leaves in 2 quarts salted water until tender, about 1 minute. Refresh under cold water and drain. Blot dry. Cut the escarole leaves to the size of the chicken breasts.

3. Lay out the chicken breasts on a work surface, wide side toward you. Place an escarole leaf, a slice of prosciutto, and a couple of slices of fontina on top. Starting at the bottom wide edge, roll the chicken breast into a tight cylinder. Pin it closed with tooth-

picks. Stuff and roll all the breasts in this fashion. Season with more salt and pepper.

4. Dip each rollatino in flour, shaking off the excess. Heat the oil in a large nonstick frying pan with an ovenproof handle. Lightly brown the rollatini on all sides over medium-high heat, working in several batches if necessary to avoid crowding the pan. Pour off any excess fat. Place the pan with the rollatini in the oven and bake until cooked, 15 to 20 minutes.

5. Transfer the rollatini to a cutting board and remove the toothpicks. Cut each rollatino crosswise into ½-inch slices. (An electric knife works great for slicing.) Fan the slices out on plates or a platter. The Braised New Potatoes with Garlic and Bay Leaves on page 199 would make a good accompaniment.

Note: To further reduce the fat in this recipe, you could omit browning the rollatini in olive oil before baking them in the oven.   *Serves 4*

318 CALORIES PER SERVING; 43 G PROTEIN; 12 G FAT; 4 G SATURATED FAT; 6 G CARBOHYDRATE; 308 MG SODIUM; 122 MG CHOLESTEROL

CHICKEN WITH ASPARAGUS, LEMON, AND PARMESAN

Asparagus sprinkled with Parmesan cheese is a popular vegetable in Florence—especially in springtime, when the first of the crop comes into season. That gave me the idea for a more substantial dish, a chicken, asparagus, and Parmesan sauté. (This is a good place to use up the chicken tenderloins reserved from other recipes.) Time-conscious cooks will appreciate the fact that this dish can be made in its entirety in a single pan.

PREPARATION TIME: 15 MINUTES   COOKING TIME: 20 MINUTES

1 pound asparagus stalks
salt
1 tablespoon extra-virgin olive oil
1½ pounds skinless boneless chicken breasts, cut
   crosswise into ½-inch strips
freshly ground black pepper
1½ tablespoons all-purpose unbleached white flour

1 medium onion, thinly sliced
1 cup dry white vermouth or white wine
1 cup Chicken Broth (page 239)
1 to 2 tablespoons fresh lemon juice
3 to 4 tablespoons freshly grated Parmigiano-
   Reggiano cheese

1. Snap the asparagus stalks (see box). Discard the stem ends. Cut the stalks sharply on the diagonal into 2-inch pieces. Bring 3 cups lightly salted water to a boil in a 12-inch nonstick frying pan. Cook the asparagus until crisp-tender, about 3 minutes. Drain the asparagus in a colander, refresh under cold water, and drain again. Rinse out the pan.

2. Heat half the olive oil in the pan. Season the chicken pieces with salt and pepper and toss with the flour. Lightly brown the chicken pieces on all sides over medium-high heat, 1 to 2 minutes per side. Transfer the chicken to a plate lined with paper towels to drain.

3. Add the remaining olive oil to the pan. Add the onion and cook over medium heat until soft but not brown, about 4 minutes. Return the chicken to the pan, add the vermouth, and bring to a boil. Add the broth. Reduce the heat and gently simmer the chicken until cooked and tender and until the wine and broth have reduced to a thick, flavorful sauce, about 10 minutes.

4. Stir in the asparagus and the lemon juice and cook for 1 minute. Correct the seasoning, adding salt or lemon juice to taste. Just before serving, sprinkle the chicken and asparagus with the Parmesan. Serve at once.

Serves 4

431 CALORIES PER SERVING; 60 G PROTEIN; 12 G FAT; 3 G SATURATED FAT; 9 G CARBOHYDRATE; 315 MG SODIUM; 148 MG CHOLESTEROL

How to Snap Asparagus

The easiest way to snap asparagus is to grasp each stalk firmly by the cut end and bend the stalk over: it will snap at the natural point of tenderness.

CHICKEN WITH BALSAMIC VINEGAR

Balsamic vinegar owes its sweetness to the fact that it's made with grape must (partially fermented juice), not wine. This leaves a considerable amount of residual sugar in the vinegar, which makes it ideal for reducing for sauces. Simple but incredibly flavorful, this is high-flavor, low-fat Italian cooking at its best.

PREPARATION TIME: 10 MINUTES   COOKING TIME: 10 TO 15 MINUTES

1½ pounds boneless, skinless chicken breasts
salt and freshly ground black pepper
2 to 3 tablespoons all-purpose unbleached white
**   flour for dredging, or as needed**

1 tablespoon extra-virgin olive oil
1 cup balsamic vinegar
1 cup Chicken Broth (page 239)
2 tablespoons finely chopped flat-leaf parsley

1. Cut each chicken breast (if whole) into halves and trim off any fat or sinews. (For a neater appearance, remove the tenderloins and reserve them for other recipes.) Season each half breast with salt and pepper and lightly dust with flour, shaking off the excess.

2. Heat the oil in a nonstick frying pan. Lightly brown the breasts on both sides over high heat, about 2 minutes per side. Add the vinegar and bring to a boil. Reduce the heat to medium and simmer until the vinegar is reduced by two-thirds.

3. Add the chicken broth and continue simmering, uncovered, until the chicken is tender, about 10 minutes. Transfer it to a platter. Boil the sauce until reduced, thick, and flavorful, about 10 minutes. Add salt and pepper to taste. Spoon the sauce over the chicken and sprinkle with the parsley. Serve at once.

Serves 4

391 CALORIES PER SERVING; 54 G PROTEIN; 10 G FAT; 2 G SATURATED FAT; 17 G CARBOHYDRATE; 220 MG SODIUM; 144 MG CHOLESTEROL

TURKEY PICCATA

When I set out to write this book, I despaired of being able to include some of my favorite Italian dishes. Such as veal piccata. After all, how could you possibly cut enough fat in a dish that consists of scaloppine dipped in an egg-and-cheese batter and pan-fried in oceans of butter? My first step was to use lean turkey breast instead of veal. Then I cut the number of egg yolks in the batter. (For a dish even lower in fat, you could eliminate them completely.) Finally, I cook the scaloppine in olive oil instead of butter. I think you'll be pleasantly surprised at how tasty a low-fat version can be.

PREPARATION TIME: 15 MINUTES   COOKING TIME: 10 MINUTES

1½ pounds turkey scaloppine (see Note)
1 whole egg plus 4 egg whites, or ¾ cup egg
   substitute
¼ cup all-purpose unbleached white flour, plus
   ¾ cup for dredging
⅓ cup freshly grated Parmigiano-Reggiano cheese

salt and freshly ground black pepper
1½ to 2 tablespoons extra-virgin olive oil
¼ cup fresh lemon juice
¼ cup Chicken Broth (page 239)
2 tablespoons drained capers
lemon wedges for serving

1. Rinse the turkey and pat dry. If necessary, place each scaloppine between sheets of plastic wrap and pound with a scallopine pounder or the side of a cleaver to a thickness of ⅛ inch.

2. Make the batter: Lightly beat together the egg and whites in a shallow bowl. (Beat just to mix.) Stir in ¼ cup flour, the cheese, and salt and pepper. The batter should be just a little thicker than heavy cream: if necessary, thin with 1 or 2 tablespoons of water. Place the remaining ¾ cup flour in another shallow bowl or on a paper towel.

3. Just before serving, preheat the oven to 400°F. Heat half the olive oil in a nonstick skillet over a medium-high heat. Season the scaloppine with salt and pepper. Lightly dust each scaloppine with flour, shaking off the excess. Using 2 forks, dip each scaloppine in the batter, shaking off the excess. Pan-fry the scaloppine until cooked, 1 to 2 minutes per side, adding olive oil as needed. As the scaloppine are

cooked, transfer them to an ovenproof serving platter and keep warm in the oven.

4. When all the scaloppine are cooked, discard any oil and add the lemon juice, broth, and capers to the pan. Boil this sauce until reduced to about 6 tablespoons and slightly thickened, about 2 minutes. Add salt and pepper to taste. Pour the sauce over the scaloppine and serve at once, with lemon wedges on the side.

Note: Many butcher shops sell turkey scaloppine. If not, it's easy to cut your own from boneless, skinless turkey breast. Cut the breast across the grain into ¼-inch slices. It's important to cut across the grain, so the scaloppine will be tender. Place each slice between 2 sheets of plastic wrap and pound with a scaloppine pounder or the side of a cleaver.

Serves 4

319 CALORIES PER SERVING; 43 G PROTEIN; 14 G FAT; 4 G SATURATED FAT; 2 G CARBOHYDRATE; 1,022 MG SODIUM; 125 MG CHOLESTEROL

TUSCAN ROAST PHEASANT

Pheasant is the perfect bird for health-conscious eaters, offering rich flavor with dramatically less fat than chicken. Once available only to hunters, pheasant can now be found at gourmet shops, specialty butchers, and many supermarkets. And because virtually all of the pheasant sold in the United States is farm-raised, you never have to worry about an unpleasantly strong gamy flavor. This recipe uses a wet-roasting technique: the wine keeps the bird from drying out. Note: Pancetta is Italian bacon. I use just a little for flavor. You could further reduce the fat in the dish by substituting prosciutto for the pancetta or omitting it entirely.

PREPARATION TIME: 15 MINUTES   COOKING TIME: 1¼ HOURS

2 fresh pheasants
2 to 3 teaspoons extra-virgin olive oil
salt and freshly ground black pepper
1 tablespoon chopped fresh rosemary
1 tablespoon chopped fresh thyme

2 cloves garlic, minced
2 thin slices pancetta (Italian bacon), each cut in half crosswise (optional)
1 cup dry white wine, or as needed
2 tablespoons good-quality brandy or grappa

1. Prepare the pheasants for roasting. Normally they are sold ready to cook, but sometimes you will need to pull out the tiny pin feathers around the wings and legs. Do this with tweezers or pliers. Remove any lumps of fat from the cavities. Preheat the oven to 350°F.

2. Brush the outside of the pheasants with olive oil. Season the inside and outside with salt and pepper. Mash together the rosemary, thyme, and garlic in a mortar and pestle or mix in a small bowl. Place half this mixture in the cavities of the birds (a little in the front cavity, more in the rear cavity). Spread the remaining mixture over the outside of the birds. If using the pancetta, place 2 half strips over each pheasant breast. Truss the birds with string.

3. Place the pheasants on their sides on a rack over the pan. Roast in the oven for 30 minutes, turning the birds from one side to the other after 15 minutes.

4. Add the wine to the pan and continue roasting the birds for another 20 minutes, turning once. (If too much wine in the pan evaporates, add a little more.) Turn the pheasants on their backs (breasts up) and increase the oven temperature to 450°F. Roast the birds in this position for 6 to 8 minutes to brown the skin.

5. Remove the pheasants from the oven and cut each one in half with a large sharp knife or poultry shears. Place the halves, cut side down, in the roasting pan with the wine. Pour the brandy over them. Roast for 3 to 4 minutes more, or until there are no traces of pink in the meat.

6. Transfer the pheasant halves to plates or a platter. Strain the pan juices into a sauce boat for serving on the side. Polenta or risotto would make an excellent accompaniment.   *Serves 4*

805 CALORIES PER SERVING; 91 G PROTEIN; 40 G FAT; 11 G SATURATED FAT; 1 G CARBOHYDRATE; 165 MG SODIUM; 0 MG CHOLESTEROL

MEAT DISHES

OSSO BUCO

BRAISED VEAL SHANKS

The mere mention of osso buco is enough to set a Milanese's mouth watering. Nothing tastes better on a cold winter night than a steaming plate of veal shanks braised with wine and vegetables. Cooking the dish will warm your kitchen. The aroma will perfume your whole house. The only remotely challenging aspect to this recipe is finding a butcher who sells osso buco. Note: the initial boiling helps melt away some of the fat in the shanks.

PREPARATION TIME: 30 TO 40 MINUTES   COOKING TIME: 2 TO 3 HOURS

4 veal shanks (about 3 pounds)
1 tablespoon extra-virgin olive oil, plus a little oil for brushing
1 large onion, finely chopped
2 carrots, peeled and finely chopped
2 stalks celery, finely chopped
2 cloves garlic, minced
½ cup chopped flat-leaf parsley
3 large ripe tomatoes, peeled, seeded, and chopped, or 1 28-ounce can imported peeled plum tomatoes, drained of their can juice and chopped in the food processor (about 2 cups)

2 tablespoons tomato paste
1 cup dry white wine
4 to 5 cups water or, for a richer sauce, Chicken Broth (page 239)
1 herb bundle comprising a bay leaf, a sprig of rosemary, a sprig of flat-leaf parsley, and a few sage leaves
salt and freshly ground black pepper
the finely grated fresh zest of 1 lemon for serving

1. Using a paring knife, cut any visible pieces of fat off the veal shanks. Place the shanks in a large pot with cold water. Bring to a boil and cook for 3 minutes. Rinse the shanks under cold water and drain. Preheat the oven to 350°F.

2. Heat the olive oil in a large, ovenproof sauté pan. Add the onion, carrot, celery, garlic, and half the parsley and cook over medium heat until lightly browned, about 6 minutes. Stir in the chopped tomatoes and cook for 1 minute. Stir in the tomato paste and cook for 1 minute.

3. Add the veal shanks and white wine and bring to a boil, stirring with a wooden spoon. Add 4 cups water, the herb bundle, salt, and pepper and bring the mixture back to a boil. Cover the pan tightly and place it in the oven. Combine the remaining parsley and the lemon zest in a small bowl and stir to mix.

4. Bake the veal shanks until they are falling-off-the-bone tender, stirring from time to time to make sure nothing burns, 2 to 3 hours. Uncover the pan the last 45 minutes to allow any excess liquid to evaporate. You should wind up with about 2 cups

Osso Buco

sauce. Correct the seasoning, adding salt and pepper to taste.

5. Serve the braised lamb shanks over rice or an-other absorbent grain. Sprinkle each shank with the parsley-lemon mixture and serve at once.

Serves 4

393 CALORIES PER SERVING; 45 G PROTEIN; 13 G FAT; 3 G SATURATED FAT; 15 G CARBOHYDRATE; 230 MG SODIUM; 155 MG CHOLESTEROL

A NEW VEAL MARSALA

Veal marsala was one of the first Italian dishes I learned to make. Thanks to its simplicity and speed (ten minutes' preparation time and not much more for cooking), it remains popular at our house on work nights. What's "new" about this veal marsala is the addition of shiitake mushrooms and the use of a new dairy product called low-fat half-and-half. The latter is made by the Land O Lakes Company and is available at some supermarkets. If unavailable, you could add 2 to 3 tablespoons evaporated skim milk.

PREPARATION TIME: 10 MINUTES   COOKING TIME: 10 TO 15 MINUTES

1 pound veal scaloppine (8 scaloppine)
salt and freshly ground black pepper
about ¼ cup all-purpose unbleached white flour
1½ tablespoons extra-virgin olive oil
½ red onion, finely chopped (about ¾ cup)
6 ounces shiitake mushrooms, stemmed and
    cut in half

1½ cups marsala wine
3 tablespoons low-fat half-and-half or evaporated
    skim milk
1 tablespoon chopped flat-leaf parsley or rosemary

1. Season the scaloppine on both sides with salt and pepper and lightly dust with flour, shaking off the excess. (I like to do the dusting—actually more rubbing than dusting—on a paper towel.)

2. Heat half the olive oil in a nonstick skillet over high heat. Quickly sear the scaloppine on both sides, about 30 seconds per side, working in several batches, if needed, to avoid crowding the pan. Transfer the veal to a platter.

3. Heat the remaining oil in the skillet. Add the onion and mushrooms and cook over medium heat until just beginning to brown, about 4 minutes. Return the veal to the pan. Add the marsala and half-and-half and bring to a boil. Reduce the heat and gently simmer the veal until it is very tender and the sauce is reduced and thick, 8 to 10 minutes. Correct the seasoning, adding salt and pepper to taste. To reinforce the marsala flavor, you can add a fresh splash of marsala at the end. Sprinkle the parsley on top and serve at once. *Serves 4*

347 CALORIES PER SERVING; 24 G PROTEIN; 12 G FAT; 3 G SATURATED FAT; 17 G CARBOHYDRATE; 144 MG SODIUM; 102 MG CHOLESTEROL

INVOLTINI OF BEEF

Many countries have a version of stuffed, braised beef rolls. This one comes from the Locanda del Gallo restaurant in the sleepy town of Acaja, near the west coast of Apulia. The easiest way to cut the beef is to have your butcher slice it on a meat slicer. You want slices that are about 6 inches long, 3 inches wide, and ¼ inch thick.

PREPARATION TIME: 20 MINUTES   COOKING TIME: 40 MINUTES

12 thin slices of beef (about 1 pound) (have it cut
   from the top or bottom of the round)
salt and freshly ground black pepper
2 cloves garlic, coarsely chopped
½ red onion, finely chopped
1 tomato, peeled, seeded, and finely chopped
⅓ cup coarsely grated Sardo, Pecorino, Romano,
   or other tangy sheep's-milk cheese
1½ tablespoons extra-virgin olive oil

FOR THE SAUCE:
1 onion, finely chopped
3 cloves garlic, very finely chopped
½ cup dry white wine
½ cup beef broth or Chicken Broth (page 239)
2 red ripe tomatoes, peeled, seeded, and finely
   chopped
1 bay leaf
3 tablespoons chopped flat-leaf parsley

1. Place each piece of beef between sheets of plastic wrap and pound with a scaloppine pounder or the side of a cleaver to flatten and tenderize the meat. Arrange the meat slices on a work surface and sprinkle with salt and pepper, the coarsely chopped garlic, the red onion, the 1 chopped tomato, and the Sardo cheese. Roll up the beef slices into compact rolls. Pin the rolls closed with toothpicks.

2. Heat half the oil in a large nonstick frying pan over high heat. Lightly brown the rolls on all sides, seasoning with salt and pepper. (This will take about 5 minutes.) Transfer the rolls to a plate.

3. Make the sauce: Add the remaining oil to the pan. Add the onion and garlic and cook over medium heat until just beginning to brown. Return the beef rolls to the pan. Add the wine and bring to a boil. Stir in the broth, the 2 chopped tomatoes, and the bay leaf.

4. Gently simmer the beef rolls, covered, for 30 to 40 minutes, or until tender. Uncover the pan the last 10 minutes to allow the sauce to cook down. Correct the seasoning, adding salt and pepper to taste. Remember to remove the bay leaf and the toothpicks (needlenose pliers work well for this) before serving. Sprinkle with the parsley and serve at once.

Makes 12 rolls, enough to serve 4 to 6

304 CALORIES PER SERVING;* 27 G PROTEIN; 16 G FAT; 5.2 G SATURATED FAT; 6.8 G CARBOHYDRATE; 224 MG SODIUM; 72 MG CHOLESTEROL

Analysis is based on 4 servings.

BEEF BRAISED IN BAROLO

The wine country around Barolo boasts some of the most stunning vineyards in the world. The vines seem not so much trained to grow down the vertiginously steep hillsides as coiffed with a giant comb. The soil, climate, and steep topography conspire to produce intense, powerful wines that go well with the stewed and braised meats so beloved in the region. You don't need to use a super-costly Barolo for this recipe (to drink with it, maybe), but try to use a wine from the region. Traditionally, the beef would be braised and served by itself, but I've added vegetables to reduce the overall proportion of meat.

PREPARATION TIME: 20 MINUTES   COOKING TIME: 2½ TO 3 HOURS

1 eye-of-the-round roast (about 3 pounds), trimmed of fat and sinew
3 cloves garlic, each cut into 6 slivers
2 sprigs fresh rosemary
1½ tablespoons olive oil
salt and freshly ground black pepper
1 onion, finely chopped
1 carrot, peeled and finely chopped

2 stalks celery, finely chopped
¼ cup chopped flat-leaf parsley
1 bottle Barolo or other powerful, dark-red wine

FOR THE GARNISH:
18 pearl onions, peeled
18 baby carrots, peeled
12 baby potatoes, or 6 small red potatoes, scrubbed

1. Preheat the oven to 350°F. Using the tip of a paring knife, make 18 tiny slits all over the roast. Insert a sliver of garlic and a few leaves from one sprig of rosemary in each hole.

2. Heat half the oil in a large, deep, ovenproof casserole. Season the roast with salt and pepper and brown it on all sides over high heat. Transfer the beef to a platter and blot with paper towels. Discard the oil.

3. Add the remaining oil to the pan and heat. Add the chopped onion, carrot, and celery and half the parsley. Cook over medium heat until soft but not brown, about 4 minutes, stirring often. Return the beef to the pan. Add the wine and the remaining rosemary sprig and bring to a boil.

4. Tightly cover the pan and place it in the oven. Cook the beef for 1½ hours. Add the pearl onions, baby carrots, and potatoes. Cover the pan and continue braising until the beef and vegetables are tender, 1 to 1½ hours more. If the vegetables become tender before the beef, transfer them to a platter with a slotted spoon.

5. Transfer the beef to a carving board and let stand for 5 minutes. Cut it crosswise into ¼-inch slices. Arrange the slices on a platter with the vegetables. Boil the braising liquid down until reduced to 1½ cups. Season it to taste with salt and pepper. Strain it on top of the beef and serve at once.

Serves 6

479 CALORIES PER SERVING; 54 G PROTEIN; 12 G FAT; 4 G SATURATED FAT; 8 G CARBOHYDRATE; 238 MG SODIUM; 126 MG CHOLESTEROL

WHEAT BERRIES WITH BEEF

Here's the Italian version of what a Latino would call picadillo *or a North American would call hash. I sampled it in Ostuni in Apulia, where it was made with a local grain called* farro *(emmer). Wheat berries are quite similar and are more widely available in this country. This is an ideal recipe for people who are trying to incorporate more grains into their diet and increase the ratio of plant-based foods to meats. The beef serves more as a flavoring than principal ingredient. I like to chop the beef myself to ensure getting the leanest possible cut.*

PREPARATION TIME: 10 MINUTES   COOKING TIME: 1 HOUR

1 cup wheat berries
1 tablespoon extra-virgin olive oil
1 small onion, finely chopped
1 stalk celery, finely chopped
1 carrot, peeled and finely chopped
1 clove garlic, finely chopped
½ pound lean beef or veal, finely chopped
1 cup dry white wine

2 cups puréed canned imported peeled plum tomatoes with their juices (see Note)
1 bay leaf
3 tablespoons minced flat-leaf parsley
½ to 1 cup Chicken Broth (page 239) or Basic Vegetable Broth (page 241) or water, or as needed

1. Rinse the wheat berries. Cook them in a pressure cooker until tender, about 20 minutes. If you don't have a pressure cooker, soak the wheat berries in cold water for at least 4 hours or overnight. Cook them, covered, in a large pot in 3 quarts briskly simmering water until tender, 1 to 1½ hours. Rinse the wheat berries in a colander and drain well.

2. Heat the olive oil in a sauté pan. Add the onion, celery, carrot, and garlic and cook over medium heat until just beginning to brown, about 5 minutes. Add the beef and cook until crumbly and cooked, chopping the meat into small pieces with the edge of a metal spatula or wooden spoon. Add the wheat berries and wine and bring to a boil. Cook until the wine has almost evaporated. Add the puréed tomatoes, bay leaf, and half the parsley and bring to a boil.

3. Reduce the heat and gently simmer the mixture until the wheat berries and beef are very tender and the sauce is reduced and richly flavored, 30 to 40 minutes. If the mixture dries out too much, add ½ to 1 cup broth. Correct the seasoning, adding salt and pepper to taste. To serve, discard the bay leaf and sprinkle the remaining parsley on top.

Note: The best way to purée the tomatoes is to place them, juices and all, in the food processor.

Serves 4

318 CALORIES PER SERVING; 18 G PROTEIN; 6 G FAT; 1 G SATURATED FAT; 40 G CARBOHYDRATE; 326 MG SODIUM; 32 MG CHOLESTEROL

OXTAILS OR SHORT RIBS SMOTHERED IN ONIONS AND BRAISED IN WINE

In the course of writing this book, I've thought a great deal about the difference between cooking in Italy and in North America. It's not only about flavors and ingredients. It's also about a notion of time. Italians are willing to devote much more time on a daily basis to food preparation than most North Americans are. As a result, Italians still enjoy the sort of long, slow, oven-braised dishes so characteristic of country cooking that have almost disappeared in the United States. Here's a recipe for braised oxtails, a cut of meat that is tough and cheap but incredibly flavorful. The same preparation can be used for another wonderful tough, cheap, flavorful cut of beef: short ribs. This is a great dish to make when you're home on a cold, rainy or snowy day: the oven warms your kitchen and the soulful aromas will fill your whole house. The initial boiling of the oxtails helps melt away some of the fat.

PREPARATION TIME: 30 MINUTES   COOKING TIME: 3 TO 4 HOURS

3 pounds oxtails
1 tablespoon extra-virgin olive oil
3 medium onions, thinly sliced
1 28-ounce can imported peeled plum tomatoes, finely chopped, with their juices (see Note)
1 tablespoon tomato paste
3 cups dry white wine, or as needed (or for a less traditional but tremendously flavorful touch, dry red wine)

1 bay leaf
1 sprig rosemary
⅓ cup finely chopped flat-leaf parsley
salt and freshly ground black pepper
1½ pounds small potatoes, cut in halves or quarters (to obtain 1-inch pieces)

1. Using a paring knife, cut any visible pieces of fat off the oxtails. Place the meat in a large pot with cold water. Bring to a boil and cook for 3 minutes. Rinse the meat under cold water and drain. Preheat the oven to 350°F.

2. In a large ovenproof pot with a tightly fitting lid, heat the olive oil. Add the onions and cook until nicely browned and richly caramelized, about 20 minutes. You'll want to start on high heat, reducing the heat to medium after a few minutes, then to low, to prevent the onions from burning.

3. Stir the oxtails into the onions. Add the tomatoes, tomato paste, wine, bay leaf, rosemary sprig, half the parsley, and salt and pepper. Bring the mixture to a boil, scraping the bottom of the pan with a wooden spoon to dissolve any congealed onion juices. Tightly cover the pot and place it in the oven.

4. Braise the oxtails, covered, for 2 hours. Remove the pan from the heat and skim off any fat that has risen to the surface. Stir in the potatoes (and more wine if needed to keep the mixture moist).

5. Cover the pan and continue baking until the oxtails and potatoes are very tender, about 1 hour. Uncover the pot the last 30 minutes to allow the pan juices to cook down to a thick gravy. Remove the bay leaf and the rosemary sprig. Correct the seasoning, adding salt and pepper to taste. I like to serve the braised oxtails right in the pan in which they were cooked, but you can also transfer them to a platter. Sprinkle the remaining parsley on top and serve at once.

Note: The best way to purée the tomatoes is to place them, juices and all, in the food processor.

Serves 6

327 CALORIES PER SERVING; 14 G PROTEIN; 7 G FAT; 0.4 G SATURATED FAT; 35 G CARBOHYDRATE; 253 MG SODIUM; 31 MG CHOLESTEROL

VARIATION: BRAISED BEEF SHORT RIBS

Prepare as above, using 3 pounds beef short ribs instead of oxtail. Trim any visible fat off the short ribs. Use red wine instead of white.

ROSEMARY-ROASTED PORK LOIN

Visit a weekly market in Umbria or Tuscany and you're sure to find a crowd lined up in front of the mobile rotisserie. This truck travels from market to market, selling porchetta, *savory slices of a young pig that has been stuffed and rubbed with herb paste and roasted in a wood-fired oven. I've cut the pork down to a manageable size (a pork loin) in the following recipe and trimmed a lot of fat.*

PREPARATION TIME: 15 MINUTES   COOKING TIME: 1½ TO 2 HOURS

8 cloves garlic
2 tablespoons fresh rosemary leaves, plus 4 sprigs fresh rosemary
4 fresh sage leaves, or 1 teaspoon dried
salt and freshly ground black pepper to taste
1 3-pound boneless pork loin roast

1 tablespoon extra-virgin olive oil
1 cup dry white wine, plus ¼ cup for deglazing the pan
1 cup Chicken Broth (page 239), Basic Vegetable Broth (page 241), or water, or as needed

1. Preheat the oven to 400°F. Pound the garlic, rosemary, and sage to a smooth paste in a mortar and pestle or purée in a spice mill. Add salt and pepper to taste.

2. Insert a long, slender object, such as sharpening steel, through the roast, from one end of the loin to the other. The idea is to make a tunnel through the center. Stuff half the herb paste into this tunnel, working from both ends, pushing it in with your fingers. Rub the roast with the olive oil, season with salt and pepper, and rub the remaining herb paste on top of the roast. Tie the rosemary sprigs on the roast lengthwise with butcher's string.

3. Place the roast on a rack in a roasting pan in the oven. Roast at 400°F. for 20 minutes. Reduce the heat to 325°, add the 1 cup wine and the broth to the roasting pan, and continue roasting until the pork is cooked, 1¼ to 1½ hours. Add broth and wine as nec-

essary to keep about ½ inch liquid in the roasting pan. Baste the pork often with the pan juices. (This is most easily done with a bulb baster. When the pork is cooked, the internal temperature will register about 160°F. Transfer the roast to a carving board, cover with foil, and let stand for 5 minutes.

4. Meanwhile, strain the pan juices into a gravy separator. (Deglaze the roasting pan by placing it over a top burner at high heat, adding the ¼ cup wine, and bringing it to a boil. Simmer for 2 minutes, scraping the bottom of the pan to dissolve any congealed juices.) Add this mixture to the gravy separator. Pour off the pan juices into a sauce boat, leaving the fat behind. Season the juices with salt and pepper.

5. To serve, remove the string and rosemary sprigs. Slice the roast widthwise and serve with the pan juices on the side.   *Serves 6 to 8*

143 CALORIES PER SERVING;* 12 G PROTEIN; 6.6 G FAT; 2 G SATURATED FAT; 2 G CARBOHYDRATE; 187 MG SODIUM; 36 MG CHOLESTEROL

Analysis is based on 6 servings.

Vegetable Dishes

Stuffed Artichokes

The Italian love for artichokes can scarcely be overstated. Italians have as many ways to prepare artichokes as we do potatoes.
I've called for small artichokes in this recipe, but you could also use full-size globe artichokes (see Note).

PREPARATION TIME: 30 MINUTES   COOKING TIME: 15 MINUTES

6 small artichokes
½ lemon, plus 1 teaspoon grated fresh lemon zest
  for the stuffing
salt

FOR THE STUFFING:
1 tablespoon extra-virgin olive oil
1 small onion, finely chopped

1 stalk celery, finely chopped
1 ounce prosciutto, finely chopped
1 cup toasted bread crumbs, preferably homemade
  (page 247)
3 tablespoons minced flat-leaf parsley
¼ cup freshly grated Parmigiano-Reggiano cheese
salt and freshly ground black pepper

1. Cut the ends off the artichoke stems, leaving about 1 inch of stem. Rub the cut end with lemon. Cut off the top third of each artichoke and rub with lemon. Cut each artichoke lengthwise in half and scrape out the "choke" (the fibrous center) with a melon baller. Rub the artichokes with lemon as you work to keep them from discoloring. Put the trimmed artichokes in a bowl of cold water with a squeeze of lemon juice until you're ready to cook them.

2. Cook the artichokes in 4 quarts boiling salted water until tender, 6 to 8 minutes. Drain in a colander, rinse under cold water, and drain again. Arrange the artichoke halves, cut side up, in an attractive baking dish.

3. Prepare the stuffing: Heat half the olive oil in a nonstick frying pan. Add the onion, celery, and pro-

sciutto and cook over medium heat until soft but not brown, about 4 minutes. Stir in the bread crumbs, the parsley, half the Parmesan, and salt and pepper to taste. Distribute the stuffing evenly among the cavities of the artichoke halves. The recipe can be prepared ahead to this stage and stored in the refrigerator for several hours.

4. Preheat the oven to 400°F. or heat the broiler. Just before serving, drizzle the remaining olive oil over the stuffed artichokes or lightly spray with oil. Sprinkle with the remaining Parmesan cheese. Bake the artichokes until thoroughly heated and the stuffing is lightly browned, 10 to 15 minutes. The artichokes can be served either hot or at room temperature.

Stuffed Artichokes

Note: To make this dish using full-size globe artichokes, cut them lengthwise in quarters. Trim off the tough parts of the leaves and the fibrous choke. Arrange the artichoke quarters in a baking dish, leaf side down, and mound the stuffing where the choke used to be.

Makes 12 pieces

79 CALORIES PER PIECE; 4 G PROTEIN; 3 G FAT; 0.8 G SATURATED FAT; 11 G CARBOHYDRATE; 193 MG SODIUM; 4 MG CHOLESTEROL

VENETIAN BRAISED ARTICHOKES

This is one of the easiest ways to prepare artichokes and one of the best. Variations of the dish are found from Venice to Palermo. Instructions on trimming artichokes are found on page 84.

PREPARATION TIME: 15 MINUTES   COOKING TIME: 10 MINUTES

4 large artichokes
1 lemon, cut in half
1 tablespoon extra-virgin olive oil
1 small onion, peeled and cut into 12 wedges
2 cloves garlic, thinly sliced

¼ teaspoon hot pepper flakes (optional)
2 cups dry white wine
salt and freshly ground black pepper
1 tablespoon fresh lemon juice, or to taste
3 tablespoons finely chopped flat-leaf parsley

1. Cut each artichoke into quarters. Trim off the outside of the stem, the tough parts of the leaves, and the fibrous choke. Rub the artichokes with lemon as you work to keep them from browning. Put the trimmed artichokes in a bowl of cold water with a squeeze of lemon juice until you're ready to cook them.

2. Heat the olive oil in a sauté pan. Add the onion and garlic and cook over high heat until beginning to brown, 1 to 2 minutes. Add the artichokes and pepper flakes (if using) and sauté for 1 minute. Add the wine, salt, and pepper and bring to a boil.

3. Reduce the heat to medium and simmer the artichokes until tender, about 10 minutes. Add the lemon juice and parsley the last 2 minutes. The cooking liquid should reduce to a syrupy glaze. If the artichokes are tender before the sauce is reduced, transfer them to a platter. Boil the sauce until thick and syrupy. Add salt and pepper to taste. Spoon the sauce over the artichokes and serve at once.

Serves 4

184 CALORIES PER SERVING; 5 G PROTEIN; 4 G FAT; 0.5 G SATURATED FAT; 18 G CARBOHYDRATE; 123 MG SODIUM; 0 MG CHOLESTEROL

ROSEMARY-ROASTED CARROTS

Like so much other Italian cooking, this recipe is simplicity itself. But I know of no other cooking method that produces tastier carrots (or other root vegetables). High-heat roasting is a great way to intensify the flavor of vegetables, evaporating the water in them to concentrate the flavor and caramelizing the natural sugars.

PREPARATION TIME: 10 MINUTES   COOKING TIME: 20 TO 30 MINUTES

1 pound carrots
1 head garlic
1 tablespoon extra-virgin olive oil

2 sprigs fresh rosemary, or 1 tablespoon dried
salt and freshly ground black pepper

1. Preheat the oven to 450°F. If using whole carrots, peel them and cut them into 2-inch sections. Break the garlic into individual cloves, leaving the skin intact on each. Place the carrots, garlic, olive oil, rosemary, salt, and pepper in a roasting pan or baking dish just large enough to hold them. Toss to mix.

2. Roast the carrots, stirring from time to time, until browned and tender, 20 to 30 minutes. Serve at once. *Serves 4*

95 CALORIES PER SERVING; 2 G PROTEIN; 4 G FAT; 0.5 G SATURATED FAT; 15 G CARBOHYDRATE; 75 MG SODIUM; 0 MG CHOLESTEROL

BRAISED NEW POTATOES WITH GARLIC AND BAY LEAVES

This dish offers a perfect example how Italians use one or two seasonings to create a dish with symphonic flavors. The potatoes are studded with slivers of bay leaf, which gives them a futuristic appearance. To make a low-fat version of this dish (the original was roasted in butter), I had the idea to braise the potatoes in chicken broth. For extra richness, you could brush the potatoes with a little melted butter or olive oil and still wind up with a low-fat dish. NOTE: THE BAY LEAVES ARE FOR FLAVOR AND SHOW ONLY. BE SURE TO HAVE EVERYONE REMOVE THEM BEFORE EATING.

PREPARATION TIME: 15 MINUTES   COOKING TIME: 1 HOUR

8 small red potatoes (about 1 pound), scrubbed
2 fresh bay leaves
8 cloves garlic, peeled
1 cup Chicken Broth (page 239) or Basic
   Vegetable Broth (page 241), or as needed

salt and freshly ground black pepper
1 tablespoon melted butter or extra-virgin olive oil

1. Preheat the oven to 400°F. Make 2 lengthwise cuts in the top of each potato, each about ¼ inch deep. Cut the bay leaves crosswise into ¼-inch slivers. Place a sliver of bay leaf in each slit. Place the potatoes in a roasting pan just large enough to hold them. (A loaf pan works well.) Add the garlic cloves, the chicken broth, and a little salt and pepper.

2. Braise the potatoes, uncovered, until soft, 45 to 60 minutes. During this time, most of the stock will evaporate or be absorbed into the potatoes, but a little should remain to form a sauce. If using the butter, brush it on top of the potatoes. Serve at once, with the sauce and garlic spooned on top. The garlic is edible; *the bay leaves are not.* HAVE EVERYONE REMOVE THEM BEFORE EATING THE POTATOES.   *Serves 4*

153 CALORIES PER SERVING; 3 G PROTEIN; 4 G FAT; 2 G SATURATED FAT; 28 G CARBOHYDRATE; 284 MG SODIUM; 12 MG CHOLESTEROL

SWEET AND SOUR CIPPOLINI

Cippolini are small flat onion-like bulbs that have an elegant, shalloty flavor. They were once available only at Italian greengrocers, but you can now find them in gourmet shops, natural-foods stores, and many supermarkets. If you can't find cippolini, use pearl onions.

PREPARATION TIME: 15 MINUTES   COOKING TIME: 10 MINUTES

1 pound *cippolini* or pearl onions
salt
1 tablespoon extra-virgin olive oil

3 tablespoons balsamic vinegar, or to taste
2 tablespoons honey
1 clove

1. Cook the *cippolini* in their skins in a pot of boiling salted water until just tender, 6 to 8 minutes. Rinse well, refresh under cold water, and drain. Peel the *cippolini* with a paring knife.

2. Heat the olive oil in a nonstick frying pan. Add the *cippolini* and cook over high heat until lightly browned, about 3 minutes. Add the vinegar, honey, and clove and continue cooking until the pan juices are reduced to a thick, sweet, syrupy glaze, 3 to 5 minutes. Remove the clove before serving.

Serves 4

116 CALORIES PER SERVING; 1 G PROTEIN; 4 G FAT; 0.5 G SATURATED FAT; 21 G CARBOHYDRATE; 6 MG SODIUM; 0 MG CHOLESTEROL

STUFFED ONIONS IN THE STYLE OF SAN GIMIGNANO

San Gimignano is one of the most scenic hill towns in Tuscany, a medieval walled city with tall towers (once used for hanging and drying dyed fabrics) that create an almost Manhattanesque silhouette against the Tuscan sky. I watched these stuffed onions being made through the back door of a restaurant kitchen and was invited in to try them. They make a wonderful accompaniment to the Rosemary-Roasted Pork Loin on page 193.

PREPARATION TIME: 15 MINUTES   COOKING TIME: 20 MINUTES

3 medium onions (each weighing about 6 ounces), unpeeled
salt
1 carrot, peeled and cut into ¼-inch dice
spray oil (or a little olive oil)
1 tablespoon extra-virgin olive oil
1 medium zucchini or yellow squash, scrubbed and cut into ¼-inch dice

1 red bell pepper, cored, seeded, and cut into ¼-inch dice
4 basil leaves, thinly sliced, or ½ teaspoon dried
3 tablespoons freshly grated Parmigiano-Reggiano cheese (optional)
freshly ground black pepper
2 tablespoons dried bread crumbs (optional)

1. Cook the onions in their skins in boiling salted water to cover until tender, about 15 minutes. Add the carrots the last 2 minutes. Drain the onions and carrots, rinse with cold water, and let cool.

2. Using a sharp knife, cut ¼ inch off the top and bottom of each onion (so it will sit straight without wobbling), then cut the onion in half crosswise. Slip off the skin. Gently remove the inside layers of the onions to create a hollow cup. Cut the inside layers into ¼-inch dice and reserve for the stuffing. Work gently and carefully, as the onion will have a tendency to fall apart. Place the onion halves in an attractive ovenproof baking dish lightly sprayed or brushed with oil.

3. Prepare the stuffing: Heat half the olive oil in a nonstick frying pan. Add the diced onion, carrot, zucchini, and bell pepper. Cook over medium heat until the vegetables are just tender, 3 to 5 minutes. Stir in the basil, Parmesan (if using), and black pepper. Correct the seasoning, adding salt if needed. Stuff this mixture into the onion halves. Sprinkle the bread crumbs on top, if using, and drizzle with the remaining olive oil. The onions can be prepared ahead to this stage.

4. Just before serving, preheat the oven to 400°F. Bake the onions until thoroughly heated, about 10 minutes.   *Makes 6 pieces*

79 CALORIES PER PIECE; 2 G PROTEIN; 3 G FAT; 0.3 G SATURATED FAT; 12 G CARBOHYDRATE; 7 MG SODIUM; 0 MG CHOLESTEROL

ZUCCHINI WITH MINT

We don't often think of mint as a traditional Italian seasoning, but fresh mint is popular throughout southern Italy, including Sicily, where it's used for seasoning everything from tuna to vegetables. Here's a zucchini recipe, elegant in its simplicity, that can be made in 5 minutes. Try to choose smallish zucchini (6 to 8 ounces each): they're firmer and sweeter than the larger ones.

PREPARATION TIME: 10 MINUTES   COOKING TIME: 5 MINUTES

1 pound zucchini
1 tablespoon extra-virgin olive oil
1 clove garlic, smashed with the side of a knife or cleaver and peeled

12 fresh mint leaves, thinly slivered, or
   2 teaspoons dried mint
salt and freshly ground black pepper
1 teaspoon fresh lemon juice (optional)

1. Scrub the zucchini and cut into matchstick slivers or ¼-inch slices. Heat the olive oil in a nonstick frying pan. Add the garlic and cook over medium heat until fragrant, about 1 minute.

2. Add the zucchini, mint, salt, and pepper and continue cooking until the zucchini is tender, 2 to 4 minutes. The zucchini should give off their own juices to make a little sauce. If they seem too dry, add

1 to 2 tablespoons water. Correct the seasoning, adding salt and pepper to taste and the lemon juice if desired.

Note: If you don't have fresh or dried mint in the house, open a mint tea bag. This dish could also be prepared using other herbs, such as basil, oregano, and rosemary.　　　　　　　　　　　*Serves 4*

49 CALORIES PER SERVING; 1 G PROTEIN; 3 G FAT; 0.5 G SATURATED FAT; 4 G CARBOHYDRATE; 4 MG SODIUM; 0 MG CHOLESTEROL

BROCCOLI RABE WITH GARLIC AND LEMON

Broccoli rabe (also known as cima di rape *or* rapini*) is a popular Italian vegetable in the cabbage family with tiny green budlike flowers, jagged dark-green leaves, and slender stems. Its flavor and texture hint at broccoli (only milder), with the leafy succulence of spinach. This makes it the perfect vegetable for people who find broccoli too strong. Jam-packed with vitamins and minerals, broccoli rabe used to be found only at Italian and Asian markets. (Asians know it as Chinese broccoli.) Today, it's available at most supermarkets. Here are two ways of enjoying this distinctive vegetable.*

PREPARATION TIME: 15 MINUTES   COOKING TIME: 8 MINUTES

1 pound broccoli rabe
salt
1 to 1½ tablespoons extra-virgin olive oil
2 cloves garlic, crushed with the side of a knife or
  cleaver and peeled

1 teaspoon grated fresh lemon zest
2 teaspoons fresh lemon juice, or to taste
freshly ground black pepper

1. Holding the broccoli rabe by the stems, wash it in a deep bowl of cold water by plunging it up and down. Change the water, as necessary, until completely free of grit or sand. Trim any large tough stems off the broccoli rabe (save them for soup or stock).

2. Bring 2 quarts salted water to a boil in a large saucepan. Add the broccoli rabe and cook until just tender, 2 to 3 minutes. Drain in a colander, refresh under cold water, and drain well. Blot the broccoli rabe dry and cut crosswise into 1-inch pieces and store covered in the refrigerator for up to 4 hours.

3. Just before serving, heat the olive oil in a nonstick frying pan. Add the garlic cloves and cook over high heat until just beginning to brown, about 2 minutes. Add the broccoli rabe, lemon zest, lemon juice, and salt and pepper. Cook until thoroughly heated, about 2 minutes. Correct the seasoning, adding salt or lemon juice to taste.

Serves 4

40 CALORIES PER SERVING; 3 G PROTEIN; 4 G FAT; 0.5 G SATURATED FAT; 6 G CARBOHYDRATE; 25 MG SODIUM; 0 MG CHOLESTEROL

BROCCOLI RABE WITH SULTANAS AND PINE NUTS

Sultanas (yellow raisins) and pine nuts give this broccoli rabe recipe a Sicilian touch of sweetness, while the hot pepper flakes provide a gentle heat.

PREPARATION TIME: 15 MINUTES   COOKING TIME: 8 MINUTES

1 pound broccoli rabe
salt
1 to 1½ tablespoons extra-virgin olive oil
1 clove garlic, crushed with the side of a knife or
   cleaver and peeled

¼ to ½ teaspoon hot pepper flakes
1½ tablespoons toasted pine nuts
2 tablespoons sultanas (yellow raisins)
freshly ground black pepper
2 teaspoons lemon juice (optional)

1. Holding the broccoli rabe by the stems, wash it in a deep bowl of cold water by plunging it up and down. Change the water, as necessary, until completely free of grit or sand. Trim any large tough stems off the broccoli rabe (save them for soup or stock).

2. Bring 2 quarts salted water to a boil in a large saucepan. Add the broccoli rabe and cook until just tender, 2 to 3 minutes. Drain in a colander, refresh under cold water, and drain well. Blot dry. The recipe can be prepared ahead to this stage.

3. Just before serving, heat the olive oil in a nonstick frying pan. Add the garlic, pepper flakes, pine nuts, and sultanas and cook until the garlic is fragrant and the pine nuts begin to brown, about 2 minutes. Add the broccoli rabe and continue cooking until thoroughly heated, about 2 minutes. Correct the seasoning, adding salt and pepper to taste. Add a little lemon juice if a touch of tartness is needed.

Serves 4

93 CALORIES PER SERVING; 4 G PROTEIN; 6 G FAT; 0.8 G SATURATED FAT; 10 G CARBOHYDRATE; 25 MG SODIUM; 0 MG CHOLESTEROL

CAULIFLOWER WITH POOR MAN'S "PARMESAN"

Italy, at least the north of Italy, is one of the prosperous regions in Europe. It's hard to imagine an age when grating cheese would have been considered an unaffordable luxury, but such was the case in southern Italy until the early part of this century. Cheese may have been in short supply, but two staples of the southern Italian diet—anchovies and stale bread—were not. Ingenious cooks combined them to make the following poor man's "Parmesan," which makes a delectable topping for all sorts of vegetables.

PREPARATION TIME: 15 MINUTES   COOKING TIME: 15 MINUTES

1½ tablespoons extra-virgin olive oil
1 clove garlic, minced
2 to 4 anchovy fillets, rinsed, blotted dry, and
  minced

¾ cup dry toasted bread crumbs
salt
1 small or ½ large head cauliflower

1. Heat the oil in a large nonstick skillet. Add the garlic and anchovies and cook over medium heat until just beginning to brown, 2 to 3 minutes. Stir in the bread crumbs. Reduce the heat to medium low and cook the mixture until crisp, toasted, and aromatic, about 10 minutes, stirring often.

2. Bring 4 quarts lightly salted water to a boil in a large pot. Stem the cauliflower and break it into small florets. Boil the cauliflower until tender, about 5 minutes, then drain well in a colander.

3. Stir the cauliflower into the crumb mixture and cook over high heat until thoroughly heated, about 2 minutes. Serve at once.   *Serves 4*

167 CALORIES PER SERVING; 8 G PROTEIN; 7 G FAT; 1 G SATURATED FAT; 21 G CARBOHYDRATE; 321 MG SODIUM; 2 MG CHOLESTEROL

FAVA BEAN MASH WITH BITTER GREENS

This dish kept turning up on a trip through southern Italy. One restaurant made it with chicory, another with dandelion greens.
Yet a third restaurant used arugula. I've even found an Umbrian version made with broccoli rabe and fava beans.
I've tried to incorporate the different versions into a single recipe that can be prepared ahead and makes an
attractive vegetable dish. The main recipe includes instructions for cooking the beans from scratch.
Perfectly tasty results can be obtained with canned beans in a lot less time (see Note).

PREPARATION TIME: 20 MINUTES   COOKING TIME: 1½ HOURS (IF COOKING BEANS
FROM SCRATCH), 10 MINUTES (IF USING CANNED BEANS)

1¼ cups dried fava beans or small lima beans
1 medium onion, peeled and quartered
1 carrot, peeled and cut into 1-inch pieces
1 celery stalk, cut into 1-inch pieces
1 slice dense white bread, crusts removed, diced
½ clove garlic, minced
1 tablespoon extra-virgin olive oil
¼ to ½ cup Basic Vegetable Broth (page 241) or
   Chicken Broth (page 239)
salt and freshly ground black pepper

FOR THE GREENS:
salt
1 pound broccoli rabe, dandelion greens, or
   chicory, or 2 bunches arugula
1 tablespoon extra-virgin olive oil
2 cloves garlic, smashed with the side of a knife or
   cleaver and peeled

1. Spread the beans on a baking sheet and pick through them, removing any twigs, stones, or misshapen beans. Soak the beans for at least 4 hours, preferably overnight, in cold water to cover.

2. The next day, drain and rinse the beans. Place them in a large, heavy, deep pot with the onion, carrot, celery, and 2 quarts water. Bring the beans to a boil. Reduce the heat to medium, and gently simmer the beans, loosely covered, until soft, about 1½ hours. Drain the beans in a colander. Note: The cooking time can be shortened considerably by using a pressure cooker.

3. Purée the beans (with the cooking vegetables), the bread, and garlic in a food processor. Add the olive oil and enough vegetable broth to obtain a light, fluffy purée. Add salt and pepper to taste. Spoon this purée into an attractive ovenproof baking dish just large enough to hold a ½-inch-deep layer of purée. (I use an 8-inch oval dish. For ease in cleaning, lightly spray the dish with oil first.)

4. Prepare the greens: Bring 2 quarts salted water

to a boil in a large saucepan. Wash the greens in a deep bowl of cold water, holding them by the stems, plunging them up and down. Change the water, as necessary, until completely free of grit or sand. Trim any tough stems off the greens. If using broccoli rabe, dandelion greens, or chicory, cook them in the boiling salted water until just tender, 2 to 3 minutes. Drain in a colander, refresh under cold water, and drain well. Blot them dry and cut crosswise into ½-inch strips. If using arugula, skip the parboiling.

5. Heat the olive oil in a nonstick frying pan. Add the garlic and cook over high heat until just beginning to brown, about 1 minute. Add the greens and cook until thoroughly heated, about 2 minutes. Correct the seasoning, adding salt and pepper to taste. Spoon the greens over the bean purée. If all the ingredients are hot, you can serve them right away. Alternatively, bake the dish in a 400°F. oven until the ingredients are thoroughly heated, about 10 minutes.

Note: To make this dish with canned beans, use 2 15-ounce cans cannellini (white kidney) beans. Drain the beans in a strainer and rinse well. Start the recipe at step 3.

Serves 6 to 8

225 CALORIES PER SERVING;* 12 G PROTEIN; 6 G FAT; 0.8 G SATURATED FAT; 35 G CARBOHYDRATE; 53 MG SODIUM; 0 MG CHOLESTEROL

Analysis is based on 6 servings.

FENNEL GRATIN

Many Americans live their entire lives without having tasted fennel. Gennaro Villella can hardly imagine a meal without it. The Umbrian-born founding chef of the restaurant Fantino at the Ritz-Carlton Hotel in New York slices fennel into salads, simmers it in soups, and even poaches it in sugar syrup to make an offbeat dessert. Here's a more traditional preparation from Umbria: a creamy fennel gratin that makes a great cool-weather side dish or vegetarian entrée. This recipe features a nontraditional element, a butterless béchamel sauce. (For more information on butterless béchamel, see page 54.)

PREPARATION TIME: 25 MINUTES   COOKING TIME: 25 MINUTES

1 large or 2 medium fennel bulbs
 (1¼ to 1½ pounds)
2 cups skim, 1 percent, or 2 percent milk
1 teaspoon salt

FOR THE BÉCHAMEL SAUCE:
3 tablespoons all-purpose unbleached white flour
⅛ teaspoon freshly grated nutmeg, or to taste
1 bay leaf

½ onion
1 clove
2½ cups 2 percent or whole milk or low-fat half-
 and-half
1 clove garlic
1 stalk celery, trimmed
freshly ground white pepper
½ cup freshly grated Parmigiano-Reggiano cheese
spray oil

1. Trim the stems, base, and outside leaves off the fennel. Cut the bulb crosswise into ¼-inch-thick slices. Place the fennel in a deep, heavy saucepan with the milk, salt to taste, and enough water (3 to 4 cups) to cover the fennel completely. Loosely cover the pan. Simmer the fennel over medium heat until very tender, 10 to 15 minutes.

2. Prepare the béchamel sauce: Have ready a bowl of cold water. Place the flour and nutmeg in a large nonstick saucepan. Cook over medium heat, stirring steadily with a wooden spoon, until the flour has a pleasant, toasted aroma, about 3 minutes. Do not let it brown or burn. Plunge the pot in the bowl of water to stop the cooking. Let the flour cool completely. Pin the bay leaf to the onion with the clove. Whisk the cold milk into the flour, a little at a time, to create a smooth mixture free of lumps. Return the mixture to the saucepan with the onion, garlic, and celery. Gradually bring the mixture to a boil, whisking steadily. Reduce the heat and gently simmer the

sauce until thick and well flavored, about 10 minutes. (It should thickly coat the back of a spoon.) Add salt and pepper (and a little more nutmeg if desired) to taste. Remove the pan from the heat and fish out and discard the onion, garlic, and celery. Whisk in half the Parmesan.

3. Spray a 12-inch baking dish with oil and spoon ⅓ of the béchamel sauce into the baking dish. Arrange the fennel slices on top, slightly overlapping. Spoon the remaining sauce on top and sprinkle with the remaining Parmesan. The recipe can be prepared ahead to this stage.

4. Preheat the oven to 400°F. Bake the fennel gratin until thoroughly heated and browned on top, about 20 minutes. Serve at once.

Note: For a crustier gratin, you can sprinkle the top with 2 to 3 tablespoons toasted bread crumbs before baking.   *Serves 6*

169 CALORIES PER SERVING; 11 G PROTEIN; 5 G FAT; 3 G SATURATED FAT; 21 G CARBOHYDRATE; 659 MG SODIUM; 14 MG CHOLESTEROL

POTATO TOMATO GRATIN

Potatoes and tomatoes make a delicious combination, the acidity of the latter cutting the starchiness of the former. In this recipe, they're layered with a little olive oil and cheese in a casserole. The potatoes poach in the liquid from the tomatoes. I like the touch of richness imparted by a little heavy cream. (Who doesn't!) But don't worry if your fat budget precludes cream—the casserole will still be delicious without it.

PREPARATION TIME: 20 MINUTES   COOKING TIME: 1 TO 1¼ HOURS

spray olive oil
1 pound starchy potatoes, like Idahos, peeled and
   thinly sliced
salt and freshly ground black pepper
2 to 4 tablespoons freshly grated Parmigiano-
   Reggiano cheese

1 tablespoon extra-virgin olive oil
1 to 2 tablespoons heavy cream (optional)
1 pound red ripe tomatoes, thinly sliced
3 tablespoons toasted bread crumbs

1. Preheat the oven to 400°F. Lightly spray a 6 × 10-inch baking dish with oil. Arrange a layer of potato slices in the bottom, using about one-third of the potatoes. Sprinkle with salt, pepper, and a little cheese. Drizzle a little olive oil and heavy cream (if using) on top. Add a layer of tomatoes, using about one-third of the tomatoes. Sprinkle with a little more salt, pepper, cheese, oil, and cream. Repeat the process twice with the remaining potatoes and tomatoes. (The top layer should be tomatoes.) Sprinkle the bread crumbs on top.

2. Bake the casserole until the potatoes are very soft, 1 to 1¼ hours. Serve hot or at room temperature.

Serves 4 to 6 as a side dish

197 CALORIES PER SERVING;* 5 G PROTEIN; 5 G FAT; 1 G SATURATED FAT; 34 G CARBOHYDRATE; 118 MG SODIUM; 2 MG CHOLESTEROL

Analysis is based on 4 servings.

MASHED POTATOES WITH SUN-DRIED TOMATOES

Italians often pair potatoes and tomatoes—perhaps because the two foods aren't native to Italy, both having been imported from the New World. The following recipe uses broth for moistening the potatoes, with just a little olive oil added at the end for flavor.

PREPARATION TIME: 10 MINUTES   COOKING TIME: 10 TO 15 MINUTES, PLUS 30 MINUTES SOAKING TIME FOR THE TOMATOES

8 dried tomato halves (page 242) or 12 to 15 store-bought dried tomato halves
1 cup warm Chicken Broth (page 239), Basic Vegetable Broth (page 241), or low-fat buttermilk

2 pounds starchy dry potatoes, like Idahos
1 to 2 tablespoons extra-virgin olive oil
salt and freshly ground black pepper

1. Soak the dried tomatoes in the broth in a bowl until soft, about 30 minutes. Remove the tomatoes with a slotted spoon and squeeze out the broth with your fingers over the bowl. Reserve the broth. Transfer the tomato halves to a cutting board and thinly slice.

2. Peel the potatoes and cut into 1-inch pieces. Place the potatoes in cold, lightly salted water and bring to a boil. Briskly simmer the potatoes until very tender, 10 to 15 minutes. Drain in a colander. Return the potatoes to the pot and cook over low heat for a few minutes to dry them out. Mash the potatoes with a potato masher.

3. Stir in the tomatoes, half the oil, and enough broth to obtain light, fluffy mashed potatoes. Add salt and pepper to taste. Just before serving, drizzle the remaining oil over the potatoes.

Serves 4 to 6

235 CALORIES PER SERVING;* 5 G PROTEIN; 4 G FAT; 0.6 G SATURATED FAT; 67 G CARBOHYDRATE; 267 MG SODIUM; 5 MG CHOLESTEROL

*Analysis is based on 4 servings.

SICILIAN STUFFED EGGPLANT

MELANZANA ALLA SICILIANA

The Italian word for eggplant is melanzana, *from the Latin words* malum insanum (literally, "mad apple"). *In the Middle Ages, eggplants were believed to cause madness, a fear that may have been based on the plant's close parentage with several highly toxic plants, including deadly nightshade. Times have changed: today, eggplant is almost synonymous with Italian cooking. I like to prepare this dish with baby eggplants (each 3 to 4 inches long), so you can serve individual halves as an antipasto or a vegetable side dish. Baby eggplants are available at Italian markets, specialty greengrocers, and many supermarkets. But larger eggplants could be prepared the same way.*

PREPARATION TIME: 20 MINUTES   COOKING TIME: 1 HOUR,
INCLUDING 30 MINUTES BAKING TIME FOR THE EGGPLANTS

1 to 1¼ pounds eggplant (preferably 4 to 6 baby eggplants), unpeeled
1 tablespoon extra-virgin olive oil
1 medium onion, finely chopped
1 stalk celery, finely chopped
1 Italian pepper or cubanelle (a small light-green pepper), or ½ green bell pepper, cored, seeded, and finely chopped
2 cloves garlic, finely chopped
1 large or 2 medium red ripe tomatoes, finely chopped (about 1 cup), with their juices

6 pitted black olives, chopped
1 tablespoon drained capers
6 basil leaves, thinly slivered, or 3 tablespoons chopped flat-leaf parsley
a few drops red wine vinegar or fresh lemon juice (optional)
2 tablespoons freshly grated Parmigiano-Reggiano cheese
salt and freshly ground black pepper

1. Preheat the oven to 400°F. Roast the eggplants in a baking dish in the oven until very tender (squeezably soft on the sides), 20 to 40 minutes (depending on the size of the eggplants). Transfer the eggplants to a cutting board to cool. Cut each in half lengthwise and scoop out the flesh with a spoon, taking care not to pierce the shell. Reserve the shells and chop the flesh.

2. Meanwhile, prepare the filling: Heat the olive oil in a large nonstick frying pan. Add the onion, celery, pepper, and garlic and cook over medium heat until just beginning to brown, about 5 minutes. Add the tomato, olives, capers, and chopped eggplant flesh and cook until the eggplant is soft and most of the tomato juices have been absorbed, about 5 minutes. Stir in the basil and vinegar (if using) and cook for 1 minute. Remove the pan from the heat and stir in the cheese and salt and pepper to taste: the filling should be highly seasoned. Stuff the filling into the eggplant shells. The eggplants can be served hot or at room temperature. (As part of an antipasto, they'd probably be served at room temperature.) To warm, bake them in a 400°F. oven until thoroughly heated, about 10 minutes.   *Serves 8 as an appetizer,*
4 as a vegetable side dish

58 CALORIES PER SERVING;* 2 G PROTEIN; 3 G FAT; 0.6 G SATURATED FAT; 7 G CARBOHYDRATE; 92 MG SODIUM; 1 MG CHOLESTEROL

Analysis is based on 8 servings as an appetizer.

TOMATOES STUFFED WITH PIPERATA AND GOAT CHEESE

Piperata refers to a savory sauté of peppers and onions. It's found in one form or other throughout the northern Mediterranean, from Spanish sofrito to French pipérade. Piperata can be served as a contorno (vegetable side dish) in its own right, but I like to use it as a stuffing for tomatoes. Stuffed tomatoes can also be served as part of an antipasto.

PREPARATION TIME: 20 MINUTES   COOKING TIME: 15 MINUTES

8 roma (plum) tomatoes
salt and freshly ground black pepper

FOR THE *PIPERATA*:
1 tablespoon extra-virgin olive oil, plus
   ½ tablespoon for drizzling
1 onion, finely chopped

1 clove garlic, minced
½ red or yellow bell pepper, finely diced
½ green bell pepper, finely diced
2 tablespoons chopped flat-leaf parsley
salt and freshly ground black pepper
1 ounce soft creamy goat cheese or thinly sliced
   Pecorino Romano

1. Preheat the oven to 400°F. Cut a ½-inch slice off the top (end opposite the stem) of each tomato. Trim the bottoms as necessary so that the tomatoes stand upright. Using a melon baller or small spoon, hollow out each tomato. Coarsely chop the tomato tops and flesh. Season the inside of the tomatoes with salt and pepper.

2. Prepare the *piperata:* Heat 1 tablespoon olive oil in a nonstick frying pan. Add the onion, garlic, bell peppers, and parsley. Cook over medium heat until soft but not brown, about 4 minutes. Add the chopped tomato flesh and cook until the tomato juices evaporate, about 2 minutes. Add salt and pepper to taste. Stuff this mixture into the tomatoes and place a piece of cheese on top. The recipe can be prepared ahead to this stage and stored in the refrigerator.

3. Bake the stuffed tomatoes until the sides are soft and the topping is browned, 10 to 15 minutes. Serve hot or at room temperature.

Makes 8 pieces, enough to serve 4 to 8

72 CALORIES PER TOMATO; 2 G PROTEIN; 4 G FAT; 0.9 G SATURATED FAT; 9 G CARBOHYDRATE; 25 MG SODIUM; 2 MG CHOLESTEROL

EGGPLANT ALLA PARMIGIANA

Is there any dish that better symbolizes the generosity, the belt-looseningly bounty of Italian cuisine than eggplant parmigiana? Talk about a nutritional nightmare, however: breaded, deep-fried eggplant slices layered with slices of cheese and baked in a sea of oily tomato sauce. My low-fat version uses a technique called "bake-frying," but I believe you'll find it as tasty as the original and a lot easier to digest. Also, I call for smoked mozzarella, which has more flavor than regular mozzarella, so a little goes further.

PREPARATION TIME: 20 MINUTES   COOKING TIME: 20 TO 30 MINUTES

1 large or 2 medium eggplants (about 1¼ pounds), unpeeled
coarse salt
1 cup all-purpose unbleached white flour
1 cup egg substitute (or 2 eggs plus 4 egg whites; 1 egg plus 6 whites; or 8 egg whites), lightly beaten with a fork
1½ cups fine dry bread crumbs (or as needed)
½ teaspoon dried oregano
2 tablespoons finely chopped flat-leaf parsley

freshly ground black pepper
spray olive oil or 1 to 2 tablespoons extra-virgin olive oil
3 to 4 cups of your favorite low-fat tomato sauce (I like the Sugo di Pomodoro on page 59 or the Roasted Vegetable Sauce on page 53)
¾ cup freshly grated smoked mozzarella cheese
¼ cup freshly grated Parmigiano-Reggiano (or more mozzarella)

1. Cut the eggplants crosswise into ¼-inch slices. Lightly sprinkle the slices with coarse salt on both sides and arrange on a baking sheet. Let stand until a darkish liquid starts oozing from the eggplant slices—the bitter juices. This will take about 30 minutes. Rinse the eggplant slices under cold water and blot dry on paper towels. This technique is called disgorging the eggplants and it draws out the bitter juices.

2. Preheat the oven to 400°F. Have the flour in one shallow bowl, the egg mixture in another, and the bread crumbs in another. Stir the oregano and half the parsley into the crumbs. Lightly season each eggplant slice on both sides with pepper and dip it into the flour, shaking off the excess, then the egg mixture. Next, dip each piece in bread crumbs, shaking off the excess. (Use a pair of tongs or forks for dipping to keep the crumb mixture off your fingers.)

3. Spray or brush a baking sheet (preferably non-stick) with oil. Arrange the eggplant slices on the baking sheet. Brush or spray the tops of the slices

with oil. Place the eggplant in the oven and bake until the slices are crusty and golden brown on the outside and soft and tender inside, about 10 minutes per side.

4. Spoon a little tomato sauce in the bottom of an attractive 12-inch baking dish. Arrange one-third of the eggplant slices on top. Spoon one-third of the sauce on top and sprinkle with one-third of the cheeses. Arrange half the remaining eggplant slices on top with half the remaining sauce and cheeses. Make one final layer of eggplant, sauce, and cheeses. The recipe can be prepared several hours or even days ahead to this stage. If your fat budget allows it, drizzle 1 teaspoon olive oil on top.

5. Bake the eggplant in the oven until the sauce is bubbly and the top becomes crusty, 20 to 30 minutes. Serve at once.

Serves 6 to 8 as an appetizer, 4 as an entrée

248 CALORIES PER SERVING;* 14 G PROTEIN; 6 G FAT; 3 G SATURATED FAT; 35 G CARBOHYDRATE; 995 MG SODIUM; 14 MG CHOLESTEROL

Analysis is based on 6 servings as an appetizer.

Pastry Desserts

Amazing Low-Fat Cannoli

This popular Sicilian dessert might seem like an unlikely candidate for a low-fat makeover—after all, what could be worse for you than a tube of fried dough stuffed with whipped ricotta cheese? But my low-fat version will shatter into a thousand buttery flakes, just like traditional cannoli. The secret? The pastry tubes are made with Chinese wonton wrappers, which are baked instead of fried. The recipe is extremely easy to make, but you must start the night before to drain the cheese.

PREPARATION TIME: 25 MINUTES (BUT REMEMBER TO START THE NIGHT BEFORE)   COOKING TIME: 10 MINUTES

FOR THE FILLING:
2 pints no-fat or low-fat ricotta cheese
6 tablespoons sugar, or to taste
1 teaspoon rosewater
½ teaspoon vanilla extract

TO FINISH THE CANNOLI:
spray oil
12 4-inch wonton wrappers

1 teaspoon cornstarch dissolved in 1 teaspoon water
1 tablespoon melted butter or canola oil or more spray oil
1 tablespoon chopped, toasted pistachio nuts

1. The night before, place the ricotta in a yogurt strainer or cheesecloth- or paper-towel-lined strainer over a bowl. Drain overnight in the refrigerator. Discard the whey.

2. Preheat the oven to 400°F. Lightly spray 12 cannoli tubes with spray oil. Starting with the corner of one wonton wrapper in the center, roll the wrapper around the tube. Glue the opposite corner to the tube with a dab of cornstarch paste. Brush the outside of the cannoli with melted butter or oil, or spray with more oil. Roll up all the wrappers the same way. Bake the cannoli until golden brown and crisp, about 4 to 6 minutes. Let cool slightly, then slide the pastry shells off the tubes. Let the shells cool to room temperature on a wire rack.

3. Finish the filling: In a large bowl, combine the drained ricotta, sugar, rosewater, and vanilla and whisk to mix. Correct the sweetness, adding sugar or rosewater to taste. Transfer the filling to a piping bag fitted with a ½-inch star tip. The recipe can be prepared several hours ahead to this stage. Store the shells in an airtight container. Store the filling in the refrigerator, up to 24 hours.

4. Just before serving, pipe the ricotta mixture into the pastry shells, a little into each end. As you withdraw the piping tube, make a rosette at each end. Sprinkle the ends with chopped pistachios and serve at once.

Amazing Low-Fat Cannoli

Note: The perfumed flavoring called rosewater is available in Middle Eastern grocery stores and gourmet shops. If it's unavailable, substitute vanilla or maraschino liqueur.

Makes 12 cannolis, enough to serve 6 to 12

284 CALORIES PER SERVING;* 18 G PROTEIN; 8 G FAT; 1 G SATURATED FAT; 33 G CARBOHYDRATE; 814 MG SODIUM; 7 MG CHOLESTEROL

Analysis is based on 6 servings.

TIRAMISU

In the late 1980s, tiramisu burst from relative obscurity to international superstardom. The reason? Tiramisu (which literally means "pick me up") has everything a dessert lover could ask for: espresso and brandy-soaked ladyfingers, a silken cream filling, a flavor scale that runs from the bass notes of coffee and cocoa to the clarion tones of cinnamon and vanilla. My reduced-fat version replaces some of the mascarpone (Italian clotted cream) with low-fat pastry cream. For an even lower-fat version of the dish, you could substitute reduced-fat cream cheese for the mascarpone. The traditional brand of ladyfingers for this dish is Vincenzo, which are available at Italian markets and gourmet shops. If unavailable, use slices of sponge cake.

PREPARATION TIME: 30 TO 40 MINUTES　　　COOKING TIME: 10 MINUTES, PLUS 2 TO 3 HOURS CHILLING

FOR THE CREAM FILLING:
1 cup skim milk
1 3-inch cinnamon stick
1 2-inch piece vanilla bean, cut in half
¼ cup sugar, plus 3 tablespoons for beating the egg whites
1½ tablespoons cornstarch
1 egg, plus 2 egg whites
1½ teaspoons finely grated fresh lemon zest
¼ cup mascarpone (2 ounces) or low-fat or no-fat cream cheese, at room temperature
¼ teaspoon cream of tartar

TO FINISH THE TIRAMISU:
2 dozen ladyfingers or one *pane di Spagna* (sponge cake) (page 218), cut into ¼-inch slices
¼ cup cold espresso coffee
2 tablespoons good-quality brandy or rum
1 tablespoon water
2 tablespoons sugar, or to taste
3 to 4 tablespoons unsweetened cocoa powder

1. Prepare the cream filling: Combine the milk, cinnamon, vanilla, and 1 tablespoon of the sugar in a saucepan and gradually bring to a boil, stirring often. (Stirring prevents the milk from scorching.) Meanwhile, in a mixing bowl, whisk together 3 tablespoons sugar and the cornstarch. Add the whole egg and the lemon zest and whisk to mix.

2. Whisk the scalded milk into the egg mixture in a thin stream. Return the mixture to the pan and bring to a boil, whisking steadily. Reduce the heat and cook until thickened, about 2 minutes. The mixture should bubble. Remove the pan from the heat and remove and discard the vanilla bean and cinnamon stick. Whisk in the mascarpone.

3. Beat the 2 egg whites and cream of tartar until firm and glossy but not dry, adding the remaining 3 tablespoons sugar as the whites stiffen. Fold the whites into the warm custard mixture. Let cool to room temperature.

4. Arrange a layer of 12 of the ladyfingers in the bottom of an attractive serving dish or platter (about 12 inches across). Combine the espresso, brandy, water, and 2 tablespoons sugar in a small bowl. Whisk until the sugar is dissolved. (Add sugar to taste.) Brush half this mixture on the ladyfingers, using a pastry brush. Spread half the mascarpone mixture on top and sprinkle with half the cocoa. (Place the cocoa in a sifter or sift it through a strainer.)

5. Place a second layer of ladyfingers on top. Brush with the remaining espresso mixture, and spread with the remaining mascarpone mixture. Refrigerate the tiramisu for 3 to 4 hours to allow the flavors to blend. Just before serving, sift the remaining cocoa on top.

Serves 6

311 CALORIES PER SERVING; 10 G PROTEIN; 7 G FAT; 3 G SATURATED FAT; 52 G CARBOHYDRATE; 170 MG SODIUM; 200 MG CHOLESTEROL

SPONGE CAKE

Pane di Spagna (literally, "bread from Spain") is used as a base ingredient in many Italian desserts—for example, in Zuppa Inglese (page 225) and Tiramisu (page 217). Here's a reduced-fat version adapted from my High-Flavor, Low-Fat Desserts book. Orange-flower water—reminiscent of the Moorish influence on Sicilian cooking—is available in Middle Eastern markets and gourmet shops.

PREPARATION TIME: 15 TO 20 MINUTES   COOKING TIME: 30 MINUTES

spray oil
2 to 3 tablespoons fine toasted bread crumbs
1 cup cake flour, sifted 2 times
2 tablespoons unsalted butter
2 eggs, plus 4 egg whites
⅔ cup sugar

1 tablespoon orange-flower water or orange liqueur
2 teaspoons vanilla extract
2 teaspoons finely grated fresh lemon zest

1 9-inch cake pan (preferably nonstick)

1. Preheat the oven to 350°F. Lightly spray the inside of the cake pan with oil and freeze for 5 minutes. Line the bottom of the pan with a circle of baking parchment. Respray the pan with oil and freeze again. Sprinkle the inside of the pan with the bread crumbs, banging the pan upside down to shake out the excess. Freezing the pan allows you to apply 2 thin coats of oil.

2. Sift the flour into a large bowl. Melt the butter in a saucepan over medium-high heat. Cook the butter until it turns hazelnut brown and immediately remove from the heat.

3. Combine the eggs, egg whites, sugar, orange-flower water, vanilla, and lemon zest in a mixer and beat until very thick and foamy. Start beating the mixture on low speed, gradually increasing the speed to medium, then to high. The whole process will take 8 to 10 minutes. When the eggs are sufficiently beaten, the mixture will be pale yellow and tripled in volume. It will fall from a raised whisk in a thick, silky ribbon.

4. Sift the flour into the egg mixture in three batches, gently folding in each batch with a rubber spatula. Take about ½ cup of the batter and whisk it into the melted butter. Return the mixture to the pan and fold just to mix. It's important to fold gently and just enough to mix: excess folding will deflate the eggs and harm their leavening ability. Spoon the batter into the prepared cake pan.

5. Bake the cake until the top of the cake feels firm, the sides of the cake start to pull away from the pan, and a skewer inserted in the center comes out clean, about 20 minutes. Remove the pan from the oven and let cool slightly. Invert the cake onto a wire rack and gently tap the pan to unmold it. Let the cake cool to room temperature.   *Serves 8 to 10*

178 CALORIES PER SERVING;* 5 G PROTEIN; 5 G FAT; 2 G SATURATED FAT; 29 G CARBOHYDRATE; 61 MG SODIUM; 62 MG CHOLESTEROL

Analysis is based on 8 servings.

FRESH FIG TARTLETS

These attractive tartlets are completely Italian in spirit, but they call for one thoroughly un-Italian ingredient: eggroll wrappers. Readers of my High-Flavor, Low-Fat Desserts book will be familiar with the use of eggroll wrappers to make crisp, almost fat-free tartlet shells.

These tartlets taste best assembled just prior to serving. Fortunately, if you have all the components ready, this takes only five minutes.

PREPARATION TIME: 25 MINUTES   COOKING TIME: 20 MINUTES

FOR THE CRUST:
1 tablespoon butter, melted, or spray oil
6 eggroll wrappers (available in the produce
    section of most supermarkets)
1 recipe Pastry Cream (page 220) (can be prepared
    while the crusts are cooling)
1 tablespoon marsala wine or grappa
18 ripe figs (I like the look of purple figs, but you
    can also use green)

FOR THE GLAZE:
3 tablespoons commercial strawberry glaze
    or 3 tablespoons red currant jelly
1 tablespoon chopped toasted pistachio nuts
    (optional)

6 3½-inch tartlet pans

1. Preheat the oven to 400°F. Brush the tartlet pans with melted butter or spray with oil. Use the eggroll wrappers to line the pans, pushing the dough into the ridges in the sides, trimming off the excess with scissors. Brush the insides of the shells with melted butter or spray with oil. Bake until crisp and golden-brown, 6 to 8 minutes, or as needed. Transfer the shells to a wire rack to cool.

2. Meanwhile, prepare the pastry cream and let cool. Whisk in the marsala.

3. Stem the figs and cut each one lengthwise into quarters. If using red currant jelly for the glaze, melt it in a small saucepan with 1 or 2 tablespoons water, whisking with a wire whisk.

4. To assemble the tartlets, spoon or pipe the pastry cream into the tartlet shells. Stand the fig quarters upright in the cream. Brush the tops of the figs with glaze and sprinkle with pistachio nuts, if using.

Note: Fresh figs are a summer fruit. At other times of the year, a similar tart could be made with fresh strawberries or blackberries.   *Serves 6*

236 CALORIES PER SERVING; 5 G PROTEIN; 4 G FAT; 2 G SATURATED FAT; 47 G CARBOHYDRATE; 118 MG SODIUM; 42 MG CHOLESTEROL

PASTRY CREAM

Here's a low-fat version of crema pasticceria. *It contains only 1 egg yolk, but the vanilla bean and lemon and orange zest provide all the flavor you could wish for.*

PREPARATION TIME: 10 MINUTES   COOKING TIME: 5 MINUTES

1¼ cups skim milk
1 2-inch piece vanilla bean, cut in half
3 strips orange zest (remove it with a vegetable peeler)
3 strips lemon zest (remove it with a vegetable peeler)
1 2-inch piece cinnamon stick
⅓ cup sugar
1½ tablespoons cornstarch
1 to 2 eggs

1. Combine the milk, vanilla bean, orange and lemon zests, cinnamon stick, and 2 tablespoons of the sugar in a saucepan and gradually bring to a boil, stirring often. (Stirring prevents the milk from scorching.) Meanwhile, in a mixing bowl, whisk together the remaining sugar and the cornstarch. Add the eggs and whisk to mix.

2. Whisk the scalded milk into the egg mixture in a thin stream. Return the mixture to the pan and bring to a boil, whisking steadily. Reduce the heat and cook until thickened, about 2 minutes. The mixture should bubble.

3. Remove the vanilla bean, citrus zest, and cinnamon stick with tongs Press a piece of plastic wrap on top of the cream to prevent a skin from forming. Make a slit in the top to allow the steam to escape. Let cool to room temperature.   *Makes 1½ cups*

85 CALORIES PER ¼-CUP SERVING; 3 G PROTEIN; 1 G FAT; 0.3 G SATURATED FAT; 16 G CARBOHYDRATE; 37 MG SODIUM; 36 MG CHOLESTEROL

LEMON RASPBERRY TARTLETS

In my family I'm known as the sourpuss because of my fondness for lemons. I can't resist a good lemon pie.
This tart features a topping of fresh raspberries in place of the cloying sweetness of the usual meringue.
Again, I use Chinese wonton wrappers to make a quick, crisp, virtually fat-free crust.

PREPARATION TIME: 30 MINUTES   COOKING TIME: 15 MINUTES

FOR THE CRUST:
spray oil or 1 tablespoon butter, melted
6 eggroll wrappers (available in the produce
    section of most supermarkets)

FOR THE FILLING:
1½ cups sugar
2 tablespoons plus 1 teaspoon cornstarch
    (7 teaspoons in all)

2 eggs, plus 2 egg whites (or another egg)
1½ cups fresh lemon juice (5 to 6 lemons)
1½ tablespoons finely grated fresh lemon zest
2 pints fresh raspberries
confectioners' sugar for sprinkling

6 3½-inch tartlet pans

1. Preheat the oven to 400°F. Prepare the tartlet shells: Lightly spray the tartlet pans with spray oil (or brush with melted butter). Use the eggroll wrappers to line the pans, pushing the dough into the ridges in the sides. Trim off the excess with scissors. Lightly spray the insides of the tartlet shells with oil or brush with butter. Bake until crisp and golden brown, 6 to 8 minutes, or as needed. Transfer the shells to a wire rack to cool.

2. Meanwhile, prepare the lemon filling: Combine the sugar and cornstarch in a mixing bowl and whisk to mix. Whisk in the eggs and egg whites. Bring the lemon juice and lemon zest to a boil in a heavy saucepan. Whisk this mixture in a thin steam into the egg mixture. Return the mixture to the pan and bring to a boil, whisking steadily. Reduce the heat and simmer for 1 minute or until thickened. Transfer the lemon mixture to a bowl and let cool to room temperature. The tartlets can be made ahead to this stage, but they must be assembled at the last minute. Store the shells in an airtight container, and the filling in the refrigerator.

3. Not more than 5 minutes before serving, spoon the lemon filling into the crusts. Arrange the fresh raspberries on top and sprinkle the tartlets with confectioners' sugar. Serve at once.   *Serves 6*

315 CALORIES PER SERVING; 5 G PROTEIN; 2 G FAT; 95 G SATURATED FAT; 73 G CARBOHYDRATE; 60 MG SODIUM; 71 MG CHOLESTEROL

RICOTTA CHEESECAKE

For me this Italian dessert will always be associated with Boston's Italian neighborhood, the North End. I remember buying lovely ricotta cheesecakes at a tiny bakery (long since defunct) on Salem Street. They were sweet and creamy, fragrant with pine nuts and candied citrus peel, and free of the stick-to-the-roof-of-your-mouth cloy one sometimes encounters with New York–style cheesecakes. (I couldn't resist putting a little cream cheese in the following recipe—a non-Italian touch, perhaps, but it helps give the low-fat ricotta a little more richness.) If your fat budget allows it, use low-fat ricotta and cream cheese, not no-fat. They have substantially more flavor. No-fat cheese will, however, work in a pinch.

PREPARATION TIME: 15 MINUTES   COOKING TIME: 1 HOUR

¼ cup marsala or other sweet wine
½ cup saltanas (yellow raisins)
2 pounds low-fat or no-fat ricotta cheese
½ pound low-fat cream cheese, at room
   temperature
1 cup sugar
3 tablespoons all-purpose unbleached white flour
¼ teaspoon salt
2 eggs, plus 5 egg whites, or 1 cup plus
   2 tablespoons egg substitute

2 teaspoons finely grated fresh lemon zest
2 teaspoons finely grated fresh orange zest
1 tablespoon vanilla extract
¼ cup diced candied orange peel, lemon peel, or a
   mixture of both
¼ cup toasted pine nuts

1 8-inch springform pan, lightly sprayed with oil

1. Pour the marsala over the raisins in a small bowl and let soak until soft, about 10 minutes. Drain well.

2. Preheat the oven to 350°F. (The rack should be set in the upper third of the oven.) Bring 1 quart water to a boil. Wrap a piece of foil around the bottom and sides of the springform pan. (This prevents water from leaking in.)

3. Purée the ricotta in a food processor, scraping down the sides several times. Add the cream cheese and purée until smooth. Add the sugar, 2 tablespoons of the flour, and the salt and purée. Add the eggs, egg whites, lemon and orange zests, and vanilla and purée. Toss the raisins and candied orange peel with the remaining 1 tablespoon flour in a small bowl. Add the raisins, peel, and pine nuts to the batter and run the machine in short bursts to mix. (Do not

purée: you want these ingredients to remain intact.) Pour the mixture into the prepared pan. Tap the pan a few times on the work counter to knock out any bubbles.

4. Set the pan in a roasting pan in the oven. Add 1 inch boiling water to the pan and bake the cheesecake until set, 40 to 60 minutes. To test for doneness, gently poke the side of the pan—when the top no longer jiggles, the cheesecake is done. Another test: A skewer inserted in the center will come out clean when the cheesecake is done. Do not overcook or the cheesecake will become watery.

5. Transfer the cheesecake to a wire rack to cool to room temperature, then refrigerate until cold, at least 4 hours. To serve, run the tip of a small knife around the inside of the pan. Unfasten the sides. Cut into wedges for serving.   *Serves 12 to 16*

261 CALORIES PER SERVING;* 16 G PROTEIN; 7 G FAT; 1 G SATURATED FAT; 34 G CARBOHYDRATE; 257 MG SODIUM; 47 MG CHOLESTEROL

Analysis is based on 12 servings.

CHOCOLATE HAZELNUT BISCOTTI

Chocolate and hazelnuts are classic dessert flavorings in Piedmont, particularly in Turin, where they're combined to make both a pudding and a gelato called gianduia (pronounced "jan-DOO-ee-ya"). If you've never tasted the combination, you'll be amazed how complex the resulting flavor is. The easiest way to skin hazelnuts is to roast them in a hot oven for a few minutes, then rub them in a clean dish towel.

PREPARATION TIME: 25 MINUTES   COOKING TIME: 45 MINUTES

½ cup shelled hazelnuts
2 eggs, plus 2 egg whites
1 cup sugar
3 tablespoons canola oil
1 tablespoon hazelnut liqueur (such as Frangelico), or amaretto liqueur

1¼ cups all-purpose unbleached white flour
½ cup unsweetened cocoa powder
¼ cup cornstarch
¼ cup stone-ground cornmeal
¼ teaspoon salt (optional)
1½ teaspoons baking powder

1. Preheat the oven to 400°F. Place the hazelnuts in a roasting pan and roast until fragrant and the skins start to blister, 5 to 8 minutes. Wrap the nuts, a few at a time, in a clean dish towel and rub them between the palms of your hands to loosen the skin. Toss the nuts between your fingers to shake away the skins. Return any hard-to-peel nuts to the oven for additional roasting. (Don't worry if you don't get every last piece of skin off. The purpose of the roasting is as much to intensify the flavor of the nuts as to remove the skins.)

2. Reduce the oven temperature to 350°F. Combine the eggs, egg whites, sugar, oil, and liqueur in a mixing bowl and whisk until smooth. Sift in the dry ingredients. Add the hazelnuts and stir just to mix. You should wind up with a soft, pliable dough.

3. Transfer the dough to the back of a baking sheet and roll it into a log about 16 inches long.

Gently pat it into a rectangle 5 to 6 inches wide and ½ inch high, tapering at the edges. Score the top of the rectangle with a knife, making shallow cuts on the diagonal every ½ inch.

4. Bake the biscotti for 25 minutes, or until the tops are firm to the touch. Remove the pan from the oven and let cool for 3 minutes.

5. Using a serrated knife, cut each rectangle into ½-inch slices, following the lines you scored on top. Place the slices, cut side down, on the baking sheet and bake for 10 minutes. Turn the biscotti and bake for 10 minutes more, or until crusty.

6. Transfer the biscotti to a wire rack to cool to room temperature, then store in an airtight container. The traditional way to eat biscotti is to dip them in coffee or wine, but I also like to munch them straight.   *Makes 32 to 36 biscotti*

74 CALORIES PER PIECE; 2 G PROTEIN; 3 G FAT; 0.3 G SATURATED FAT; 12 G CARBOHYDRATE; 22 MG SODIUM; 12 MG CHOLESTEROL

CUSTARD, FRUIT, AND FROZEN DESSERTS

INDIVIDUAL ZUPPA INGLESES

You don't need a degree in Italian gastronomy to know that zuppa inglese means "English soup." And that it's not really soup at all, but a sort of trifle made by layering liqueur-soaked sponge cake with fresh fruit and custard. I like to serve zuppa inglese in individual wineglasses (see photo opposite), but you could certainly use a large glass bowl. This is another dessert that actually tastes best made a few hours ahead of time to allow the flavors to blend.

PREPARATION TIME: 25 MINUTES (NOT INCLUDING MAKING THE CAKE)
COOKING TIME: 5 MINUTES, PLUS THE TIME FOR THE CUSTARD TO COOL

FOR THE CUSTARD SAUCE:
2 cups skim milk
1 2-inch piece vanilla bean, cut in half
1 2-inch piece cinnamon stick
5 tablespoons sugar
2 tablespoons cornstarch
2 eggs, plus 1 egg white
1 teaspoon finely grated fresh lemon zest

1 sponge cake (page 218) or angelfood cake, cut into 1-inch cubes (you'll need 6 to 8 cups diced cake)
3 to 4 tablespoons maraschino liqueur or kirsch
1½ cups diced fresh ripe fruit, including peaches, plums, pears, or apricots
1½ cups fresh berries, including sliced strawberries and/or whole blueberries, raspberries, and blackberries
8 sprigs fresh mint

1. Prepare the custard sauce: Combine the milk, vanilla bean, and cinnamon stick and 2 tablespoons of the sugar in a saucepan and gradually bring to a boil, stirring often. (Stirring prevents the milk from scorching.) Meanwhile, in a mixing bowl whisk together the remaining 3 tablespoons sugar and the cornstarch. Add the eggs, egg white, and lemon zest, and whisk to mix. Whisk the scalded milk into the egg mixture in a thin stream. Return the mixture to the pan and bring to a boil, whisking steadily. Reduce the heat and cook until slightly thick, about 2 minutes. The mixture should bubble.

Remove the vanilla bean and cinnamon stick with tongs. Press a piece of plastic wrap on top of the cream to prevent a skin from forming. Make a slit in it to allow the steam to escape. Let the cream cool to room temperature, then chill.

3. Place a layer of cake cubes in the bottom of 8 large wine goblets or compote glasses. Sprinkle with maraschino liqueur. Spoon in a layer of custard sauce and top with fresh fruit and berries. Sprinkle with more maraschino. Continue layering the cake, custard, and fruit until all are used up, sprinkling with maraschino as you go. The zuppa ingleses can be prepared several hours ahead of time. Store in the refrigerator covered with plastic wrap. Just before serving, garnish each serving with a sprig of fresh mint.

Note: A great recipe for a low-fat sponge cake is found on page 218. To save time, you could use store-

Individual Zuppa Ingleses

bought cake. (I'd use store-bought angelfood, as few sponge cakes are as low in fat as mine.) Maraschino is a liqueur made not from cloying maraschino cherries, but from *marascas*, wild sour cherries from northeast Italy. The *marasca* has a nutty flavor reminiscent of almonds. It's well worth the trouble of finding real maraschino—look for it in Italian spirit shops and specialty liquor stores. *Serves 8*

298 CALORIES PER SERVING; 9 G PROTEIN; 6 G FAT; 2.7 G SATURATED FAT; 50 G CARBOHYDRATE; 115 MG SODIUM; 115 MG CHOLESTEROL

PANNE COTTA

Panne cotta (literally, "cooked cream") is a dessert of astonishing simplicity, a sort of Jell-O made with milk and heavy cream.
When properly prepared, it will be set—but quivering, not so hard that you can bounce a spoon off of it. My low-fat
version uses skim milk—plus a nontraditional ingredient: sweetened condensed skim milk for richness. The
real flavor comes from the spices and seasonings: vanilla, cinnamon, almond extract, and lemon zest.
For a pretty presentation, serve panne cotta on pools of fruit sauce.

PREPARATION TIME: 10 MINUTES   COOKING TIME: 10 MINUTES

1½ envelopes gelatin, softened over 3 tablespoons
   cold water
2 cups skim milk
1 cup sweetened condensed skim milk (for an even
   lower-fat dessert, use no-fat sweetened
   condensed milk)
1 piece vanilla bean, 2 inches long, split,
   or 1 teaspoon vanilla extract

1 teaspoon finely grated fresh lemon zest
1 3-inch cinnamon stick, or ½ teaspoon ground
   cinnamon
½ teaspoon almond extract
spray oil

6 ½-cup ramekins

1. Sprinkle the gelatin over the water in a small bowl. Let stand until spongy, about 5 minutes.

2. Combine the skim milk, condensed milk, vanilla bean, lemon zest, and cinnamon stick in a heavy saucepan. Heat the mixture to simmering but do not let it boil. Simmer the seasonings in the milk over low heat for 10 minutes. Remove the pan from the heat and whisk in the gelatin and almond extract.

3. Spray the ramekins with oil. Strain the *panne cotta* mixture into the ramekins. Let cool to room temperature, then cover with plastic wrap and refrigerate until firm (at least 4 hours, as long as overnight).

4. To serve the *panne cotta*, run the tip of a paring knife around the inside of the ramekins. Put a dessert plate over a ramekin, invert, and give a little shake: the *panne cotta* should slide out easily. Serve with the raspberry or peach sauce on pages 228, 229.

Serves 6

202 CALORIES PER SERVING; 8 G PROTEIN; 5 G FAT; 3 G SATURATED FAT; 32 G CARBOHYDRATE; 109 MG SODIUM; 19 MG CHOLESTEROL

FRUIT SAUCES

Use these colorful fruit sauces the way an artist would paint: to create shimmering pools or whimsical squiggles of color.
I always try to keep a few fruit sauces on hand in squirt bottles. Refrigerated, they'll keep for one or two weeks.

STRAWBERRY SAUCE

PREPARATION TIME: 5 MINUTES

1 quart ripe strawberries, hulled
2 tablespoons strawberry preserves

2 to 4 tablespoons confectioners' sugar
1 tablespoon fresh lemon juice, or to taste

Purée the berries and strawberry preserves in a food processor or blender, adding sugar or lemon juice to taste. Strain the sauce into a bowl.

Makes about 2 cups (¼ cup per serving)

18 CALORIES PER SERVING; 0 G PROTEIN; 0 G FAT; 0 G SATURATED FAT; 5 G CARBOHYDRATE; 1 MG SODIUM; 0 MG CHOLESTEROL

RASPBERRY SAUCE

PREPARATION TIME: 5 MINUTES

3 cups fresh raspberries or 1 10-ounce package frozen, thawed
2 to 4 tablespoons confectioners' sugar, or as needed

1 tablespoon fresh lemon juice, or to taste

Purée the berries in a food processor, adding sugar and lemon juice to taste. Run the machine in brief bursts. Don't overpurée, or you'll crush the raspberry seeds, which would make the sauce bitter. Strain the sauce into a bowl.

Makes about ¾ cup (3 tablespoons per serving)

61 CALORIES PER SERVING; 1 G PROTEIN; 0.5 G FAT; 0 G SATURATED FAT; 15 G CARBOHYDRATE; 0 MG SODIUM; 0 MG CHOLESTEROL

BLACKBERRY SAUCE

PREPARATION TIME: 5 MINUTES

3 cups fresh blackberries or 1 10-ounce package
 frozen, thawed
2 to 4 tablespoons confectioners' sugar, or as
 needed

1 tablespoon fresh lemon juice, or to taste
1 tablespoon black currant liqueur (optional)

Purée the berries in a food processor, adding sugar, lemon juice, and black currant liqueur to taste. Run the machine in brief bursts. Don't overpurée, or you'll crush the blackberry seeds, which would make the sauce bitter. Strain the sauce into a bowl.

Makes about ¾ cup (3 tablespoons per serving)

72 CALORIES PER SERVING; 1 G PROTEIN; 0.4 G FAT; 0 G SATURATED FAT; 18 G CARBOHYDRATE; 0 MG SODIUM; 0 MG CHOLESTEROL

PEACH SAUCE

PREPARATION TIME: 5 MINUTES

2 ripe peaches (about 1 pound—enough to make
 2 cups diced peaches)
2 tablespoons confectioners' sugar, or to taste
1 tablespoon fresh lemon juice, or to taste

2 to 4 tablespoons fresh orange juice or water
 (enough to thin the sauce to a pourable
 consistency)

Peel the peaches and cut the flesh off the stones. Purée in a food processor, adding sugar and lemon juice to taste and enough orange juice or water to obtain a pourable consistency. Strain the peach sauce into a bowl.

Makes about 2 cups (¼ cup per serving)

20 CALORIES PER SERVING; 0 G PROTEIN; 0 G FAT; 0 G SATURATED FAT; 5 G CARBOHYDRATE; 0 MG SODIUM; 0 MG CHOLESTEROL

FRUIT "ASPICS"

GELATINA DI FRUTA

Da Guido is one of the finest restaurants in Piedmont. And one of the best-hidden! To get there, we embarked on a labyrinthine journey, down winding country roads, through deserted villages (at nighttime, no less). Once there, we embarked on what can only be described as a ten-course food odyssey, complete with a truffle tasting. (It turns out there's a subtle difference in taste between the truffles that grow under different types of trees.) Among the many dishes that stand out in my mind is a dessert of startling simplicity—the description "fruit aspic" or "fruit gelatin" fails to convey how light, refreshing, and welcome at the end of a copious meal such a simple confection can be. Feel free to vary the fruits depending on what's in season.

PREPARATION TIME: 20 MINUTES   COOKING TIME: 15 MINUTES, PLUS CHILLING TIME

1½ envelopes unflavored gelatin
2 cups fresh orange juice (the juice must be freshly squeezed)
½ cup fresh raspberries, picked over and washed
½ cup fresh blueberries, picked over and washed
½ cup fresh blackberries, picked over and washed (or other berry)

3 to 5 tablespoons sugar, or to taste
spray oil
fresh Blackberry Sauce or Peach Sauce (page 229) or both for serving

6 ½-cup ramekins

1. Sprinkle the gelatin over ½ cup of the orange juice in a small metal bowl. Let stand until spongy, about 10 minutes. Place the bowl in a pan of simmering water to melt the gelatin.

2. Meanwhile, combine the raspberries, blueberries, and blackberries in a mixing bowl and gently toss with the sugar. Let stand for 15 minutes, or until the berries start to become juicy.

3. Warm the remaining 1½ cups orange juice in a saucepan over medium heat. Do not let it boil. Stir the gelatin mixture into the orange juice, followed by the berries. Gently stir until all the sugar is dissolved. Let the mixture cool to room temperature.

4. Meanwhile, lightly spray the insides of the ramekins with spray oil. Line the bottom of each with a small circle of baking parchment and lightly spray with oil again. Ladle the fruit mixture into the ramekins and place in a baking pan in the refrigerator. Cover and chill until firm, at least 8 hours, preferably overnight.

5. To serve, run the tip of a paring knife around the inside of the ramekins. Put a dessert plate over a ramekin, invert, and give a little shake: the fruit aspic should slide out easily. Pool the fruit sauce around the aspics. (If using two sauces, you can marble them with the point of a knife.)   *Serves 6*

149 CALORIES PER SERVING; 3 G PROTEIN; 0.7 G FAT; 0 G SATURATED FAT; 35 G CARBOHYDRATE; 4 MG SODIUM; 0 MG CHOLESTEROL

FRESH BERRIES WITH LOW-FAT ZABAGLIONE

The frothy egg dessert known as zabaglione has a curious history. It is named for Baglioni, a fifteenth-century general who defended Florence against a warring neighboring city. Reduced to cooking with eggs and sweet wine (the enemy having captured his provision wagon), the general's chef invented a sweet dessert, which he called zuppa baglioni—"Baglioni's soup." In time the term was shortened to zabaglione (pronounced "tsa-bah-LYO-nay"). Traditionally, zabaglione is a heart-stoppingly rich dessert sauce made with wine and beaten egg yolks. Here's a low-fat version that uses 2 eggs and 2 egg whites instead of the traditional 6 to 8 yolks.

PREPARATION TIME: 15 MINUTES   COOKING TIME: 5 MINUTES

6 cups mixed berries, including strawberries, raspberries, blackberries, and/or blueberries

FOR THE ZABAGLIONE:
2 eggs, plus 2 egg whites
¾ cup Moscato or marsala wine
¼ cup sugar

1. Wash, stem, hull, if necessary, and dry the berries, cutting any large berries, like strawberries, into slices. Toss the berries in a mixing bowl and spoon them into 6 wineglasses or martini glasses. The recipe can be prepared ahead to this stage.

2. Prepare the zabaglione: Bring 4 cups water to a boil in a large, wide saucepan and reduce the heat to a gentle simmer. Combine the egg, egg whites, wine, and sugar in a large metal mixing bowl. Place the bowl with the zabaglione mixture over the pan of simmering water. Beating steadily with a whisk, cook the mixture until thick, moussy, and doubled in volume, 3 to 5 minutes. When the zabaglione is ready, the whisk will leave a clean trace on the bottom of the bowl. Do not overcook, or the mixture will curdle. Remove the bowl from the heat and spoon the zabaglione over the fruit. Serve at once.

Serves 6

144 CALORIES PER SERVING; 4 G PROTEIN; 2 G FAT; 0.6 G SATURATED FAT; 24 G CARBOHYDRATE; 59 MG SODIUM; 71 MG CHOLESTEROL

Peaches in Asti Spumante or in Moscato

The mere mention of Asti Spumanti is enough to make many North American wine lovers curl their lips with disdain. But the sweet sparkling wine from Piedmont has a wide following in Italy, where its perfumed bouquet and fruity flavor are prized at the conclusion of a meal. This simple dessert takes literally seconds to make, but the contrast of flavors is stunning. Because of its simplicity, you must use fragrant ripe peaches that are at the height of their ripeness. Moscato is a nonsparkling sweet wine. Use it if you prefer a dessert without fizz.

PREPARATION TIME: 10 MINUTES

2 to 3 ripe peaches
1 cup fresh raspberries, washed, stemmed, and
  patted dry with paper towels

3 cups Asti Spumante wine or Moscato wine
4 sprigs fresh mint

1. Peel and pit the peaches. (To pit a peach, cut it in half to the stone around the lengthwise circumference. Twist the halves in opposite directions to separate the peach into halves. Pry out the stone with a spoon.) Dice the peaches and place them in wineglasses.

2. Add the raspberries and Asti Spumante wine to cover. Garnish each glass with a sprig of mint.

Serves 4

154 CALORIES PER SERVING; 1 G PROTEIN; 0.2 G FAT; 0 G SATURATED FAT; 1.3 G CARBOHYDRATE; 0 MG SODIUM; 0 MG CHOLESTEROL

PEPPERED STRAWBERRIES

For most North Americans, pepper belongs to the realm of savory seasonings. Italians are more broad-minded in their thinking, adding pepper to desserts and confections as diverse as biscotti, spice cakes, and fruit dishes. The peppery bite in this strawberry dessert is as tasty as it is unexpected.

PREPARATION TIME: 10 MINUTES

1 quart fresh strawberries (about 3 cups sliced)
¼ cup sugar, or to taste
2 to 3 tablespoons Strega or other Italian liqueur (see Note)

2 to 3 tablespoons orange-flavored liqueur
½ teaspoon coarsely ground black pepper, or to taste
3 cups vanilla frozen yogurt (optional)

1. Wash, drain, and hull the strawberries and cut them lengthwise into ¼-inch slices. Place in a large glass bowl.

2. Shortly before serving, mix in the sugar, liqueurs, and pepper. Let the mixture stand until the juices start to come out of the strawberries, about 10 minutes. If using the frozen yogurt, scoop it into martini glasses or bowls and spoon the strawberry mixture over it. If not, just spoon the strawberries into the glasses or bowls. Grind a little more fresh pepper on top and serve at once.

Note: Strega is an angelica-and-spice-based liqueur made in Benevento in southern Italy and sold in long, slender bottles. If it's unavailable, use another Italian liqueur.

Serves 4 to 6

137 CALORIES PER SERVING;* 1 G PROTEIN; 0.6 G FAT; 0 G SATURATED FAT; 28 G CARBOHYDRATE; 2 MG SODIUM; 0 MG CHOLESTEROL

Analysis is based on 4 servings.

MARINATED RAISINS

Raisins flavored with citron and grappa and tied into neat bundles in grape leaves are a symbol of welcome in southern Italy. It certainly seemed that way when I found such a treat in my room at the Excelsior Vittoria, one of the grand old hotels in Sorrento. Grappa is a potent spirit distilled from grape skins and seeds. If unavailable use cognac or a good-quality brandy. If grape leaves are unavailable, simply pack the raisins in small jars or crocks. (You don't want to use the pickled grape leaves sold in jars for this recipe: they'd be too salty.) Be sure to use grape leaves that haven't been treated with pesticides.

PREPARATION TIME: 15 MINUTES   MARINATION TIME: 6 TO 8 HOURS

1 pound raisins
¼ cup citron, cut into ⅛-inch dice

½ cup grappa
8 fresh or dried grape leaves (optional)

1. In a nonreactive bowl, mix together the raisins, citron, and grappa. Cover the bowl and let the raisins steep in the grappa for at least 6 hours, preferably overnight, stirring occasionally.

2. If using the grape leaves, lay them on a work surface and place a couple of spoonfuls of raisin mixture in the center of each. Fold the sides, top, and bottom over the raisins to make a neat bundle. Tie each bundle with string. Alternatively, pack the raisins into small jars or crocks.

Serves 6 to 8

277 CALORIES PER SERVING;* 2 G PROTEIN; 0.4 G FAT; 0.1 G SATURATED FAT; 61 G CARBOHYDRATE; 9 MG SODIUM; 0 MG CHOLESTEROL

Analysis is based on 6 servings.

PEACH GELATO

No one makes better ice cream than the Italians. This fact is not lost on the French, who have welcomed Italian gelato makers in Paris since the seventeenth century and continue to enjoy their icy fare today. What makes gelato so satisfying yet so light is its emphasis on fresh fruit and fruit juices, with only a little cream or other dairy products added for richness. I discovered that a thoroughly non-Italian ingredient—no-fat sweetened condensed milk—could provide the same richness as heavy cream but without a gram of fat. Below are a few of my favorite gelati.

PREPARATION TIME: 15 MINUTES   COOKING TIME: 10 MINUTES, PLUS COOLING AND FREEZING TIME

2 to 3 ripe peaches (enough to make 2 cups purée)
1½ cups water
½ cup sugar, or to taste

½ cup no-fat sweetened condensed milk
1 to 2 tablespoons fresh lemon juice
sprigs of fresh mint for garnish

1. To peel the peaches, plunge them into 2 quarts boiling water in a saucepan for 1 minute. Rinse under cold water and slip off the skins. Cut the flesh off the stones and dice. Purée the peach flesh in a food processor and put it through a strainer: you should have about 2 cups purée.

2. Combine the water, sugar, and condensed milk in a heavy saucepan and bring to a rolling boil. When the sugar is completely dissolved and the mixture is syrupy, remove the pan from the heat and let cool to room temperature. Stir in the peach purée and lemon juice. Taste the mixture for sweetness, adding sugar or lemon juice as necessary.

3. Freeze the mixture in an ice cream machine, following the manufacturer's instructions. Gelato tastes best served freshly frozen (i.e., a little soft). Serve the gelato in martini glasses, garnishing each with a spring of mint.

Makes about 1 quart, enough to serve 6 to 8

143 CALORIES PER SERVING;* 2 G PROTEIN; 0 G FAT; 0 G SATURATED FAT; 39 G CARBOHYDRATE; 27 MG SODIUM; 2 MG CHOLESTEROL

Analysis is based on 6 servings.

VARIATIONS

STRAWBERRY GELATO: Wash and hull 1 quart strawberries. Purée the berries in a blender. Prepare the above gelato, substituting strawberries for the peaches.

RASPBERRY GELATO: Wash 1 quart raspberries. Purée the berries in a blender, being careful not to over-purée, which would crush the seeds and make the gelato bitter. Prepare the above gelato, substituting raspberries for the peaches.

PEAR GELATO: Peel and core 4 very ripe pears, rubbing each with cut lemon as it is peeled to prevent browning. Add the pears to the boiling water-sugar-milk mixture and poach until very soft. Purée the mixture in a blender or processor. Add the lemon juice, let the mixture cool to room temperature, and correct the seasoning, adding sugar or lemon juice to taste. Freeze as described above.

GIANDUIA (CHOCOLATE HAZELNUT) GELATO

Gianduia (pronounced jan-DOO-ya) is a classic combination of chocolate and toasted hazelnuts associated with the Piedmont city of Turin. If you think chocolate and hazelnuts are good by themselves, wait until you try them together.

PREPARATION TIME: 15 MINUTES   COOKING TIME: 10 MINUTES, PLUS COOLING AND FREEZING TIME

½ cup hazelnuts
1 cup sugar, or to taste
3 cups water
½ cup unsweetened cocoa powder

½ cup no-fat sweetened condensed milk
2 tablespoons hazelnut liqueur (such as Frangelico), plus 2 tablespoons for serving

1. Preheat the oven to 400°F. Toast the hazelnuts in a roasting pan until fragrant and the skins begin to split (about 5 minutes). Transfer the nuts to a clean dish towel and rub them between your hands to remove the skins. (Don't worry if you can't get all the skins off—the idea is to remove the majority.) Let the nuts cool completely. Place nuts in a food processor with ¼ cup of the sugar and grind to a fine powder, running the machine in short bursts.

2. Combine the water, the remaining ¾ cup sugar, the cocoa powder, and the condensed milk in a heavy saucepan and bring to a rolling boil, whisking as needed. When the sugar is completely dissolved and the mixture is syrupy, remove the pan from the heat and let cool to room temperature. Stir in the hazelnut mixture and the 2 tablespoons hazelnut liqueur.

3. Freeze the mixture in an ice cream machine, following the manufacturer's instructions. Serve the gelato in martini glasses, splashing additional hazelnut liqueur on top.

Makes about 1 quart, enough to serve 6 to 8

319 CALORIES PER SERVING;* 5 G PROTEIN; 8 G FAT; 1 G SATURATED FAT; 59 G CARBOHYDRATE; 32 MG SODIUM; 3 MG CHOLESTEROL

Analysis is based on 6 servings.

LEMON-LIME GRANITA

Granita is, perhaps, the most refreshing dessert on the face of the planet. It consists of nothing more than frozen fruit juice, sugar, and water, scraped into icy crystals as it freezes. These tiny crystals (granita literally means "tiny seed") melt on the tongue like snowflakes, releasing tiny bursts of flavor. This recipe offers the tropical touch of lime (after all, the author lives in Miami), but you could certainly make a traditional lemon granita by using all lemon juice and zest.

PREPARATION TIME: 10 MINUTES   COOKING TIME: 5 MINUTES, PLUS 2 HOURS FREEZING TIME

2 cups water
⅔ cup sugar, or to taste
6 tablespoons fresh lemon juice

6 tablespoons fresh lime juice
2 teaspoon finely grated fresh lemon zest
2 teaspoons finely grated fresh lime zest

1. Combine the water and sugar in a shallow non-reactive bowl and whisk until the sugar crystals are dissolved. Stir in the citrus juice and zest. Taste the mixture for sweetness, adding sugar or citrus juice as desired. Transfer the granita to the freezer.

2. Freeze the granita, scraping the mixture with a fork three or four times as it freezes to break it into ice crystals. Scrape again just before serving to loosen the crystals.   *Serves 6*

97 CALORIES PER SERVING; 0 G PROTEIN; 0 G FAT; 27 G CARBOHYDRATE; 3 MG SODIUM; 0 MG CHOLESTEROL

BASIC RECIPES

CHICKEN BROTH

Brodo (broth) is the foundation of much of great low-fat Italian cooking (or even great high-fat Italian cooking).
Below is the recipe for the chicken broth used in this book. The cooked chicken meat can be used for stuffings and salads.

PREPARATION TIME: 10 MINUTES   COOKING TIME: 1 HOUR

1 3½- to 4-pound chicken
1 bay leaf
1 large onion, quartered (unpeeled)
1 clove
2 carrots, peeled and cut into 1-inch pieces

2 stalks celery, cut into 1-inch pieces
2 cloves garlic, peeled and cut in half
2 sprigs flat-leaf parsley
1 sprig rosemary
4 quarts cold water, or as needed

1. Remove the skin and lumps of fat from the chicken and wash the bird inside and out. Pin the bay leaf to one of the onion quarters with a clove. Place all the ingredients for the broth in a stockpot with enough cold water to cover the chicken.

2. Bring the broth to a boil and skim off any foam that rises to the surface. Lower the heat and gently simmer for 1 hour, adding cold water as necessary to keep the chicken covered and skimming the broth often with a flat ladle to remove any fat or impurities that rise to the surface, especially after you've added water. (The cold water brings the fat to the top.)

3. Ladle the broth through a strainer lined with paper towels into a large container and let cool to room temperature. Transfer the broth to 1- and 2-cup containers and refrigerate or freeze. (Broth will keep for 4 to 5 days in the refrigerator; for several months in the freezer.) The chicken can be pulled off the bone and used for stuffings and salads.

Note: Chicken broth can be made with 1½ pounds chicken parts or bones (such as backs or thighs).
Makes 10 to 12 cups

VARIATION: ROASTED CHICKEN AND VEAL BROTH

Roasting the bones gives you a darker, richer broth.

Cut the chicken into 8 pieces. Roast the chicken and veal on a rack on a baking sheet in a 400° F. oven until darkly browned, about 1 hour. Add the vegetables after 30 minutes and roast them as well. Transfer the chicken, veal, and vegetables to a stockpot, leaving the fat behind on the baking sheet. Add 1 cup dry white wine and bring to a boil. Add water to cover and proceed from step 2 of the recipe above.

Chicken Broth

FISH BROTH

If you've ever wondered why Italian fish stews have such an incredible depth of flavor, look no further than this recipe. In Italy, fish broth would be made with small, bony rockfish, like gallinella (sea hen) and scorfano (rascasse or wraisse). In this country, use the frames (bones) and heads of any nonoily or dark-fleshed fish. Good candidates include snapper, grouper, halibut, sole, turbot, cusk, hake, sea bass, and striped bass. The more different types of fish you use, the richer your broth will be. In a pinch, you can use bottled clam juice in place of fish broth. Or chicken or vegetable broth.

PREPARATION TIME: 10 MINUTES   COOKING TIME: 30 MINUTES

2 pounds frames, scraps, or heads from fine-flavored white fish
1 tablespoon extra-virgin olive oil
1 medium onion, finely chopped
1 small leek, trimmed, washed, and finely chopped (see box on page 46)
2 stalks celery, finely chopped
1 clove garlic, minced

1 tablespoon tomato paste
1 tomato, finely chopped
1 herb bundle comprising a bay leaf, a sprig of rosemary, a sprig of flat-leaf parsley, and a sprig of fresh thyme
5 cups cold water, or enough to cover the fish and vegetables

1. Remove any gills from the fish frames and wash thoroughly to eliminate all traces of blood. Using a cleaver, cut the frames into 3-inch pieces.

2. Heat the olive oil in a large saucepan or small stockpot. Add the onion, leek, celery, and garlic and cook over medium heat until soft and translucent but not brown, about 4 minutes. Add the tomato paste and cook for 1 minute. Add the tomato and cook for 1 minute. Add the fish frames, increase the heat to high, and cook until the fish starts to turn opaque, about 2 minutes. Add the herb bundle and cold water to cover.

3. Bring the broth to a boil and skim off any white foam that rises to the surface. Reduce heat and gently simmer the stock until richly flavored, 20 to 30 minutes, skimming often.

4. Ladle the broth through a strainer lined with paper towels into a large container and let cool to room temperature. (If the flavor of the broth is not concentrated enough, continue boiling the stock without the bones, until it is reduced to the taste and consistency you desire.) Transfer the broth to 1- and 2-cup containers and refrigerate or freeze. (Broth will keep for 4 to 5 days in the refrigerator; for several months in the freezer.)   *Makes 4 to 5 cups*

BASIC VEGETABLE BROTH

Here's a broth for vegetarians. It's even easier to make than chicken or fish broth, because it requires almost no skimming. Almost any vegetable or vegetable trimming is a candidate for stock: tomatoes, fennel tops, corncobs, zucchini, summer and winter squash, red and yellow bell peppers, green beans, mushrooms, collard greens, and kale stalks. Use strong-tasting vegetables—such as green peppers, eggplants, turnips, and cabbage—in moderation, as their flavor can become overpowering. Avoid beets, which will turn a stock red, and asparagus and artichokes, which will make it bitter.

PREPARATION TIME: 10 MINUTES   COOKING TIME: 1 HOUR

1 large onion, quartered (unpeeled)
1 leek, trimmed, washed, and cut into 1-inch
   pieces (see box on page 46)
2 carrots, peeled and cut into 1-inch pieces
2 stalks celery, cut into 1-inch pieces
2 tomatoes, cut into 1-inch pieces
6 cloves garlic, unpeeled, cut in half
2 quarts chopped vegetables or vegetable trimmings
   (see above for some suggested vegetables)

2 tablespoons tomato paste
1 herb bundle comprising a bay leaf, a sprig of
   rosemary, a sprig of flat-leaf parsley, and a sprig
   of thyme
3 quarts water
sea salt and freshly ground black pepper

1. Combine all the ingredients except the salt and pepper in a stockpot and bring to a boil. Reduce the heat and simmer the broth, uncovered, until richly flavored, about 1 hour. Add water as necessary to keep the vegetables covered. (A certain amount of evaporation will take place—this helps concentrate the flavor.) Skim the broth once or twice and season with salt and pepper at the end.

2. Pour the broth through a strainer, pressing with the back of a spoon to extract as much liquid as pos-sible from the vegetables. Let the broth cool to room temperature, then refrigerate or freeze. For a thicker, richer broth, force the liquid and vegetables through a vegetable mill or purée in a blender, then strain.

Note: I like to freeze 1-cup portions of vegetable broth, so I always have the right amount on hand.

*Makes 2 to 3 quarts (yield will vary,
depending on the vegetables used, the size
of the pot, and the length of the cooking time)*

DRIED TOMATOES

The hot, dry climate of Sicily makes it possible to dry tomatoes outdoors in the sun. Few of us have backyards with the right climatic conditions for drying tomatoes, but it's easy to make your own in the oven. Homemade dried tomatoes taste much better than the commercial. Plum tomatoes are the traditional fruit for drying, but you can also dry regular tomatoes.

PREPARATION TIME: 10 MINUTES   COOKING TIME: 8 TO 12 HOURS

12 ripe roma (plum) tomatoes or 6 large round tomatoes
sea salt and freshly ground black pepper

3 cloves garlic, minced
1 tablespoon chopped fresh rosemary or basil
1 tablespoon extra-virgin olive oil

1. Preheat the oven to 200°F. Wash and dry the tomatoes. If using plum tomatoes, cut them in half lengthwise. If using regular tomatoes, cut in half widthwise and cut out the stem. Arrange the tomatoes on a nonstick baking sheet. Generously sprinkle each tomato with salt, pepper, garlic, and rosemary and drizzle with a little olive oil.

2. Bake the tomatoes at 200°F. until shrunken, wrinkled, and almost dry, 8 to 14 hours. (If you trust your oven, you can bake the tomatoes overnight. But try it first during the daytime hours, so you can make sure the tomatoes don't burn.) Don't let the tomatoes brown, and don't let them dry out completely or they'll be tough.

3. Let the tomatoes cool to room temperature, then transfer to a jar. Some people like to add olive oil to cover. (You can use the resulting tomato oil in salads or over steamed vegetables.) Keep dried tomatoes in the refrigerator.

Makes 24 small or 12 large pieces

21 CALORIES PER PLUM TOMATO PIECE; 1 G PROTEIN; 1 G FAT; 0 G SATURATED FAT;
3 G CARBOHYDRATE; 124 MG SODIUM; 0 MG CHOLESTEROL

HOW TO PEEL AND SEED A TOMATO

Many people like to peel and seed tomatoes before adding them to pasta dishes. Why? Cooked tomato skins can form red filaments that get caught in your teeth when you eat them. And some people feel that the watery pulp that holds the seeds dilutes the flavor of the sauce. One general word of advice: Never refrigerate tomatoes. If they're not completely ripe when you buy them, they will continue to ripen at room temperature. Refrigeration stops the ripening process. If the tomatoes are ripe, refrigerating will make them mealy.

And now, to peel a tomato. Using the tip of a paring knife, cut the stem end out of the tomato and score a shallow × in the rounded end. Plunge the tomato in rapidly boiling water for 15 to 60 seconds. (The riper the tomato, the shorter the time required to loosen the skin.)

Let the tomato cool on a plate until you can comfortably handle it, then pull off the skin with your fingers. It should slip off in broad strips.

To seed a tomato, cut it in half crosswise and squeeze each half in the palm of your hand, cut side down, to wring out the seeds and liquid. Work over a bowl and strainer. Push the pulp through the strainer with the back of a spoon. Reserve the tomato liquid that collects in the bowl for sauces, soups, or even drinking.

1 good-size ripe tomato (8 to 10 ounces)
yields ¾ to 1 cup peeled, seeded, chopped flesh

How to Cook Beans

Italians love beans and have ready access to fresh favas, cannellini, and other beans. In this country, most of us have to settle for dried beans or canned beans. The latter certainly are convenient and can be used in any recipe calling for beans in this book. Their drawback is that most brands are very salty. If using canned beans, drain them in a colander and rinse well with cold water.

If you have the time, you may wish to start with dried beans. Below is the basic method, plus a chart for approximate cooking times (on page 245). If you like your beans on the firmer side, cook them uncovered, but watch that the cooking water doesn't evaporate to a level below the beans. If you like them on the softer side, cook loosely covered. Always add the salt or any acidic flavorings— such as wine, vinegar, or tomatoes—at the end: these ingredients cause the skins of the beans to toughen if added at the beginning. Cooking times vary according to the freshness of the beans.

1 cup dried beans
1 bay leaf
1 small onion, peeled

1 clove
salt to taste

1. Spread the beans on a baking sheet and pick through them, removing any twigs, stones, or misshapen beans. Rinse the beans in a colander. Soak the beans for at least 4 hours, preferably overnight, in 8 cups water in a large bowl. (This rids the beans of some of their flatulence-causing complex starches.)

2. Drain the beans. Pin the bay leaf to the onion with the clove. Place the beans and onion in a large, heavy pot with 12 cups water. Bring the beans to a boil, reduce the heat, loosely cover the pot, and simmer for the amount of time shown in the chart on page 245. The beans should be tender, even soft, but not mushy. Add water as necessary to keep the beans submerged. Add salt to taste the last 5 minutes. Note: The cooking time can be shortened substantially in a pressure cooker (see chart).

Note: To test for doneness, squeeze a bean between your thumb and forefinger: it should crush easily. There's nothing worse than eating undercooked beans.   *Makes about 2½ cups cooked beans*

159 CALORIES PER SERVING;* 10 G PROTEIN; 1 G FAT; 0 G SATURATED FAT; 29 G CARBOHYDRATE; 2 MG SODIUM; 0 MG CHOLESTEROL

Analysis is based on 4 servings. Slight variation among the different types of beans.

BEAN COOKING TIMES
Presoaked Beans

*For beans that have been soaked for at least 4 hours. Add about 1 hour
of regular cooking time or 10 minutes of pressure cooking for unsoaked beans.*

TYPE OF BEAN	REGULAR COOKING TIME	IN A PRESSURE COOKER
chickpeas	1½ to 2 hours	10 minutes
fava beans	1½ to 2 hours	15 minutes
cannellini beans	1 to 1½ hours	10 minutes
white kidney beans	1 to 1½ hours	10 minutes
lima beans	50 minutes	5 minutes
lentils (require no presoaking)	20 minutes	4 minutes

Note: The above times are approximate. Check the beans after the indicated amount of time. You may need 15 to 20 minutes additional cooking (2 to 3 minutes in a pressure cooker).

How to Soak, Wash, and Trim Dried Porcini

Porcini are large, rotund mushrooms from the Italian woodlands. Their earthy aroma and rich, meaty flavor are hallmarks of Italian cuisine. Fresh porcini are available irregularly at Italian markets and gourmet shops, and through mail-order outlets, such as Comptoir Exotique. (See mail-order sources, page 248.)

But porcini are often used in their dried state; indeed, drying seems to intensify the flavor, adding a dimension that's almost smoky. Many Italian recipes call for both fresh and dried porcini. Dried porcini are widely available at gourmet shops, natural-foods stores, and Italian markets.

Dried porcini are easy to use, but they're often quite gritty. I've developed a two-stage process for cleaning them while retaining the maximum flavor. The first step is to soak the porcini without agitating in warm water or stock for 30 minutes or until soft. The soaking liquid picks up the porcini flavor. It is strained and reserved.

The second step is to transfer the porcini to a bowl of water and agitate them quite vigorously with your fingers. This jars loose any grit. The porcini are then gently lifted out, leaving the grit behind, and the water is discarded.

PREPARATION TIME: 5 MINUTES   SOAKING TIME: 30 MINUTES

1 ounce dried porcini mushrooms
1 cup warm stock or water

2 cups cold water

1. Soak the porcini in the warm stock or water until soft, about 30 minutes. Remove the porcini with your fingers, gently wringing the stock back into the bowl. Strain the stock through cheesecloth or a coffee filter into another bowl and reserve.

2. Transfer the porcini to a bowl of cold water. Agitate the mushrooms with your fingers to wash out any grit. If the porcini are really gritty, change the water one or two more times. Lift the porcini out of the water, gently wringing with your fingers. leaving the silt behind. Gently wring out the porcini and transfer to a cutting board. Trim off any gritty parts. The porcini are now ready for adding to sauces or stews, as is the reserved porcini stock.

Makes ¾ cup reconstituted porcini

HOMEMADE BREAD CRUMBS AND TOASTED BREAD CRUMBS

Cooks are by nature a frugal lot, and Italians are no exception. Many of the recipes in this book call for bread crumbs. The final dish will taste much better if you use homemade instead of store-bought. (The latter are full of preservatives and unnecessary flavorings.) The bread will be easiest to grind if it's stale (a day or two old) but not hard. Crumbs are generally made from white bread.

stale bread, broken into 1-inch pieces

1. Grind the bread in a food processor fitted with a metal blade. Run the machine in bursts and don't overcrowd the chopping bowl. For coarse bread crumbs, grind coarsely; for fine bread crumbs, grind finely, then shake the crumbs through a strainer.

2. To make toasted bread crumbs, preheat the oven to 400°F. Spread the crumbs in a thin layer on a baking sheet and bake until golden-brown, about 5 minutes, raking with a spatula to ensure even browning. Transfer the crumbs to a bowl to cool. I like to store homemade bread crumbs in a plastic container in the freezer.

Mail-Order Sources

COMPTOIR EXOTIQUE
120 Imlay Street
Brooklyn, NY 11231
tel. 888-547-5471; 718-858-5277
Specializes is mushrooms and other exotic produce.

DEAN & DELUCA, INC.
560 Broadway
New York, NY 10012
tel. 800-221-7714
A full range of Italian products, including oils, vinegars, beans, and dried mushrooms.

GRAND BAZAAR, INC.
4151 NW 132nd Street
Miami, FL 33054
tel. 800-625-FOOD; 305-681-5191
A full range of Italian products, including oils, vinegars, beans, pastas, dried mushrooms, and anchovies.

HARVEST IMPORTS, INC.
156 Newark Avenue
Jersey City, NJ 07302
tel. 201-858-5277
Porcini, truffles, and other wild mushrooms.

INDEX

Page numbers in *italics* refer to captions for photographs.